AN INTRODUCTION TO THE MODEL PENAL CODE

AN INTRODUCTION
TO THE
MODEL PENAL CODE

Second Edition

Markus D. Dubber

OXFORD
UNIVERSITY PRESS

OXFORD
UNIVERSITY PRESS

Oxford University Press is a department of the University of Oxford. It furthers the University's objective
of excellence in research, scholarship, and education by publishing worldwide.

Oxford   New York

Auckland   Cape Town   Dar es Salaam   Hong Kong   Karachi   Kuala Lumpur   Madrid
Melbourne   Mexico City   Nairobi   New Delhi   Shanghai   Taipei   Toronto

With offices in

Argentina   Austria   Brazil   Chile   Czech Republic   France   Greece   Guatemala   Hungary
Italy   Japan   Poland   Portugal   Singapore   South Korea   Switzerland   Thailand
Turkey   Ukraine   Vietnam

Oxford is a registered trademark of Oxford University Press in the UK and certain other countries.

Published in the United States of America by
Oxford University Press
198 Madison Avenue, New York, NY 10016

Library of Congress Cataloging-in-Publication Data

Dubber, Markus Dirk, author.
An introduction to the Model Penal Code / Markus D. Dubber.—Second edition.
    pages cm
Includes bibliographical references and index.
ISBN 978-0-19-024304-3 (hardback : alk. paper)—ISBN 978-0-19-024305-0 (pbk : alk. paper)
1. American Law Institute. Model penal code. 2. Criminal law—United States. I. Title.
KF9219.D83 2015
345.73—dc23

2014037208

1 3 5 7 9 8 6 4 2

Printed in the United States of America on acid-free paper

Note to Readers

This publication is designed to provide accurate and authoritative information in regard to the subject
matter covered. It is based upon sources believed to be accurate and reliable and is intended to be
current as of the time it was written. It is sold with the understanding that the publisher is not engaged
in rendering legal, accounting, or other professional services. If legal advice or other expert assistance
is required, the services of a competent professional person should be sought. Also, to confirm that
the information has not been affected or changed by recent developments, traditional legal research
techniques should be used, including checking primary sources where appropriate.

*(Based on the Declaration of Principles jointly adopted by a Committee of the
American Bar Association and a Committee of Publishers and Associations.)*

**You may order this or any other Oxford University Press publication
by visiting the Oxford University Press website at www.oup.com**

CONTENTS

CONTENTS

PREFACE

This is the second edition of a short book that first saw the light of day under the title *Criminal Law: Model Penal Code* (Foundation Press 2002). The present version retains the book's original aim, approach, and structure as a companion to the Model Penal Code that reflects, and reflects on, the Code's attempt to present an accessible, comprehensive, and systematic account of American criminal law. In this way, the book seeks to realize the Code's full potential as a key to American criminal law for law students and teachers, and for anyone else with an interest in getting a sense of the basic contours of American criminal law.

Herbert Wechsler's Model Penal Code, despite recent efforts by the American Law Institute to reconsider some of its provisions (notably on sentencing and sexual offenses), has remained essentially unchanged since its publication in 1962. Given the U.S. Supreme Court's continued reluctance to constitutionalize the basic principles of substantive criminal law, the Model Penal Code remains the closest approximation of a common thread that connects a diverse collection of over fifty American criminal law jurisdictions, each featuring its own—more or less ambitious—criminal code.

At the same time, the Model Penal Code is one of the world's most sophisticated criminal codes, which serves as an excellent platform for comparative analysis, particularly with code-based civil law systems that are often difficult to place alongside opinion-based common law systems. In particular, the Code's now classic provision on mens rea—with its mental states quartet of purpose, knowledge, recklessness, and negligence—has drawn attention in jurisdictions well beyond the borders of the United States as an attempt to clarify an issue as central to any criminal law system as it is vexing.[1]

While the book's basic approach has remained unchanged, the content has been thoroughly revised, resulting in changes large and small throughout the text. Citations to primary and secondary materials have been checked, updated, and supplemented where appropriate. The comparative analysis found sporadically throughout the original version of the book has been expanded in places to provide additional context.

The American Law Institute's ongoing revision of the Code's sentencing and sexual offense provisions has been taken into account, though it has little, if any, effect on the book's approach or content as it does not concern itself with the Code's overall structure or, more specifically, the structure and content of the Code's "general part" (part I). This part sets out the "general provisions" of criminal liability, which are the focus of virtually every introductory criminal law course (as well as the bulk of criminal law scholarship) and so, not coincidentally, of the present book as well.

---

1. See, e.g., Thomas Weigend, Zwischen Vorsatz und Fahrlässigkeit, 93 ZStW 657 (1981) (Germany); Bernd Schünemann, Geleitwort, in Markus D. Dubber, Einführung in das US-amerikanische Strafrecht vii (2005) (same); Codifying the Criminal Law 10, 20–21, 49 (2004) (Ireland); Ian Leader-Elliot, Benthamite Reflections on Codification of the General Principles of Criminal Liability: Towards the Panopticon, 9 Buff. Crim. L. Rev. 391, 397 (2006) (Australia & UK); Martin L. Friedland, My Life in Crime and Other Academic Adventures 175, 281 (2007) (Canada).

ACKNOWLEDGMENTS

I am very happy to acknowledge those who helped me write this book. On the first edition, Guyora Binder, Rosanna Cavallaro, Lutz Eidam, Sara Faherty, Shubha Ghosh, Stuart Green, Thomas A. Green, Kent Greenawalt, Tatjana Hörnle, Cornelius Nestler, Paul Robinson, Robert Steinfeld, Louis Swartz, Robert Weisberg, and Leo Zaibert, along with my criminal law students in Ann Arbor and Buffalo, gave helpful comments, suggestions, and encouragement. On the second edition, Dragana Rakic contributed exemplary research assistance and Vanessa Zhang provided exceptional administrative support.

The first edition was dedicated to the memory of Herbert Wechsler, the driving force behind the Model Penal Code (among many other things). The second edition is dedicated to the memory of my father.

INTRODUCTION

This book is a brief introduction to American criminal law through the lens of the American Law Institute's Model Penal Code. It does not cover the Code in its entirety. Instead it illustrates how the Model Penal Code fits together, both as a code of criminal law and as still the most systematic account of American criminal law we have.

Like virtually all criminal law textbooks and casebooks, this book focuses on the general principles of criminal liability rather than on specific offenses.[1] In other words, it deals with the so-called general part of criminal law, rather than its special part. Specific offenses will make an appearance, but only to illustrate the application of the general part, which applies across the special part.

Although the book is written primarily with American law students in mind, others looking for an accessible introduction to American criminal law as a codified subject may find it useful as well. Throughout, the discussion is lightly footnoted, with occasional references to

---

1. This limitation also reflects the relative influence of the Model Penal Code's general and special parts: not surprising in a *model* code, the general part—and in particular the Code's scheme of "kinds of culpability," or modes of mens rea—was meant to have, and did have, a greater impact than its special part, which was intentionally left incomplete to leave room for variations among jurisdictions. Drug offenses, notably, were excluded altogether, along with other "special topics" such as "alcoholic beverages, gambling and offenses against tax and trade laws." The American Law Institute is currently considering a revision of the Code's anachronistic sexual offense provisions. See American Law Institute, Model Penal Code: Sexual Assault and Related Offenses (Tentative Draft No. 1) (Apr. 30, 2014); see also Deborah W. Denno, Why the Model Penal Code's Sexual Offense Provisions Should Be Pulled and Replaced, 1 Ohio St. J. Crim. L. 207 (2003).

primary and secondary sources, including some comparative materials and supplemental Code resources such as preparatory drafts and the multi-volume Commentaries published by the American Law Institute in the 1980s.

§ 1 A KEY TO THE MODEL PENAL CODE AND TO AMERICAN CRIMINAL LAW

To understand the structure of the Code is to understand the Code. And to understand the Code goes a long way toward understanding American criminal law. The key to the Model Penal Code therefore turns out also to be the key to American criminal law.

Oddly enough, the Model Penal Code, although hailed as "the principal text in criminal law teaching"[2] and "the point of departure for criminal law scholarship,"[3] still needs an introduction; since its completion in 1962, it largely has been left to speak for itself, with mixed results. The Code is remarkably precise, but it is not easy reading. (More than once the Code drafters traded comprehensibility for comprehensiveness, as we will see.) It did not help matters that the Code found itself dissected into snippets of various shapes and sizes sprinkled in among the assortment of materials that make up a traditional criminal law casebook.

I still remember when I first encountered the Model Code in my first-year criminal law class. After wading through a series of more or less entertaining cases from a spattering of jurisdictions and a smattering of decades, which did not even pretend to add up to a coherent body of

2. Sanford H. Kadish, The Model Penal Code's Historical Antecedents, 19 Rutgers L.J. 521, 521 (1988).

3. Id. If one wants to get an overview of scholarly perspectives on various aspects of the Code, the symposia on the Code are a good place to start. See Symposium on the Model Penal Code, 63 Colum. L. Rev. 589 (1963); The 25th Anniversary of the Model Penal Code, 19 Rutgers L.J. 519 (1988); The Model Penal Code Revisited, 4 Buff. Crim. L. Rev. 1 (2000); Model Penal Code Second Commentary, 1 Ohio St. J. Crim. L. 157 (2003); Symposium, Model Penal Code: Sentencing, 7 Buff. Crim. L. Rev. 1 (2003); Christopher Slobogin, Introduction to the Symposium on the Model Penal Code's Sentencing Proposals, 61 Fla. L. Rev. 665 (2009).

doctrine, we ran smack into the Code's mens rea provisions.[4] Suddenly there were detailed and complex definitions of concepts such as "purpose" and "recklessness," carefully crafted to fit into some general scheme of things that we could only guess at. Suddenly words mattered; words even retained their meaning from one rule to the next! Everything was connected to everything else, and everything seemed to be provided for, somewhere, somehow. It was only a matter of time before the complete edifice of criminal law would emerge before us, with its principles, rules, and exceptions interwoven in a rational and systematic way.

Alas, that time never came. The mirage of coherence vanished almost as soon as it had appeared. Before we knew it, we were back reading opinions from throughout space and time, which often enough seemed to have only one thing in common: they all appeared in one and the same, our, casebook.

Very quickly the Model Code turned from a beacon of hope into a source of annoyance. Rather than making sense of the mess, it added to it. Now we were responsible not only for the law of fifty-two jurisdictions (including federal criminal law and the District of Columbia), but fifty-three.[5]

What originally had appeared as the Model Code's strength now simply complicated things unnecessarily. Not only did the "MPC rules" on this or that add to the existing pile of "common law" rules, but their meticulous detail seemed to stem less from a drive to systematize than from a less benign urge to inflict gratuitous pain on overworked law students.

And why did we have to bother with this fantasy jurisdiction anyway? What was the point of torturing us with the intricate rules of a

---

4. § 2.02. Unless otherwise indicated, all citations are to the Official Draft of the Model Penal Code, Model Penal Code (Official Draft and Explanatory Notes: Complete Text of Model Penal Code as Adopted at the 1962 Annual Meeting of the American Law Institute at Washington, D.C., May 24, 1962) (American Law Institute 1985), and to the American Law Institute's official commentaries on the Code, Model Penal Code and Commentaries (Official Draft and Revised Comments 1980–1985) [hereinafter Commentaries].

5. Fifty-four if you count the cadre of English cases, old and new, that continue to appear in American criminal law casebooks.

piece of model legislation that, unlike the Uniform Commercial Code we encountered in contracts, had not been adopted in toto by a single jurisdiction?

In other words: never mind what the Model Penal Code says; why should it matter?

This book addresses both questions, the *what* and the *why*. In fact, it is based on the assumption that the answer to both questions is the same: the Model Code's nature as a systematic code of criminal law. Once one grasps the Code's system, the answers to particular questions of doctrine fall into place. At the same time, to grasp the Code's system is to appreciate its usefulness for anyone trying to get a handle on the often-chaotic rules of American criminal law, from students to teachers and scholars, and from lawyers to judges and legislators.

This book thus aims to make good on the Model Penal Code's promise of coherence, something teachers usually do not have the time to do in a course already overflowing with rules from here and there and on this and that. As a systematic backdrop, a conceptual backbone, the Model Code can fulfill its potential as a tool for teaching and learning American criminal law.[6] You will not find the entirety of American criminal law in the Code, nor anywhere else for that matter— there is just too much of it. There are so-called common law rules that tend to differ from jurisdiction to jurisdiction, from law school to law school, and even from criminal law class to criminal law class. In this chaos, the Code can provide a safe haven, or at least a brief respite, for the bewildered student of criminal law.

If there is such a thing as a common denominator in contemporary American criminal law, it is the Model Penal Code.[7] And that is how this

---

6. Note that the federal constitution does not fit the bill. Unlike criminal procedure, substantive criminal law has not been thoroughly constitutionalized. See generally William J. Stuntz, Substance, Process, and the Civil-Criminal Line, 7 J. Contemp. Legal Issues 1 (1996); Markus D. Dubber, Toward a Constitutional Law of Crime and Punishment, 55 Hastings L.J. 509 (2004).

7. That is a big "if." Given the enormous variation among code-based American jurisdictions, any reference to "American criminal law" (or to some supposed American "common law" of crimes) must be taken with several grains of salt. In fact, one might think of contemporary American criminal law as an exercise in internal, or domestic, *comparative* law. See Markus D. Dubber, Comparative Criminal Law, in Oxford

book treats the Code, rather than as yet another source of alternative rules on whatever topics a criminal law course can accommodate.

Criminal law casebooks devote considerable space to the Model Penal Code, mostly by inserting Code sections, and sections of sections, between their primary sources: appellate court opinions. This book supplements these casebooks by stringing the excerpts together and placing them into the context of the Code as a whole. That way the connections between otherwise disjointed selections will become clearer, something that in turn will help students make better sense of the selections themselves.

The criminal law, and most criminal law exams, come down to a single basic question: *Who is liable for what?*[8] The Model Penal Code provides a key to the answer. That key lies in the Code's structure. That is why to get a handle on the Model Penal Code is also to get a handle on criminal law. Even though the particular answers along the way may differ from jurisdiction to jurisdiction, the general path of analysis is the same. (If it were not, there would be no point in teaching "criminal law," as opposed to Indiana criminal law, federal criminal law, and so on.[9]) And there is no better tool in American criminal law for grasping the analysis of criminal liability than the Model Penal Code.

An important reason that the Model Code is the key to American criminal law in fact, and not only in theory, is that so much of American criminal law derives from it, one way or another. Most obvious is the Code's influence in the forty or so jurisdictions that recodified their criminal law on its basis, including New York, Texas, Illinois,

Handbook of Comparative Law 1287 (Mathias Reimann & Reinhard Zimmermann eds., 2006).

8. Antony Duff prefers the question "Who can be *held* liable for what *by whom*?," at least for purposes of criminal law theory. R.A. Duff, "I Might Be Guilty, But You Can't Try Me": Estoppel and Other Bars to Trial, 1 Ohio St. J. Crim. L. 245, 245 (2003).

9. That is not to say that teaching jurisdiction-specific criminal law courses would be a bad idea. See, e.g., Markus D. Dubber, New York Criminal Law: Cases & Materials (2008). Whether that means the Model Penal Code is obsolete as a teaching tool is another question. See Chad Flanders, The One-State Solution to Teaching Criminal Law, or Leaving the Common Law and the MPC Behind, 8 Ohio St. J. Crim. L. 167 (2010); see also Anders Walker, The New Common Law: Courts, Culture, and the Localization of the Model Penal Code, 62 Hastings L.J. 1633 (2011).

Pennsylvania, and New Jersey.[10] Even though none of these revisions adopted the Code as a whole, all of them were influenced by it to a greater or lesser extent. To get a sense of the Model Code in action, as well as to explore principled alternatives to Code approaches to particular issues, we will follow the American Law Institute's official commentaries on the Code and pay particular attention to the New York Penal Law.[11]

For added perspective, we also will take occasional glances at tort law, especially the ALI's Second Restatement, which was drafted at about the same time as the Model Penal Code, and at comparative criminal law, particularly German criminal law, the most influential criminal law system outside the realm of Anglo-American law.[12] The Model Penal Code invites comparative analysis that is otherwise complicated by the long-standing divide between "common law" and "codified" systems.

The Code continues to influence the criminal law in "non-MPC" jurisdictions as well. These include two important jurisdictions where the national recodification effort triggered by the Code failed miserably: California and federal criminal law.[13] As evidence of its nationwide impact, the Code has been cited in over 3,000 opinions from every American jurisdiction. Courts in non-MPC jurisdictions frequently draw on the Code's analysis to elucidate unsettled issues, such as the mental state requirements of particular offenses, even if they end up rejecting the particular solution proposed by the Code drafters. As of 2004, the Code had been cited in over 150 California and over

10. Richard Singer, The 25th Anniversary of the Model Penal Code: Foreword, 19 Rutgers L.J. 519, 519 (1988).
11. See, e.g., Commentaries § 3.02, at 18; Commentaries § 3.06, at 97. On the origins of the New York Penal Law, and its relationship to the Model Penal Code, see Markus D. Dubber, New York Criminal Law: Cases & Materials (2008).
12. Cf. Commentaries § 3.02, at 11; Commentaries § 210.3, at 65.
13. The authoritative history of the federal effort is Ronald L. Gainer, Federal Criminal Code Reform: Past and Future, 2 Buff. Crim. L. Rev. 45, 92–139 (1998); see also Julie Rose O'Sullivan, The Federal Criminal "Code": Return of Overfederalization, 37 Harv. J.L. & Pub. Pol'y 57 (2014). On the failure of the California reform, see Philip Hager, Fired Scholars Defend Penal Code Revisions, L.A. Times, Sept. 22, 1969, at 3; 22 Stan. L. Rev. 160, 162 (1969) (letter of Herbert L. Packer) (both cited in Sanford H. Kadish, Fifty Years of Criminal Law: An Opinionated Review, 87 Cal. L. Rev. 943, 949 (1999)).

700 federal opinions, including some 100 Supreme Court opinions.[14] Where does a federal appellate court turn when faced with an ambiguous criminal statute? To the Model Penal Code.[15] The Supreme Court? To the Model Penal Code.[16] And a California court? To the Model Penal Code.[17]

§ 2 ORIGINS: THE ALI, LEGAL PROCESS, AND TREATMENTISM

To get a handle on the Model Penal Code, it helps to know something about where it came from and who drafted it.[18] Although it was drafted between 1952 and 1962, the origins of the Code lie in the 1930s, when the American Law Institute decided to tackle criminal law and criminal procedure. An organization of distinguished jurists, founded in 1923 "to promote the clarification and simplification of the law and its better adaptation to social needs, to secure the better administration of justice, and to encourage and carry on scholarly and scientific legal work," the ALI took one look at American criminal law and procedure at the time and was so appalled by what it saw that it decided that, unlike in other areas such as torts or contracts, more than a mere "restatement" of the law was called for. What was needed was a fresh start in the form of *model codes*. The Model Code of Criminal Procedure was completed in 1930. The Model Penal Code was next, but its drafting was postponed until after World War II.[19]

14. American Law Institute, Published Case Citations to Principles of Corporate Governance, Model Penal Code, and Uniform Commercial Code as of March 1, 2004 (http://www.ali.org/_news/annualreports/2004/AM04_08-CaseCitations04.pdf).
15. See, e.g., United States v. M.W., 890 F.2d 239 (10th Cir. 1989) (arson (18 U.S.C. § 81)).
16. See, e.g., United States v. U.S. Gypsum Co., 438 U.S. 422, 443–44 (1978) (Sherman Act).
17. People v. Carr, 97 Cal. Rptr. 2d 143 (Cal. App. 2000) (reckless burning of any structure, forest land, or property) (citing In re Steven S., 31 Cal. Rptr. 2d 644 (Cal. App. 1994)).
18. For a brief overview, see Paul H. Robinson & Markus D. Dubber, The American Model Penal Code: A Brief Overview, 10 New Crim. L. Rev. 319 (2007); see generally Markus D. Dubber, Penal Panopticon: The Idea of a Modern Model Penal Code, 4 Buff. Crim. L. Rev. 53 (2000); Sanford H. Kadish, The Model Penal Code's Historical Antecedents, 19 Rutgers L.J. 521 (1988).
19. A Model Code of Pre-Arraignment Procedure followed in 1975.

After the war, Herbert Wechsler, a Columbia law professor, was put in charge of the Model Penal Code project. Wechsler had laid out the plans for a comprehensive reform of American criminal law in a monumental 1937 article, entitled modestly and somewhat misleadingly "A Rationale for the Law of Homicide."[20] Wechsler consolidated these ideas into a program for the Model Penal Code, which began as two memoranda to the American Law Institute and ended up as a *Harvard Law Review* article.[21]

These two articles contain the blueprint for the Model Penal Code. They are required reading for anyone who wants to penetrate the depths of the Model Code and its underlying approach to the criminal law.

For everyone else, here is a quick summary. Wechsler was a leading proponent of what came to be known as the Legal Process school—a moniker derived from the phenomenally influential and, until recently, remarkably unpublished, casebook of the same name by Henry Hart and Albert Sacks.[22] Its Legal Process pedigree accounts for several features of the Model Penal Code.[23]

First, the Code is a model piece of *legislation*. Its goal was to transfer the power to make criminal law from the common-law-making judiciary to the statute-law-making legislature. "No conduct constitutes an offense unless it is a crime or violation under this Code or another statute of this State."[24] Common law crimes were no more.

Second, the Code is *comprehensive*. In its effort to guide the courts' discretion in applying the rules generated by the legislature, the Code left little to chance. Given too much wiggling room, ingenious judges

---

20. Jerome Michael & Herbert Wechsler, A Rationale of the Law of Homicide (Parts I & II), 37 Colum. L. Rev. 701, 1261 (1937); see also Jonathan Simon, Wechsler's Century and Ours: Reforming Criminal Law in a Time of Shifting Rationalities of Government, 7 Buff. Crim. L. Rev. 247 (2003) (discussing Herbert Wechsler, A Caveat on Crime Control, 27 J. Am. Inst. Crim. L. & Criminology 629 (1937)).

21. Herbert Wechsler, The Challenge of a Model Penal Code, 65 Harv. L. Rev. 1097 (1952).

22. Henry M. Hart & Albert M. Sacks, The Legal Process: Basic Problems in the Making and Application of Law (William N. Eskridge, Jr. & Phillip P. Frickey eds., 1994).

23. See generally Markus D. Dubber, The Model Penal Code, Legal Process, and the Alegitimacy of American Penality, in Foundational Texts in Modern Criminal Law 239 (Markus D. Dubber ed., 2014).

24. § 1.05(1).

might try to circumvent the prohibition of common law crimes. That is why the Code reads—and looks—as much like a criminal law textbook as it does like a code.[25] It was meant to teach criminal law to criminal justice professionals.

Third, the Code is a *code*. It attempted to construct a rational system of criminal law, rather than a compendium of existing rules. This system served certain "purposes," which the drafters, in an unusual step, made explicit.[26] Those purposes were then implemented in the "principles," "provisions," and "definitions" that make up the bulk of the Code.[27]

Fourth, the Code is *pragmatic*. Legal Process was a way of making policy first and a theory of law second. There is no point to a policy that is not implemented. And in fact, as we have seen, the Code helped shape criminal law in the majority of American jurisdictions, in one way or another.

For our purposes, the latter two characteristics are most significant because they turned the Code into the key to American criminal law. Its "principled pragmatism"[28] ensured that the Code was more than an elaborate theoretical construct, rather a model system of criminal law that could have an impact on the actual law in our statute books and courtrooms.

Wechsler was not only committed to the Legal Process way of doing things. He also subscribed to another orthodoxy of his time: treatmentism. Growing out of the beginnings of the new science of criminology at the turn of the twentieth century, treatmentism called

---

25. This feature of the Code distinguishes it from other influential modern criminal codes, and makes it a much better teaching vehicle. The German Penal Code, for instance, does not define actus reus, mens rea, causation, or consent.

26. § 1.02. Guiding officials in their application of norms can be seen as a Legal Process innovation. Legal Process scholars did not regard legal norms as self-executing, and from the start directed their attention to "Basic Problems in the Making *and Application* of Law," as the subtitle of Hart & Sacks's Legal Process materials put it (emphasis added). Having recognized the central significance of discretion in the operation of a legal system, Wechsler and his Legal Process colleagues saw the need to guide its exercise, rather than to deny its existence (never mind to forbid it, as had been proposed in the early days of modern codification).

27. See, e.g., art. 2 ("general principles of liability"); pt. I ("general provisions"); pt. II ("definition of specific crimes").

28. Herbert L. Packer, The Model Penal Code and Beyond, 63 Colum. L. Rev. 594, 594 (1963).

for the replacement of punishment with treatment. According to treatmentism, crime was a disorder that required diagnosis and treatment. Penal treatment was prescribed based on a penological diagnosis that roughly distinguished between two types of offenders: those who could be cured and those who could not. The former were subjected to rehabilitative, the latter to incapacitative, treatment.

In the treatmentist model, criminal law was not a matter of meting out just punishments, but of administering indicated treatments. A rational system of criminal law, or rather of criminal administration, was a system that prescribed and then administered the proper treatment based on a correct diagnosis. This was precisely the sort of policy challenge that the Legal Process school was designed to meet. The Model Penal Code was the result in the realm of criminal law.[29]

§ 2.1 Criminal Propensities

That the "Model Penal and Correctional Code" (to cite its full title) wholeheartedly endorsed the then-orthodoxy of treatmentism is not of merely theoretical interest. To make sense of the Code it helps to keep the centrality of treatmentism in mind.[30] Moreover, when confronted with a particularly ornery Code provision, recall that the drafters sought to "describe the character deficiencies of those subjected to [the

---

29. For a somewhat different take on the challenge, by Wechsler's fellow Legal Process traveler Henry Hart, see Henry M. Hart, Jr., The Aims of the Criminal Law, 23 Law & Contemp. Probs. 401 (1958).

30. The ALI's current project to revise certain aspects of the Model Penal Code, in particular its (relatively non-influential) sentencing provisions, attempts to update the Code by introducing what have been called "neo-retributivist" elements. James Q. Whitman, The Case for Penal Modernism: Beyond Utility and Desert, 1 Critical Analysis of Law 143 (2014) (with comments by Darryl Brown and Lindsay Farmer). Notably, this was thought to require adding "the blameworthiness of offenders" to the Code's list of sentencing factors. American Law Institute, Model Penal Code: Sentencing § 1.02(2)(a) (approved July 2007). At the same time, the revision reaffirms "the original Code's investment in utilitarian crime-reductive goals, including offender rehabilitation and the incapacitation of dangerous offenders." The revision project is limited to sentencing; no changes have been proposed to § 1.02(1), which lays out the "general purposes of the provisions governing the definition of offenses," which are most directly relevant to the subject of this book. Incidentally Hart had (unsuccessfully) suggested an alternative formulation of § 1.02(1) that would have inserted a

criminal law] in accord with the propensities that they...manifest."[31] In the end, the analysis of a case often enough comes down to this diagnosis of propensities, and of the propensity to commit crimes in particular. The concept of criminal dangerousness might come in handy, for instance, when a particular case (or exam question) requires drawing the line between preparation and attempt, or between purpose and knowledge, or in assessing the availability of defenses such as claim of right (in larceny), renunciation, or self-defense. One might reason, for instance, that "Ms. X is guilty of attempted burglary because her preparatory actions had been so extensive as to suggest a strong propensity to commit crimes, and the crime of burglary in particular." Or, perhaps, that "a finding of purposeful behavior in this case would be inappropriate since the defendant did not possess that high degree of criminal disposition, that exceptional criminal energy, which distinguishes purposeful from merely knowing conduct."[32] As Richard Posner put it succinctly, without reference to the Model Penal Code, "words like 'intent' and 'negligence' denote degrees of dangerousness, nothing more."[33]

Depending on a particular teacher's approach to the Model Code, considerations of this kind can be made more or less explicit.[34] At any rate, recalling the Code's treatmentist program—as set out clearly and forcefully in Wechsler's "Rationale of the Law of Homicide"[35] and "Challenge of a Model Penal Code"[36]—can help bring some analytic clarity to tricky questions of doctrine. It is possible to read the Model Penal Code in any number of ways; this is not surprising, given the Code's pragmatic aim of influencing criminal law reform efforts

reference to "blameworth[iness]." Henry M. Hart, Jr., The Aims of the Criminal Law, 23 Law & Contemp. Probs. 401, 441 (1958).

31. Commentaries §§ 220.1–230.5, at 157 n.99.

32. For a discussion of the related notion of "criminal energy" in German criminal law, see Tatjana Hörnle, Distribution of Punishment: The Role of a Victim's Perspective, 3 Buff. Crim. L. Rev. 175, 198–200 (1999).

33. Richard A. Posner, Economic Analysis of Law 208 (4th ed. 1992).

34. See, e.g., Herbert Wechsler, The Challenge of a Model Penal Code, 65 Harv. L. Rev. 1097, 1109 (1952) ("actor's state of mind" relevant to differentiated diagnosis whether "the individual [is] a larger menace than another man").

35. Jerome Michael & Herbert Wechsler, A Rationale of the Law of Homicide (Parts I & II), 37 Colum. L. Rev. 701, 1261 (1937).

36. Herbert Wechsler, The Challenge of a Model Penal Code, 65 Harv. L. Rev. 1097 (1952).

among its primary audience: state legislators. In fact, despite its driving treatmentist rationale, the Code since its publication has survived shifts from treatmentism as rehabilitation to treatmentism as incapacitation, and from treatmentism to retributivism, intact, adapting itself to each new orthodoxy along the way. (Another, less sympathetic, way of making this point is to say that the Code proved remarkably compatible with the dramatic—and entirely unanticipated—expansion of imprisonment in the United States since the 1960s.) This book presents the Model Penal Code as it was envisioned and designed: as a model *code*, not as it has been, could be, and quite possibly will be read thanks to its pragmatic flexibility as a *model* code.

Penal treatment supplements the Code's primary goal: the prevention of crime. The Code pursues its preventive goal in two steps. First, it tries to deter crime.[37] Second, if that attempt fails, it *treats* those it could not deter, that is, it "subject[s] to public control persons whose conduct indicates that they are disposed to commit crimes."[38] The attempt at deterrence of course fails untold times every day. And so it turns out, in fact, that treatment, despite its officially supplementary status, appears as the tail that wags deterrence's dog.

Once they have received a rough, preliminary diagnosis of criminal disposition—or dangerousness—under the provisions in the Code's first, "penal," half (which encompasses parts I and II), offenders are sent on for treatment according to the elaborate set of correctional guidelines laid out in the Code's second, "correctional," half (parts III and IV). The Code's first half gets all the attention in criminal law classes, and rightly so, as it is there that we find the stuff of criminal law, including general principles of liability (part I) and specific offenses (part II). But the first half is merely a setup for the second. The first half (the "Penal Code" proper) provides the tools for diagnosing the criminal disposition, which is then treated according to the second half (the "Correctional Code"). If you put both halves together, then and only then do you have the Model Penal and Correctional Code.[39]

---

37. § 1.02(1)(a); § 1.02, at 3 (explanatory note).
38. § 1.02(1)(b).
39. § 1.01(1).

§ 2.2 The Model Penal and Correctional Code

The Model Penal Code is only the first half of a comprehensive code of criminal and prison law that also includes a Model Correctional Code. To ignore this fact is to ignore the treatmentist orientation of the Model Penal Code and therefore to run the risk of misreading not only its general approach, but also its specific provisions. Every section in the Model Penal Code should be read with an eye toward its role in the Code's general treatment scheme.

Let us take a brief look at the overall structure of the Model Penal and Correctional Code to place our subject, the Model *Penal* Code, in the proper context. In this way, we can better appreciate the full scope of the drafters' treatmentist ambition, and the Penal Code's place within it.[40]

Part I, the general part, is devoted to "General Provisions." Offense definitions appear in part II, the special part, entitled "Definition of Specific Offenses":

Part I. General Provisions
Part II. Definition of Specific Offenses

Like the Penal Code, the Correctional Code consists of two parts:[41]

Part III. Treatment and Correction
Part IV. Organization of Correction

40. For an interesting comparative perspective on the Correctional Code's ambitions and rationale, see Bernd Schünemann, Some Comments on Parts III and IV of the Model Penal Code from a German Perspective: Fundamentals of the Statutory Regulation of Correctional Practice in Germany, 7 Buff. Crim. L. Rev. 233 (2003). The German Prison Act of 1976 [StVollzG] was passed in response to a decision by the German Constitutional Court holding that the design and administration of correctional institutions required an act of legislation rather than executive regulations and orders. BVerfGE 33, 1 (1972). In substance, the German Prison Act professes a commitment to the same "treatment objective" that animated the Model Penal Code. See StVollzG § 2.
41. The discussion of the Correctional Code (parts III & IV) relies on the original version of the Code to illustrate the Code's overall design and structure. Some of the Correctional Code's contents—including its part, article, and section headings—may be subject to change as a result of the ALI's sentencing project.

Part III lays out the principles of penal enforcement, that is to say, of "treatment and correction." It specifies how the general treatment parameters set by a court-imposed sentence are to be applied in practice, and revised if necessary.[42] Every type of sentence laid out in the Penal Code—probation, fine, imprisonment, and parole—finds its enforcement analog in the Correctional Code:[43]

Art. 301   Suspension of Sentence; Probation
Art. 302   Fines
Art. 303   Short–Term Imprisonment
Art. 304   Long–Term Imprisonment
Art. 305   Parole

To get a sense of the detail with which the Code sought to regulate the application of penal treatment, consider the range of topics covered in article 303, on "short-term imprisonment":

§ 303.1   State and Local Institutions for Short–Term Imprisonment; Review for Adequacy; Joint Use of Institutions; Approval of Plan of New Institutions

42. Every felony prison sentence is provisional. During the first year of correctional treatment, the "Commissioner of Correction" could petition the court to resentence the offender, if he was "satisfied that the sentence of the Court may have been based upon a misapprehension as to the history, character or physical or mental condition of the offender." § 7.08.

43. In arts. 6 & 7. There is one obvious exception, capital punishment, which has no analog in the realm of "treatment and correction." Cf. § 210.6. Perhaps ironically, although the Code's death penalty provision famously was placed in noncommittal brackets by its drafters, it ended up significantly shaping the Supreme Court's attempt to construct a constitutional system of capital punishment. See Markus D. Dubber, Penal Panopticon: The Idea of a Modern Model Penal Code, 4 Buff. Crim. L. Rev. 53, 71 (2000); Russell Dean Covey, Exorcizing Wechsler's Ghost: The Influence of the Model Penal Code on Death Penalty Sentencing Jurisprudence, 31 Hastings Const. L.Q. 189 (2003). This provision has since been withdrawn as part of the ALI's ongoing review of the Code's sentencing provisions. See Franklin E. Zimring, The Unexamined Death Penalty: Capital Punishment and Reform of the Model Penal Code, 105 Colum. L. Rev. 1396 (2005); Carol S. Steiker & Jordan M. Steiker, No More Tinkering: The American Law Institute and the Death Penalty Provisions of the Model Penal Code, 89 Tex. L. Rev. 353 (2009).

§ 303.2   Records of Prisoners; Classification; Transfer

§ 303.3   Segregation of Prisoners; Segregation and Transfer of Prisoners with Physical or Mental Diseases or Defects

§ 303.4   Medical Care; Food and Clothing

§ 303.5   Program of Rehabilitation

§ 303.6   Discipline and Control

§ 303.7   Employment and Labor of Prisoners

§ 303.8   Reduction of Term for Good Behavior

§ 303.9   Privilege of Leaving Institution for Work and Other Purposes; Conditions; Application of Earnings

§ 303.10   Release from Institution

The final part of the Correctional Code, "Organization of Correction," set up the administrative bureaucracy necessary to implement the detailed provisions of part III. These institutions once again mirrored the various types of treatment available:

Art. 401   Department of Correction

Art. 402   Board of Parole

Art. 403   Administration of Institutions

Art. 404   Division of Parole

Art. 405   Division of Probation

§ 2.3 The Structure of the Model Penal Code

It is important to understand the Model Penal Code's place in the overall structure of the Model Penal and Correctional Code. Even more important for our purposes, however, is to understand the Model Penal Code's structure taken by itself.

In a sense, the Model Penal Code's structure *is* the Model Penal Code. The Code wears its conceptual coherence on its sleeve. So comprehensive and integrated is the Code's conceptual structure that its table of contents could easily serve as the outline for a criminal law exam. Try doing that with codes untouched by the Model Code, such as the federal criminal code, or the California penal code.

The Model Code drafters imposed structure on chaos wherever they turned. For example, the Code systematized the special part of criminal law by categorizing offenses by the interests and institutions they are designed to protect, such as the state, the person, property, or the family.[44] Before the Code, the preferred method of organization in American criminal codes was the alphabet. In 1948, four years before the Model Code project began in earnest, Congress decided to revise the vast body of federal criminal statutes that had accumulated over a century and a half. That revision, "for which the spadework was done by the hired hands of three commercial law-book publishers, on delegation from a congressional committee desirous of escaping the responsibility of hiring and supervising its own staff,"[45] consisted of placing the existing statutes in alphabetical order. The federal criminal code, Title 18, has retained this ordering to this day, more or less.[46] Efforts to recodify federal criminal law on the basis of the Model Penal Code failed in the early 1980s.[47]

---

44. See Stuart Green, Prototype Theory and the Classification of Offenses in a Revised Model Penal Code: A General Approach to the Special Part, 4 Buff. Crim. L. Rev. 301 (2000); see also Markus D. Dubber, Theories of Crime and Punishment in German Criminal Law, 53 Amer. J. Comp. L. 679 (2005) ("protected legal interests" in German criminal law); Markus D. Dubber & Tatjana Hörnle, Criminal Law: A Comparative Approach 520–23 (2014) (comparing structure of special parts of Model Penal Code, New York Penal Law, German Penal Code).

45. Henry M. Hart, Jr., The Aims of the Criminal Law, 23 Law & Contemp. Probs. 401, 431 n.70 (1958).

46. *Less* because, in its continuous generation of federal crimes, Congress on occasion has found even the alphabet too demanding a structural device. So, for instance, the chapter on "child support" (18 U.S.C. ch. 11A) precedes that on "chemical weapons" (ch. 11B), and "importation of explosive materials" comes after "explosives" but before "extortion," (chs. 39–41). The struggle to alphabetize was not limited to American criminal law. Cf. S.F.C. Milsom, Historical Foundations of the Common Law 417 (2d ed. 1981) (remarking that English "criminal law had by the eighteenth century attained an incoherence which seemed to defy even the modest order of the alphabet"); R. Burn, Justice of the Peace and Parish Officer (1st ed. 1755) (headings include, in order, "Game; Gaming; Gaol and gaoler; Gunpowder; Habeas corpus; Hackney coaches and chairs") (cited in Milsom, supra).

47. See Ronald L. Gainer, Federal Criminal Code Reform: Past and Future, 2 Buff. Crim. L. Rev. 45 (1998).

The Code's greatest structural contribution, however, came not in the special part, but in the general part of criminal law. Before the Model Penal Code, American criminal codes had no general parts to speak of. Central concepts such as actus reus or mens rea remained undefined. Defenses were treated in the context of particular offenses, chief among them homicide and larceny, rather than as general principles of criminal liability that applied to any and all offenses. The federal criminal code, to return to our example, is still without a general part worth its name. Title 18 contains no general provision on jurisdiction, voluntariness, actus reus, mens rea, causation, mistake, entrapment, duress, infancy, justification, self-defense, or inchoate offenses.

Most important, for our purposes, the Code's structure bears within it a roadmap for the analysis of criminal liability in every case that an American lawyer, judge, or law student might come across.

The Model Penal Code's general part (part I: general provisions) includes principles that apply across the board to all offenses defined in its special part (part II: definition of specific offenses). These principles are divided into five articles:[48]

Art. 1 Preliminary
Art. 2 General Principles of Liability
Art. 3 General Principles of Justification
Art. 4 Responsibility
Art. 5 Inchoate Crimes

Article 1 deals with a number of issues at the boundary between criminal law and criminal procedure, including jurisdiction and venue,[49] the statute of limitations,[50] double jeopardy,[51] and proof requirements.[52] Most relevant for our purposes, it spells out the purposes of the Code,[53]

48. We will ignore the last two articles (6 & 7), which are dedicated to the law of sentencing. They are the subject of the ALI's ongoing Model Penal Code: Sentencing project.
49. § 1.03.
50. § 1.06.
51. §§ 1.07–.11.
52. § 1.12.
53. § 1.02.

establishes the principle of legality (in the sense of legislativity, i.e., the legislature's monopoly in criminal lawmaking)[54] and defines certain key concepts.[55]

Article 2 is the heart of the Code's general part. Here we find provisions on the core principles of criminal liability, including:

§ 2.01	actus reus
§ 2.02	mens rea (and § 2.05)
§ 2.03	causation
§ 2.04	mistake (§ 2.04(1))
§ 2.06	complicity

In addition, the drafters began addressing possible defenses to criminal liability, such as:

§ 2.04	ignorance (§ 2.04(3))
§ 2.08	intoxication
§ 2.09	duress
§ 2.10	military orders
§ 2.11	de minimis
§ 2.12	entrapment

The treatment of defenses begins in earnest in article 3, dedicated to "general principles of justification." The justification defenses covered there include:

§ 3.02	necessity
§ 3.03	public duty
§ 3.04	self-defense
§ 3.05	defense of another
§ 3.06	defense of property
§ 3.07	law enforcement
§ 3.08	special responsibility

---

54. § 1.05.
55. §§ 1.04 & 1.13.

Article 4 concludes the Code's consideration of defenses, completing the list of potential excuse defenses begun in article 2 with excuses based on the actor's nonresponsibility due to incapacity:

§ 4.01   insanity
§ 4.10   immaturity

Finally, article 5 deals with inchoate crimes. Article 5 is a code within a code, specifying the general principles of inchoate liability, including possible defenses (such as renunciation and impossibility), and defining both inchoate crimes and quasi-inchoate—possession-related—crimes at the same time:

§ 5.01   attempt
§ 5.02   solicitation
§ 5.03   conspiracy
§ 5.06   possession of dangerous instruments (and § 5.07)

Insofar as it defines specific offenses, rather than setting out general principles of liability, the article on inchoate crimes already stands with one foot in the special part.[56] That part, the second half of the Penal Code (and part II of the four-part Model Penal and Correctional Code), is devoted to the definition of offenses.[57] It is here that we find the stuff of criminal law, the crimes that make the criminal law what it is. These are divided into the following categories of criminally-protected interests:

Offenses against the existence or stability of the state[58]
Offenses involving danger to the person

56. In fact, several criminal codes revised on the basis of the Model Code place the definition of inchoate offenses not at the end of the general part, but at the beginning of the special part. See, e.g., N.Y. Penal Law arts. 100–15.

57. Though offense-specific defenses can also be found there, e.g., extreme mental or emotional disturbance (formerly known as "provocation") in the homicide provisions, § 210.3(1)(b), and claim of right in the theft provisions, § 223.1(3), to name only a few. For each of these special part defenses, one might ask whether the defense should be retained in its limited scope, rather than reconceptualized as an instance of an existing general part defense, generalized into a new general part defense, or eliminated altogether. (Consider, for instance, the controversial defense of provocation, discussed in § 16 below.)

58. Model Penal Code 123 (Proposed Official Draft 1962).

Offenses against property
Offenses against the family
Offenses against public administration
Offenses against public order and decency
Miscellaneous offenses:[59]
    Narcotics
    Alcoholic beverages
    Gambling
    Offenses against tax and trade laws

It might be interesting to take a closer look at the drafters' choice of interests worthy of penal protection, and at their assignment of particular offenses to particular interests. Why, for instance, should the criminal law be enlisted to protect "the family" as a social institution, assuming there is any way of determining what that institution consists of today? And what is abortion doing among offenses against the family, if it is to be retained in a criminal code at all?[60] New York, for example, did not follow the Model Code's lead and instead codified abortion under "offenses against the person."[61]

However, for our purposes, an overview of the Model Penal Code's protected interests will suffice.[62] As already mentioned, this book follows the practice of most introductory courses in American criminal law in focusing on the criminal law's general part, that is, on part I of the Model Code. Still, specific offenses—most notably homicide in its various permutations—will inevitably be considered when it comes to illustrating the workings of the general principles in particular cases.

59. Id. at 241.
60. § 230.3.
61. N.Y. Penal Law §§ 125.40–.60; but see id. § 125.05(1) (defining "person" as "a human being who has been born and is alive").
62. For further discussion, see Markus D. Dubber, The Model Penal Code, Legal Process, and the Alegitimacy of American Penality, in Foundational Texts in Modern Criminal Law 239 (Markus D. Dubber ed., 2014) (on the Model Penal Code's conception of crime, or rather "offense"); see also Markus D. Dubber, Theories of Crime and Punishment in German Criminal Law, 53 Amer. J. Comp. L. 679 (2005) (comparative discussion of legal interests recognized in German criminal law and J.S. Mill's "harm principle" in Anglo-American criminal law).

Even the choice of offense categories will come up, if only briefly, when we home in on the Model Code's prerequisites for criminal liability, as outlined in its purposes section, § 1.02, which include interference with the "individual or public interests" enumerated in the special part.

§ 3 THE MODEL PENAL CODE IN A NUTSHELL: SECTION 1.02

If the Model Penal Code is the key to American criminal law, then § 1.02 is the Model Penal Code in a nutshell. It compresses the Code's elaborate analytic structure into a single statement of the prerequisites of criminal liability. This is precisely what one might expect from a self-consciously systematic statement of criminal law, a *code*.[63] Section 1.02 lays out the "purposes" that the remainder of the Model Penal Code works out in detail, applying them to particular issues in the analysis of criminal liability. Section 1.02 is the Model Penal Code in miniature or, better yet, the Model Penal Code compressed.

§ 3.1 The Prerequisites of Criminal Liability: Of Crimes and Criminals

Section 1.02 tells us not only what sort of conduct is criminal, but also what sort of person is to be punished (or rather, treated) for having engaged in it. Right at the outset, it defines both the crime and the criminal, or the offense and the offender.[64]

---

63. Note, however, that other criminal codes, notably the German Penal Code, do not contain a similar provision. In fact, the German Penal Code—often held up as a code's code—lacks many of the features that Anglo-American codification proponents consider essential to the very idea of a code, including, most important, definitions of varieties of fault (or "intent"). The Model Penal Code's influential mens rea provisions are discussed in § 4.2 below.

64. This is an important distinction: the Code deals with offenses (and offenders), not all of which (or whom) are crimes (or criminals). On non-criminal offenses, so-called "violations," see §§ 1.05(1) & 2.05. On the Model Penal Code as model *offense* code, see Markus D. Dubber, The Model Penal Code, Legal Process, and the Alegitimacy of American Penality, in Foundational Texts in Modern Criminal Law 239 (Markus D. Dubber ed., 2014). For purposes of this introduction, however, we will use "crime" and "offense" interchangeably, except where the distinction matters under the Code.

This is an offense:

conduct that
unjustifiably and inexcusably
inflicts or threatens
substantial harm to
individual or public interests.[65]

And this is an offender:

a "person whose conduct indicates that [he is] disposed to commit crimes."[66]

The rest of the Code puts meat on the bones of these general definitions: while its chapters and sections elaborate the elements of the definition of *offense,* their definition and application pursues the treatmentist aim of detecting and diagnosing the *offender.* The bulk of this book mirrors this approach, by unfolding the doctrinal rules packed into § 1.02's definition of the prerequisites of criminal liability.

Before we move on to the details, it is worth pausing for a moment to consider the relation between the definitions of offenses and offenders in § 1.02. As we will see, the Code is committed to the idea that no one should be punished unless that person has committed a crime, no matter how disposed to committing crimes he or she may be. The concept of crime, in this sense, is prior to that of a criminal: one must commit a crime before one can be labeled a criminal. At the same time, it is not as though the two questions are entirely unrelated. As we saw earlier, the entire Code is designed to diagnose criminal dangerousness.[67]

---

65. § 1.02(1)(a) ("conduct that unjustifiably and inexcusably inflicts or threatens substantial harm to individual or public interests").
66. § 1.02(1)(b); see also Herbert Wechsler, The Challenge of a Model Penal Code, 65 Harv. L. Rev. 1097, 1105 (1952) (offenders' "conduct shows" them to be "sufficiently more likely than the rest of men to be a menace in the future to justify official intervention to measure and to meet the special danger he presents").
67. See Herbert Wechsler, The Challenge of a Model Penal Code, 65 Harv. L. Rev. 1097, 1105 (1952) (criminal codifiers' challenge "in making the social and psychological

Rules about whether a crime has been committed, therefore, will try to weed out those who lack that predisposition, and even to differentiate between different levels of that predisposition.[68] For this reason our exploration of the Code's definition of crimes (and criminal liability) will also have to keep in mind its definition of criminals.

The criminal law—and the Model Penal Code—is concerned first and foremost with general rules governing the question of whether a crime has been committed. These general rules provide an analytic framework of criminal liability that is applied to particular cases, in order to determine whether a particular person is criminally liable for a particular crime, that is to say, whether in the final analysis he is guilty of that crime.

§ 3.2 The Analysis of Criminal Liability: Three Levels of Inquiry

The Model Code defines a crime as "conduct that unjustifiably and inexcusably inflicts or threatens substantial harm to individual or public interests." Criminal liability thus has these three components:

1. conduct
2. without justification and
3. without excuse

To count as a crime, "conduct" must, however, meet several additional criteria. It must:

a. inflict or threaten
b. substantial harm to individual or public interests.

---

evaluations of behavior involved in legislative application of these principles upon a practicable scale").
68. See id. (crime defined as "past behavior [that] has such rational relationship to the control of future conduct that it ought to be declared a crime").

This generates the Model Penal Code's complete scheme of criminal liability:

A person is criminally liable if he engages in

1. conduct that
    a. inflicts or threatens
    b. substantial harm to individual or public interests
2. without justification and
3. without excuse.

Compare this to the scheme of criminal liability generally said to underlie the "common law." It is difficult to crystallize a single liability scheme from hundreds of years of Anglo–American common law. Still, it seems clear enough that a crime in the common law sense consists of two "offense" elements:

1. actus reus (the guilty act) and mens rea (the guilty mind).

Actus reus and mens rea are necessary, but not sufficient, prerequisites of criminal liability under the common law. Owing to the hopelessly confused common law concept of mens rea, which after centuries of judicial expansion and contraction came to encompass everything and nothing, it is difficult to say what else is needed for criminal liability exactly. It is safe to say, however, that courts from early on recognized that criminal liability required both a criminal "offense" (consisting of actus reus and mens rea) and the absence of "defenses." Particularly in the law of homicide, which has always managed to attract the lion's share of doctrinal attention, courts generally divided these defenses into two types: justifications and excuses.[69] Criminal liability thus attached to an offense committed

---

69. 4 William Blackstone, Commentaries on the Laws of England 178–88 (1769) (justifiable and excusable homicide). It is not an accident that Wechsler first sketched his plan for a fundamental revision of American criminal law in an article ostensibly dedicated to the "law of homicide." See Jerome Michael & Herbert Wechsler, A Rationale of the Law of Homicide (Parts I & II), 37 Colum. L. Rev. 701, 1261 (1937).

2. without justification and
3. without excuse.

The analytic schemes of the Model Penal Code and the common law are more or less interchangeable, depending on how one views the connection between conduct and mens rea. The Model Code defines conduct as encompassing both: conduct is "an action or omission and its accompanying state of mind."[70] Replacing "actus reus and mens rea" with "conduct," the common law scheme of criminal liability therefore looks like this:

1. conduct
2. without justification
3. and without excuse

The common law and the Model Penal Code thus turn out not to differ in their general analysis of criminal liability.[71] That is why the Model Penal Code can serve as the analytic backbone of American criminal law, common law or not. Where the Model Penal Code and the common law differ, on occasion, is at the level of particular rules. But this we will see in greater detail as we work our way through the three levels of the Model Code's analysis of criminal liability, next.[72]

---

70. § 1.13(5).
71. There are also obvious similarities to the dominant analytic scheme in the civil law tradition, first developed in German criminal law. For a detailed comparative analysis, see Markus D. Dubber & Tatjana Hörnle, Criminal Law: A Comparative Approach ch. 6 (2014).
72. The impatient can skip ahead to the conclusion, where they will find a conceptual flowchart that presents a condensed version of the Model Code's scheme for the analysis of criminal liability, with citations to relevant Code sections. See § 18 below.

[1]

CRIMINAL CONDUCT

The Model Penal Code's inquiry into criminal liability begins with the question of whether the defendant (procedurally speaking) has engaged in *conduct*. Thoughts are not punished, no matter how evil. And neither are certain movements that do not qualify as conduct. Once it is clear that some sort of conduct has occurred, we need to see if that conduct qualifies as *criminal* conduct. Conduct is criminal if and only if it matches the definition of an offense in each of its elements. These elements include, according to the Model Penal Code, conduct, attendant circumstances, and result, plus the states of mind associated with each.

Assuming the match between offense definition and conduct can be made, we move on to the next step in our inquiry into criminal liability, the question of whether the facially criminal conduct was justified. If it was not justified, we then see if it can be excused nonetheless. And only if it cannot be excused either, do we declare the defendant guilty of the crime, that is to say, criminally liable.

The next three chapters spell out the prerequisites for criminal liability mentioned in § 1.02—"conduct that unjustifiably and inexcusably inflicts or threatens substantial harm to individual or public interests"—and track the Model Penal Code along the way. Chapter 1 deals with "conduct that...inflicts or threatens substantial harm to individual or public interests" (covered in Model Penal Code art. 2). Chapter 2 moves on to consider justification defenses ("unjustifiably") (art. 3). And, finally, Chapter 3 explores the Code's treatment of excuse defenses ("inexcusably") (arts. 2 & 5).

The discussion in Chapter 1, which makes up the bulk of the book (and of the Code's general part, as well as of most introductory criminal law courses), in turn falls into three sections, each of which focuses on topics in criminal doctrine that address various aspects of the question of how one might determine what amounts to

> conduct... (§ 4)
>> [actus reus, mens rea, intoxication, mistake, complicity]
> ...that inflicts or threatens... (§ 5)
>> [causation, inchoate offenses]
> ...substantial harm to individual or public interests (§ 6).
>> [de minimis, protected interests]

§ 4 "CONDUCT ... "

Before we can match conduct to crime, we first must decide whether "conduct" of any kind has occurred. The requirement that criminal liability can be imposed only on the basis of conduct is often called the "actus reus" principle. In common law terms, only an actus can blossom into an actus reus, an "evil act," even if the actor happens to be as reus as they come.

§ 4.1 Actus Reus

The Model Penal Code is emphatic about its adherence to the act requirement. Its very first "general principle of liability" proclaims that "[a] person is not guilty of an offense unless his liability is based on conduct that includes a voluntary act or the omission to perform an act of which he is physically capable."[1]

(A) Act

To qualify as "conduct," then, behavior must be an act and it must be voluntary. The Code defines the former, but not the latter, at least not directly. An act, according to the Code, is "a bodily movement whether voluntary or involuntary."[2] So just lying around, or just thinking evil thoughts, will not a crime make. Or so it seems.

---

1. § 2.01(1).
2. § 1.13(2). If you think it makes no sense to speak of an *involuntary* act, you are in good company. See, e.g., Oliver Wendell Holmes, The Common Law 45–46 (Mark DeWolfe

Thinking evil thoughts is never enough, but lying around doing nothing may be. That is because conduct also includes "the omission to perform an act of which [one] is physically capable."[3] Doing nothing therefore constitutes conduct, perhaps surprisingly, if it is interpreted as not doing something one could have done. As we will see shortly, not doing something may even be *punished* if one not only could, but *should*, have done it.

(B) Voluntariness

The more important aspect of the act requirement is its second component, voluntariness.[4] Here the best the Code could do was provide an indirect definition, by listing acts that do not qualify as voluntary (though for each of these one might wonder whether they should count as "acts" in the first place):

    (a) a reflex or convulsion;

    (b) a bodily movement during unconsciousness or sleep;

    (c) conduct during hypnosis or resulting from hypnotic suggestion.[5]

The Code comes closest to an affirmative definition of a voluntary act when it includes among involuntary acts:

    (d) a bodily movement that otherwise is not a product of the effort or the determination of the actor, either conscious or habitual.[6]

Howe ed., 1961) (1881) ("A spasm is not an act. The contraction of the muscles must be willed."); Restatement (Second) of Torts § 2. Note, however, that the distinction between act and voluntariness within a few years of the Code's publication had attained something like constitutional significance. Robinson v. California, 370 U.S. 660 (1962) (constitutionalizing act requirement); Powell v. Texas, 392 U.S. 514 (1968) (refusing to constitutionalize voluntariness requirement).

3. We will leave aside for the moment the question of liability for possession, which also requires no bodily movement. See § 4.1(D) below.

4. Which is not to say that many cases turn on the issue of voluntariness. For an exception, see State v. Tippetts, 180 Ore. App. 350, 43 P.3d 455 (2002) (relying on MPC Commentaries to find that accused did not voluntarily supply contraband).

5. § 2.01(2).

6. Id.

This is the first, but it will not be the last, multiple negative we will come across in our exploration of the Model Penal Code. If an *involuntary* act is "a bodily movement that otherwise is not a product of the effort or the determination of the actor, either conscious or habitual," we may be permitted to infer that a *voluntary* act is "a bodily movement that [is] a product of the effort or the determination of the actor, either conscious or habitual."[7] The absence of an affirmative definition of voluntariness is no accident. The Code drafters eventually rejected this direct approach because it would raise metaphysical questions of the freedom of the will that they preferred to set aside. Interestingly, their ALI colleagues working on the Restatement of Torts at approximately the same time had no similar qualms and simply defined an act as the "external manifestation of the actor's will."[8] Whether the distinction between the Model Penal Code's non-definition definition of "voluntary act" and the Torts Restatement's definition of "act" comes out in the wash is another question.

(C) Omission

The absence of bodily movement, now labeled an "omission," also can give rise to criminal liability, the act requirement notwithstanding. Not just any omission will do: only an omission that violates an explicit obligation to act. These obligations can come in two forms:

(a) the omission is expressly made sufficient by the law defining the offense; or

(b) a duty to perform the omitted act is otherwise imposed by law.[9]

Here the Code is drawing a useful distinction between what might be called *direct* and *indirect* omission liability, a distinction the common law often obscures. Direct omission liability, covered under (a), is

---

7. § 2.01(2)(d).

8. Compare Restatement (Second) of Torts § 2. Early drafts of the Code defined "voluntary" as "responding to an inward effort of the actor, whether conscious or habitual." Tentative Draft No. 1, § 2.01(8), at 9 (May 1, 1953).

9. § 2.01(3).

imposed for violations of statutes that explicitly criminalize failures to do this or that. For example, the Model Code provides that one way of "committing" the crime of theft by deception is by "fail[ing] to correct a false impression which the deceiver previously created or reinforced."[10]

Indirect omission liability, captured under (b), sweeps much more broadly. It applies to all offenses that are not explicitly defined in terms of an omission (or "failure"), and that is the vast majority of offenses. Most dramatically, indirect omission liability extends to the most serious offense on the books: homicide. Again and again, courts have upheld manslaughter, even murder, convictions of those who "cause[d] the death of another human being,"[11] to use the Model Code's homicide definition, through inaction rather than through action.[12]

Not just anyone will be liable under an indirect omission theory for criminal offenses she engaged in by doing nothing ("commission through omission"). To be criminally liable, I must have been under a duty to do that which I did not do. But where would I find such a duty? On this subject the Code is oddly vague. Speaking of duties "otherwise imposed by law" (§ 2.01(3)(b)) excludes duties not imposed by law, and those imposed by morality or religion or some other non-legal system of norms in particular. But law comes in many shapes and sizes, and the Code does not exclude any as sources of omission duties.

More specifically, the Code does not provide that only *statutorily* defined duties should matter for purposes of indirect omission liability. It may be difficult to reconcile this position with the Code's categorical declaration that the legislature holds the monopoly on criminal lawmaking (principle of legislativity): "No conduct constitutes an offense unless it is a crime or violation under this Code or another statute of this State."[13]

---

10. § 223.3(3). A classic example of a direct omission liability offense is tax evasion. See, e.g., 26 U.S.C. § 7201 ("willful failure to file return, supply information, or pay tax").

11. § 210.1(1).

12. See, e.g., Commonwealth v. Pestinikas, 421 Pa. Super. 371 (1992) (murder); People v. Steinberg, 79 N.Y.2d 673 (1992) (manslaughter).

13. § 1.05(1); see Don Stuart, Supporting General Principles for Criminal Responsibility in the Model Penal Code with Suggestions for Reconsideration: A Canadian Perspective, 4 Buff. Crim. L. Rev. 13 (2000).

As a result, common law and statute law both qualify as sources of duties the violation of which results in criminal liability, provided that a criminal offense can be found that threatens anyone causing a certain type of harm (say, death) with criminal punishment (as is the case with homicide). Traditional common law duties include those based on certain "relationships" (parent to child, husband to wife, captain to sailor, employer to employee, and so on), on a specific mutual "contract" to provide assistance (which presumably differs from the general contractual relationship between, say, an employer and an employee), or—most ambiguously—on the one-sided "voluntary assumption of care," the bane of Good Samaritans everywhere (which presumably differs from the voluntary assumption manifested in a mutual contract).

In addition to these non-statutory sources of criminally enforceable duties, there are the duties one can find in the vast array of modern statutes, criminal or not. Some of these duties simply codify traditional common law duties. For instance, the New York Court of Appeals, in *People v. Steinberg*, managed to find a statutory source for a father's duty to prevent the death of his daughter.[14] It invoked New York's Family Court Act in support of the proposition that "[p]arents have a nondelegable affirmative duty to provide their children with adequate medical care."[15] As its title suggests, the statute invoked by the court dealt primarily with procedural matters. It did not explicitly set out parental duties, never mind parental duties the violation of which may trigger criminal liability (including, as in this case, liability for homicide).[16] The provision cited by the court in *Steinberg* appears in the general definitional section of the article on "child protective proceedings."[17]

---

14. 79 N.Y.2d 673 (1992).

15. Id. at 680.

16. The defendant was charged with murder, and convicted of manslaughter. As the presence or absence of a duty relates to the question of actus reus rather than mens rea, the court's affirmation of a duty in this case would have supported a murder conviction.

17. It defines "neglected child" as "a child less than eighteen years of age…whose physical, mental or emotional condition has been impaired or is in imminent danger of becoming impaired as a result of the failure of his parent or other person legally responsible for his care to exercise a minimum degree of care…in supplying the child with adequate food, clothing, shelter or education…, or medical, dental, optometrical or surgical

Perhaps this case illustrates that limiting criminal omission duties to statutory sources, by itself, would not do much to constrain a court's freewheeling search for duties more felt than specified. A court is likely to find a duty if it looks hard enough, even among statutes. Still, it is noteworthy that the Code, given its professed commitment to both the principle of legislativity and the act requirement, did not at least force courts eager to convict unseemly (or perhaps abnormally dangerous?) omitters to jump through this additional hoop. In the end, the court's invocation of the Family Court Act did not make much of a difference, as the parent-child relationship had been long established as a *common law* source of criminally enforceable duties.

But let us say we have found a bona fide omission duty of one kind or another. Although the Code does not say so directly, we can assume that omissions must be voluntary too, just like commissions. The Code's list of "involuntary acts" does not easily translate to nonacts (what is a reflex omission, or an omissive reflex?), but it is doubtful that the Code drafters meant to hold us criminally liable for what we do not do while sleepwalking anymore than for what we do do while sleepwalking.

At this point, it might appear that the Code's supposedly ironclad grip on the "act requirement" is about as slippery as its sense of what counts as an act is generous. But that should not be a surprise. One would expect that the Code drafters would hesitate to shackle the act requirement with dogmatic constraints. After all, an omission too can provide convincing evidence of that all-important criminal disposition in need of penal treatment.[18]

(D) Possession

The Code's flexible understanding of the act requirement becomes most obvious, however, in its rather cavalier treatment of an offense that was to become the policing tool of choice in the war on crime: possession.[19]

---

care, though financially able to do so or offered financial or other reasonable means to do so...." N.Y. Fam. Ct. Act § 1012(f)(i)(A).

18. For more on the Code's treatmentist approach, see § 2 above.

19. See Markus D. Dubber, Policing Possession: The War on Crime and the End of Criminal Law, 91 J. Crim. L. & Criminology 829 (2002); see also Andrew Ashworth, The Unfairness of Risk-Based Possession Offences, 5 Crim. L. & Phil. 237 (2011).

Possession might be many things. It might be a status, a condition, or perhaps a relationship between a person and an object. But whatever it is, it is not an act or any other type of conduct.[20] To possess something is *to be* in possession of it.[21]

One would expect that this simple, and universally acknowledged, observation would remove possession offenses from the arsenal of a system of criminal law as emphatically devoted to the act requirement as the Model Penal Code proclaims to be: "A person is not guilty of an offense unless his liability is based on conduct that includes a voluntary act or the omission to perform an act of which he is physically capable."[22] (Perhaps it doth protest too much?)

But that is not so. Possession offenses play a crucial role in the Code's scheme for identifying and treating dangerous persons. In that scheme, persons who possess certain items, "instruments of crime" or weapons, reveal themselves as suffering from a criminal disposition by the mere fact of possession.[23] For that reason, a preventive system of criminal law is entitled, even required, to step in already at this point, long before dangerous possessions have been put to any use by their presumptively dangerous possessors.[24]

Unwilling to do without this mechanism for early treatment intervention, yet unable simply to ignore the tension between possession offenses and the act requirement, the Code drafters simply cut the Gordian knot of inconsistency by *declaring* that "[p]ossession is an act."[25] Possession is an act, they said, "if the possessor knowingly procured or received the thing possessed or was aware of his control thereof for a

20. See, e.g., Regina v. Dugdale, 1 El. & Bl. 435, 439 (1853) (Coleridge, J.).
21. The nature of possession as an inchoate offense is discussed in § 5.2(A) below.
22. § 2.01(1).
23. §§ 5.06 & .07.
24. On the general presumptions of dangerousness and incorrigibility in the war on crime, see Markus D. Dubber, The Model Penal Code, Legal Process, and the Alegitimacy of American Penality, in Foundational Texts in Modern Criminal Law 239 (Markus D. Dubber ed., 2014); on the "presumption of guilt" in the Crime Control Model of the criminal process, see Herbert Packer, The Limits of the Criminal Sanction (1968).
25. See Tentative Draft No. 4, at 123 (Apr. 25, 1955): "Crimes of possession constitute an important category of offenses. But possession is neither a bodily movement nor an omission. The application of [§ 2.01(1)] must, therefore, be made clear."

sufficient period to have been able to terminate his possession."[26] In other words, possession is an act because acquisition is an act and because non-disposal is not an act, but an omission, and possession implies both acquisition and non-disposal.[27] That much, of course, is true; but it is also true of any status acquired after birth, yet no one would describe the *facts of being* overweight, forgetful, or bald as acts. At any rate, if it is the acquisition or the non-disposal they were after, the drafters might have done better to criminalize these acts directly. They did not, and neither have legislatures. It is possessing guns or drugs that is criminal, not buying them or failing to get rid of them.

So much for the actus. But what makes it reus? Perhaps its voluntariness. But that is unlikely; so many voluntary acts are perfectly benign, even saintly. No, what makes an actus reus is what makes conduct criminal: it must match the definition of a criminal offense. The act requirement is a sort of preliminary check that every defendant is subjected to before her conduct is matched against a criminal offense definition. If she fails the act test, the inquiry into criminal liability is over, and she is—procedurally speaking—acquitted.

§ 4.2 Mens Rea and Offense Elements

Let us assume, then, that the object of our inquiry into criminal liability, the defendant, has met the act requirement, in other words, that her behavior qualifies as an "act" in general. Now we must check whether her behavior satisfies the more specific requirements listed in the definition of a particular criminal offense. If there is a match between her act and the definition of an offense, we have prima facie, or facial, criminal liability. Facial criminal liability is the topic of the current chapter. Facial liability, however, is not quite the same as actual liability, or "guilt." Facial liability becomes guilt only if the defendant cannot

---

26. § 2.01(4); cf. N.Y. Penal Law § 15.00(2) (possession as *voluntary act*).
27. The failure to dispose presumably is criminal because we are all under an—undeclared—duty to get rid of things we are not supposed to possess; but of course that would be circular. Perhaps the duty is meant to attach to things that are (very? abnormally?) dangerous, but then would the duty not be too vague and too broad, besides not having been defined?

avail herself of a defense. We will cover defenses, called justifications and excuses, in Chapters 2 and 3, respectively.

In the Model Penal Code, as in modern criminal codes generally, the offenses defined in the Code's special part spell out the criminal law's general proscription of "conduct that unjustifiably and inexcusably inflicts or threatens substantial harm to individual or public interests."[28] Code drafters have several building blocks at their disposal to assemble the multitude of offenses into the edifice of criminal law with the necessary clarity and specificity to guide the behavior of potential offenders and of those persons (police officers, prosecutors, judges, jurors, etc.) charged with the assessment of potentially criminal acts and therefore, ultimately—under the Model Penal Code's approach—of potentially dangerous actors.[29] The Model Code calls these building blocks "offense elements." These offense elements are assembled into offenses, which in turn are put together (more or less systematically) to form the special part of a criminal code in general, and the Model Penal Code in particular.

(A) Element Types

In Model Penal Code language, there are three basic types of offense elements: conduct, attendant circumstance, and result (or CAR, for friends of mnemonic devices).[30] All offenses in the Code are constructed out of these elemental building blocks, which is not to say that each offense definition will include all offense element types. With these tools in hand, the drafting possibilities are limitless, or close enough to limitless for purposes of criminal law. An offense could have, but does not have to have, all three types of elements. It could include no attendant circumstances, or one, or as many as the drafters could think of. It might have a result element. Then again, it might not.

---

28. § 1.02(1)(a).

29. On the Model Penal Code as a Legal Process project aimed at assigning and then guiding discretion in the application of norms to the process participants best suited to exercise it, see § 2 above.

30. Note that "conduct" here is used in a slightly different, narrower, sense than it is in § 1.02(1)(a). In its broader, and looser sense, conduct refers to the entire offense definition. In its narrower sense, it applies only to one element of that definition.

Conduct is a different story. Given the act requirement, every offense must include at least a conduct element.[31] Although criminal law doctrine does not require this, offense definitions tend to consist of more than a bare conduct element. That is because without an attendant circumstance or a result, the offense may run afoul of the constitutional prohibition against vague criminal statutes (the principle of specificity, one of the components of the legality principle).[32]

A crime defined simply as "driving" for example would not give you a lot of notice of what exactly you are prohibited from doing and, even worse, would give police officers a lot of discretion to decide this question for you on the spot.[33] Even if "driving" was not too vague, it may well be too broad—unless the state could constitutionally prohibit anyone from driving anything anywhere.[34] "Driving under the influence of alcohol" is another story. The attendant circumstance of "under the influence of alcohol" narrows the reach of the conduct, "driving." The conduct itself might be further specified to include the driving of certain things, such as "motor vehicles." An offense such as "operating a motor vehicle under the influence of alcohol" would pass constitutional muster—it would not be too vague or too broad.[35]

We could further pinpoint our offense by throwing in a result element, such as "serious physical injury." This would transform our *conduct offense* (embellished with an attendant circumstance) into a *result offense*: "causing serious physical injury while operating a motor vehicle under the influence of alcohol." Note that only result offenses have a result element. This will be important later on, when we talk about causation.[36]

---

31. See § 1.13(5) (defining conduct as "an action or omission").
32. On vagueness, see Skilling v. United States, 561 U.S. 358 (2010) (honest services fraud); City of Chicago v. Morales, 527 U.S. 41 (1999) (gang loitering); Papachristou v. City of Jacksonville, 405 U.S. 156 (1972) (vagrancy); on specificity as an aspect of the principle of legality, see Markus D. Dubber & Tatjana Hörnle, Criminal Law: A Comparative Approach ch. 2 (2014).
33. On the two prongs of vagueness scrutiny (fair notice and arbitrary enforcement), see, e.g., Skilling v. United States, 561 U.S. 358, 402–03 (2010).
34. On the connection between vagueness and overbreadth, see, e.g., Markus D. Dubber & Tatjana Hörnle, Criminal Law: A Comparative Approach ch. 2.B (2014).
35. See, e.g., N.Y. Veh. & Traf. Law § 1192(3).
36. See § 5.1 below.

There is no need to worry about causation unless you are confronted with a result offense, which is a good thing as causation issues can be quite a headache.

It is important to keep in mind that the Code's trichotomy of offense elements is a means to an end, rather than an end in itself. That end is analytic clarity (for the sake of systematic and consistent control of discretion in the interpretation and application of legislative norms). Do not get bogged down trying to decide whether a particular word, or phrase, in an offense definition counts as one type of element or another. In most cases, it makes little difference whether you are dealing with conduct, attendant circumstance, or result. Here is the Commentaries' sensible (i.e., pragmatic) take on the point of distinguishing among the various element types:

> The "circumstances" of the offense refer to the objective situation that the law requires to exist, in addition to the defendant's act or any results that the act may cause. The elements of "nighttime" in burglary, "property of another" in theft, "female not his wife" in rape, and "dwelling" in arson are illustrations. "Conduct" refers to "breaking and entering" in burglary, "taking" in theft, "sexual intercourse" in rape and "burning" in arson. Results, of course, include "death" in homicide. *While these terms are not airtight categories, they have served as a helpful analytical device in the development of the Code.*[37]

So much for the three basic types of offense elements (or CAR). There is one more ingredient that is needed to transform a pile of offense definitions into the special part of a criminal code: mens rea or, as the Model Code drafters preferred to say, *culpability.*

(B) The Mens Rea Requirement
When it comes to mens rea, the Model Penal Code drafters insisted on two things. First, there is no such thing as mens rea. Second, mens

37. Commentaries § 5.01, at 301 n.9 (emphasis added).

rea is required. They rejected the common law's unitary concept of mens rea and replaced it with a scheme of "kinds of culpability" or mental states (§ 2.02(2)). These kinds of culpability are offense elements, too (§ 1.13(9)(b)). If you like, you can think of the offense elements we have encountered so far (conduct, circumstance, result) as *objective* offense elements, and of mental states as *subjective* offense elements. Just remember that, as we will see in a moment, this manner of speaking may be misleading insofar as at least one of the mental states hardly counts as subjective, and that at the very least the degree of subjectivity varies considerably from mental state to mental state (with purpose on one end and negligence—or strict liability, depending on your point of view—on the other). It is often said that a mental state is attached to, or accompanies, some offense element or other. That is fine, but here keep in mind that mental states, strictly speaking, are offense elements, too.

In fact, and this takes us to the Model Code's mens rea requirement, they are not just elements, but *material* elements. In § 2.02(1), the Code announces that

> [e]xcept as provided in Section 2.05, a person is not guilty of an offense unless he acted purposely, knowingly, recklessly or negligently, as the law may require, with respect to each material element of the offense.

This sounds quite emphatic, in fact just about as emphatic as the Code's endorsement of the act requirement. And as in the case of the act requirement, the Code's commitment to mens rea turns out to be much less categorical than it might seem at first glance. First, literally, even before the rule, comes a significant exception for all offenses covered in § 2.05. In that section, the Code deals not only with a newly minted category of non-criminal offenses it calls "violations," which gets all the attention (and this book is no exception), but also with a much more mundane but potentially far more significant class of offenses "defined by statutes other than the Code, insofar as a legislative purpose to impose absolute liability for such offenses or with respect to any material element thereof plainly appears."

Next, even for those offenses that fall within the scope of its mens rea requirement, the requirement only applies to "material elements." In other words, it does not—despite initial appearances—apply to all elements of an offense, but only to some (though the important ones). Offense elements, under the Code include "(i) such conduct or (ii) such attendant circumstances or (iii) such a result of conduct as (a) is included in the description of the forbidden conduct in the definition of the offense; or (b) establishes the required kind of culpability; or (c) negatives an excuse or justification for such conduct; or (d) negatives a defense under the statute of limitations; or (e) establishes jurisdiction or venue."[38] Material elements are those that do not "relate exclusively to the statute of limitations, jurisdiction, venue or to any other matter similarly unconnected with (i) the harm or evil, incident to conduct, sought to be prevented by the law defining the offense, or (ii) the existence of a justification or excuse for such conduct."[39] Leaving aside the tricky but interesting issue of mental states attaching to defenses ("justification or excuse"), which the Model Code addresses indirectly, and implicitly, through provisions on mistakes regarding various defense elements (was I really under imminent attack when I used force in supposed self-defense?) and the potentially wide, and vague, exception for elements "unconnected with ... the harm or evil, incident to conduct, sought to be prevented by the law defining the offense,"[40] the other nonmaterial elements include those related to procedural matters such as the statute of limitations as well as jurisdiction and venue. The latter exception, in particular, precluded the application of the Code's mens rea requirement to common provisions in federal criminal statutes that, in the absence of a single comprehensive treatment of jurisdictional issues in the federal criminal code's general part, include references to the supposed federal nature of the offense,

38. § 1.13(9).
39. § 1.13(10).
40. This somewhat odd ("evil"?) formulation appears, and does considerable work, in several places throughout the general part. See §§ 1.09(1)(c) & 1.10(1)(a) (double jeopardy), 2.02(6) (conditional purpose), 2.11 (consent), 2.12 (de minimis), 3.02 (necessity).

most notably to the offense's relevance to interstate commerce,[41] or perhaps the use of the mails.[42]

And finally, even if the mens rea requirement applies to the offense in question, and to a specific ("material") element of that offense, the scope—and the bite—of the requirement in the end depends on just how demanding it turns out to be (in other words, on just what the requirement requires). To this question we now turn. The answer, not surprisingly, will be: it depends, primarily on what "kind of culpability" is required.[43] Negligence, for instance, requires far less than, say, knowledge.[44]

Culpability comes in four varieties, or five, depending on who is counting: purpose, knowledge, recklessness, negligence, and strict liability. Strict liability is the fifth wheel here. The other "kinds of culpability" are often referred to as "mental states" or "states of mind." Strictly speaking, however, strict liability is not a mental state. It is a kind of liability, namely one that is "strict" precisely because it pays no attention to mental state. For purposes of strict liability, it does not matter

41. Commentaries § 1.13, at 210–11. In the absence of a general federal police power, federal criminal law—like all exercises of federal power—is limited to those subjects enumerated in the federal constitution, including the power to regulate interstate commerce. See, e.g., 18 U.S.C. § 922(g)(3) ("It shall be unlawful for any person...who is an unlawful user of or addicted to any controlled substance...to possess in or affecting commerce, any firearm or ammunition; or to receive any firearm or ammunition which has been shipped or transported in interstate or foreign commerce.").

42. So the Unabomber, Ted Kaczynski, who killed and injured several people in the 1980s and 1990s, committed the federal crime of "Transportation of an Explosive with Intent to Kill or Injure" because he "knowingly did transport and attempt to transport, and willfully did cause to be transported, in interstate commerce an explosive with the knowledge and intent that it would be used to kill, injure and intimidate an individual, and unlawfully to damage and destroy real and personal property." Indictment, United States v. Kaczynski, No. S–CR–S–96–259 (E.D. Cal. June 18, 1996) (citing 18 U.S.C. § 844(d)); see also id. ("Mailing an Explosive Device with Intent to Kill or Injure," 18 U.S.C. § 1716).

43. And, to a lesser extent, on the offense element type to which it is attached.

44. It is worth thinking about whether, under the Model Code's treatmentist approach, it is helpful to think of § 2.02(1) as setting out a mens rea requirement in the sense of a proto-constitutional norm designed to safeguard the rights of defendants. It may make more sense to think of it as setting the common analytic framework for an individualized diagnosis of criminal dangerousness.

whether the defendant had a mental state of any kind—which is not to say that he did not, just that it does not matter whether he did or not.

True, negligence also does not quite fit in with the others. That is because negligence really is not quite a mental state either. It is the *absence* of a mental state: to act negligently means not being aware of a risk of harm. But unlike strict liability, negligence at least makes some reference to a mental state—awareness—even if only in absentia. To punish negligence is to punish this absence; it is to say that the defendant *should have* been aware, even though he was not. It is his *failure* to recognize that his behavior might cause harm that renders him criminally liable.

In sum, we have three types of (objective) offense elements, and four states of mind. Now the Model Code drafters decided that each element of an offense could have attached to it a different state of mind, or one and the same. And if none of the four mental states fit the bill, there was strict liability—at least for minor ("non-criminal") offenses called "violations."

The Code drafters then went on to define the various kinds of culpability differently, depending on the type of element to which they were attached. So "purposeful" meant one thing when it accompanied a conduct or a result element, and quite another when it was attached to an attendant circumstance. "Knowingly" was one thing for conduct and an attendant circumstance, and another for a result element. The definitions of "reckless" and "negligent" were less differentiated, so undifferentiated in fact that it was unclear whether they were defined at all when they accompanied a conduct element, as opposed to an attendant circumstance or a result.[45]

Much classroom time is spent each year on the tedious, and ultimately fruitless, task of making sense of the Code's complicated taxonomy of elements and mental states, and then trying to apply it to particular offenses. (Is this a conduct element? A result? Or perhaps

---

45. See Paul H. Robinson & Jane A. Grall, Element Analysis in Defining Criminal Liability, 35 Stan. L. Rev. 681 (1983), for an in-depth exploration of this point, and the Code's mens rea scheme in general.

an attendant circumstance?) One is much better off to recognize that the Code drafters might have lost the forest for the trees here.

Let us take a step back, then, in the Code's pragmatic spirit and look at the big picture, before zooming in on the details of the Code's mens rea system. The Code drafters were eager to do away with what they saw as the common law's hopelessly confused doctrine of mens rea. They viewed that doctrine as the root of all—certainly most—evil in traditional Anglo-American criminal law. They were not the only ones, nor were they the first, to become exasperated with mens rea. Here is a fairly typical, and roughly contemporaneous, complaint about the looseness—and uselessness—of a unitary concept of mens rea, taken from Herbert Packer's classic *The Limits of the Criminal Sanction*:

> When we speak of Arthur's having the *mens rea* of murder, we may mean any one or more of the following things: that he intended to kill Victor; or that he was aware of the risk of his killing Victor but went ahead and shot him anyhow; or (more dubiously) that he ought to have known but did not that there was a substantial risk of his killing Victor or that he knew it was wrong to kill a fellow human being, or that he ought to have known it; or that he did not really think that Victor was trying to kill him; or that he did think that, but only a fool would have thought it; or that he was not drunk to the point of unconsciousness when he killed Victor; or that even though he was emotionally disturbed he was not grossly psychotic, etc., etc.[46]

So great was the Code drafters' exasperation with the traditional mens rea concept (or cluster of concepts) that they banned it from the realm of criminal law. Since then it is considered bad taste to speak of mens rea, or its cousin "intent," in the context of the Model Penal

---

46. Herbert L. Packer, The Limits of the Criminal Sanction 104–05 (1968). By the time the Model Code drafters and their contemporaries got into the act, railing against the common law's notion of mens rea already had a long, and distinguished, tradition. See, e.g., James Fitzjames Stephen's opinion in R. v. Tolson, 23 Q.B.D. 168, 185–86 (1889). For a brief historical account of common law mens rea, see Francis B. Sayre, Mens Rea, 45 Harv. L. Rev. 974 (1932).

Code. (I do not see any reason to adhere to this taboo—talking about criminal law without reference to intent makes about as much sense as talking about criminal law without mentioning punishment, incidentally another concept the drafters turned into a taboo.[47])

The Code drafters' attempt to overhaul the law of mens rea was a great success. The Code's all new, all differentiated, mens rea scheme was widely hailed as a significant advance, and rightly so. The mens rea section, § 2.02, is the heart of the Model Penal Code. For that reason alone it deserves careful attention. It is also the single most influential section in the Code, in MPC and non-MPC jurisdictions alike.

The drafters' basic claim, also not new, was that traditional mens rea jurisprudence was mistaken in assuming that each offense had only a single mens rea requirement and, even more generally, that there was only one concept of mens rea *in the entire criminal law*. At common law, there was mens rea, period. Criminal liability turned on two questions: first, was there actus reus?, and, second, was there mens rea?[48] In other words, did the defendant engage in the proscribed conduct as defined?, and, did he have the requisite "depravity of the will,"[49] "diabolic malignity,"[50] "abandoned" or "bad heart,"[51] "heart regardless of social duty, and fatally bent on mischief,"[52] "wicked heart,"[53] "mind grievously depraved,"[54] or "mischievous vindictive spirit"[55]?

By contrast, the Code drafters decided not only that different offenses had different mens rea requirements (rejecting the notion

47. See Markus D. Dubber, Penal Panopticon: The Idea of a Modern Model Penal Code, 4 Buff. Crim. L. Rev. 53, 70–73 (2000); on this point, see also Henry M. Hart, Jr., The Aims of the Criminal Law, 23 Law & Contemp. Probs. 401, 405 (1958) ("'treatment' has become a fashionable euphemism for the older, ugly word").
48. On the recognition of justification and excuse in the common law scheme, see § 3.2 above.
49. 4 William Blackstone, Commentaries on the Laws of England 21 (1769).
50. General Summary of Crimes, and Their Punishments, in 2 Laws of the Commonwealth of Pennsylvania 558, 568 (1810)
51. 4 William Blackstone, Commentaries on the Laws of England 200 (1769).
52. General Summary of Crimes, and Their Punishments, in 2 Laws of the Commonwealth of Pennsylvania 558, 562, 573 (1810).
53. Id. at 562.
54. Id.
55. Id. at 570.

of a single concept of mens rea for all of criminal law), but also that *individual offenses* might have different mens rea requirements attached to their constitutive parts, the aforementioned "elements." And so the Code's "element analysis" of mens rea was born to replace the "offense analysis" of the common law.

That is when things got complicated. The price of lucidity was complexity, and of differentiation, confusion. The common law had made do with two units of analysis: mens rea and actus reus. The Code recognized seven, and that is not even counting strict (mens-rea-less) liability. The quartet "purpose, knowledge, recklessness, and negligence" took the place of mens rea, and the trio "conduct, attendant circumstance, and result," that of actus reus.

If every element of every offense—rather than every offense—can have its very own mental state, an obvious problem arises: How can one tell which mental state attaches to which offense element? The simplest solution would be to specify the required mental states in the offense definition. However, this would lead to offense definitions so filled with mental state requirements that the offense elements would be difficult to make out, sacrificing notice, and presumably guidance, for the sake of specificity. So adultery, for instance, might become something like "knowingly engaging in an act one knows to constitute sexual intercourse with another whom one knows to be a person at a time when one is reckless with regard to one's having a spouse and with regard to that spouse's being alive, or when one is virtually certain that the other person has a spouse and where he should have been aware of a substantial likelihood that this spouse is alive."[56]

(C) Rules of Interpretation

To avoid confounding concoctions of this sort the Code drafters set up rules of statutory interpretation that allowed careful readers of criminal codes—including courts and law students—to match mental states to offense elements when confronted with offense definitions

---

56. Loosely based on N.Y. Penal Law § 255.17 ("engag[ing] in sexual intercourse with another person at a time when he has a living spouse, or the other person has a living spouse").

containing elements unaccompanied by mental states. This can be a cumbersome exercise.[57] Unfortunately, it is also a necessary evil; without having figured out precisely what the elements of an offense are and what mental state, if any, attaches to each, we cannot proceed to the real task: determining whether the defendant's behavior matches the definition of that offense, and therefore qualifies for facial liability—the topic of the present chapter.[58]

Rule 1. Recklessness Default (absence means presence I):[59] If the offense definition does not identify the mental state accompanying an offense element, apply recklessness. Example: to commit adultery in New York, that is, "engage in sexual intercourse with another person at a time when he has a living spouse, or the other person has a living spouse," one would have to have been at least reckless about the fact that the other person was married at the time. In other words, the relevant element of the offense—once the mental state is filled in by implication—would read "at a time when he was reckless regarding the possibility that the other person has a living spouse." And, as recklessness in the Model Code means conscious disregard of a substantial and unjustifiable risk that the offense element exists,[60] the offense element in full bloom reads something like this: "at a time when he consciously disregarded a substantial and unjustifiable risk that the other person has a living spouse."

It is important not to confuse this rule of statutory interpretation with a finding of fact. Rule 1 simply provides that a mental state of recklessness should be read into an offense definition in certain cases. It does not help you determine whether the defendant actually acted with that mental state. That is a substantive question of liability, not a preliminary question of interpretation.

---

57. Official Draft and Explanatory Notes 23 (1962) ("aid to drafting the definitions of specific crimes").

58. Note that in early drafts of the Code, the concept of behavior played a central role in the Code's analytic scheme. Notably, "criminal behavior" was defined as "behavior of such a kind, occurring under such circumstances and threatening or causing such results that it presents all the elements required to establish it to be a crime." Tentative Draft No. 1, § 2.01(3), at 9 (May 1, 1953).

59. § 2.02(3).

60. § 2.02(2)(c).

Another way of making this point is to think of the Model Penal Code's rules of interpretation as interpretive presumptions, not evidentiary ones. The Code's criminal possession provisions feature several evidentiary presumptions, as is common in the criminal law of possession. For instance, § 5.06(2) establishes a presumption, under certain circumstances, *from* the possession of a firearm *to* the purpose to employ it criminally.[61] The presumption in § 5.06(3) points the other way, *from* the presence of "a weapon or other instrument of crime" in a car *to* its possession by one or more of the car's occupants.

Rule 1, by contrast, can be seen as the Model Code drafters' attempt to capture and concretize in their terms the long-standing but vague common law interpretive presumption of mens rea (or intent).[62] In fact, in some jurisdictions (and in some cases) this presumption has been read to require proof of something akin to recklessness, at least absent an expression of contrary legislative intent, most obviously through the inclusion of a different mental state requirement.[63]

Rule 2. One-for-All (absence means presence II):[64] If the offense definition does not identify the mental state accompanying an offense element, but lists a mental state with respect to another element, apply that mental state, unless it is clear from the text of the statute that this is not what the legislature intended (or, more precisely, "unless a contrary purpose plainly appears").[65] Example: in a well-known Supreme Court case, *Morissette v. United States*,[66] the defendant was convicted of

---

61. §§ 5.06(2) ("Presumption of Criminal Purpose from Possession of Weapon") & 5.06(3) ("Presumptions as to Possession of Criminal Instruments in Automobiles"); on presumptions in possession criminal law, see Markus D. Dubber, Policing Possession: The War on Crime and the End of Criminal Law, 91 J. Crim. L. & Criminology 829 (2002).

62. Official Draft and Explanatory Notes 23 (1962) ("rough correspondence between this provision and the common law requirement of 'general intent' "); Commentaries § 2.02, at 244.

63. See, e.g., R. v. Buzzanga, 25 O.R. (2d) 705, 49 C.C.C. (2d) 369 (Ont. Ct. App. 1979).

64. § 2.02(4). Kenneth Simons calls this the "travel rule." Kenneth W. Simons, Should the Model Penal Code's Mens Rea Provisions Be Amended?, 1 Ohio St. J. Crim. L. 179 (2003).

65. See, e.g., State v. Lozier, 101 Ohio St. 3d 161, 803 N.E.2d 770 (2004); People v. M&H Used Auto Parts & Cars, Inc., 22 A.D.3d 135, 799 N.Y.S.2d 784 (2005).

66. 342 U.S. 246 (1952).

having committed the following offense: "Whoever embezzles, steals, purloins, or knowingly converts government property is punishable by fine and imprisonment." Does the mental state "knowingly" apply (1) only to "converts," or (2) to "government property" as well? Under the Model Code's Rule 2, the answer is (2). There is no reason to believe that whoever drafted the offense definition meant to confine the reach of "knowingly" to its immediate successor, "converts." That is also what the Supreme Court decided, though by a far more circuitous route—but, of course, the Model Penal Code was not finished until ten years later.[67] Not that the Court would have been under any obligation to consult the Model Code, even if it had been around at the time. The Court might have turned to the Code for advice, or at least inspiration, and thereby saved itself a lot of trouble. But the Model Code itself is not binding on the Supreme Court, nor for that matter on any other court. *Morissette* dealt with a federal statute. And, as we know by now, the federal criminal code, Title 18 of the United States Code, is among those American criminal codes that have remained virtually untouched by the Model Code's influence. Although even in jurisdictions that have adopted some version of some parts of the Model Penal Code, its authority is at best persuasive.

Rule 2 also includes an exception to itself (or, if you like, a way to rebut the interpretive presumption it establishes): do not apply one mental state across the board if a "contrary purpose plainly appears." So Rule 2 might not apply to the *Morissette* statute if that statute instead had read: "Whoever knowingly converts, or embezzles, steals, or purloins government property is punishable by fine and imprisonment." And it certainly would not have applied to this statute: "Whoever embezzles, steals, purloins, or knowingly converts government property is punishable by fine and imprisonment. Ignorance of the fact that the property in question is government property is immaterial."

Rule 3. Strict Liability (absence means absence, for violations).[68] If the offense definition does not identify the mental state accompanying

---

67. This did not stop Hart from mocking the Court's opinion in the case, to the point of drafting an alternative opinion by Justice Tenthjudge. See Henry M. Hart, Jr., The Aims of the Criminal Law, 23 Law & Contemp. Probs. 401, 431 n.70 (1958).
68. § 2.05.

an offense element, it means what it says: no mental state applies. Example: Rule 3 would read the New York adultery statute as a strict liability offense through and through.[69] For instance, it would not matter whether one had known, or even suspected, that "the other person has a living spouse."[70]

Note, however, that the Code would prevent this reading of our adultery statute for a different reason: it limits strict liability to a class of non-criminal offenses called "violations."[71] An offense qualifies as a violation if it is identified as such or if it is punishable only by fine, forfeiture, or some other civil penalty (such as disbarment).[72] What counts is the penalty threatened in the Code, not that actually sought or imposed in a case. (Note that there are no limits on the amount of the fine.[73]) Rule 3 thus would not apply to adultery because adultery is, at least in New York, a misdemeanor.[74] (As a Class B misdemeanor, it is punishable by imprisonment of up to three months.[75])

Unlike the Model Penal Code, many codes do not limit the application of the "no (mental state) means no" rule to minor (never mind to "non-criminal") offenses. As a result, there is no interpretative rule that bars courts from reading even the most serious crimes as strict liability offenses. Among the most prominent examples of this practice are strict liability drug possession felonies that impose severe punishments, up to and including life imprisonment without the possibility of parole, in the absence of mental state requirements with respect to such

---

69. In fact, adultery was one of the classic strict liability offenses of the common law. See, e.g., Commonwealth v. Thompson, 6 Allen 591 (Mass. 1863) (Thompson I); Commonwealth v. Thompson, 11 Allen 23 (Mass. 1865) (Thompson II).

70. For a classic set of judicial opinions pondering strict liability and the presumption of mens rea in a bigamy case, see R. v. Tolson, 23 Q.B.D. 168 (1889).

71. Actually, it also allows strict liability for other, criminal, offenses, as long as they are defined outside the criminal code and it is clear that the legislature wanted to create a strict liability offense. § 2.05(1)(b).

72. § 1.04(5).

73. For a comparative analysis of the irrelevance of fines in American criminal law, see Markus D. Dubber & Tatjana Hörnle, Criminal Law: A Comparative Approach ch. 1 (2014).

74. N.Y. Penal Law § 255.17 (Class B misdemeanor).

75. N.Y. Penal Law § 70.15(2) (sentences of imprisonment for misdemeanors and violations).

elements as the fact of possession, or the nature and the weight of the drug possessed.[76]

At any rate, the same caveat that applies to the use of Rule 2 (one-for-all) in *Morissette* also applies here. The Model Code's rules of interpretation do not control the interpretation of other codes—they apply only to the Code itself. That is not to say that courts will not look to them for inspiration, but they do not have to follow them, or pay any attention to them, for that matter. The New York adultery statute differs from *Morissette* in that the New York Penal Law, unlike the federal criminal code, was fundamentally revised on the basis of the Model Penal Code. But New York did not adopt the Model Code wholesale. The drafters picked and chose, and often changed what they chose. And among the Code provisions they chose to change was Rule 3. The New York Penal Law does contain a general presumption against strict liability, but it does not limit strict liability to non-criminal offenses and, in fact, expressly recognizes strict liability crimes, without limitation, provided the statute clearly shows that the legislature meant to create a strict liability crime.[77]

A final note on strict liability and statutory interpretation. The Code's move from offense analysis to element analysis, its shift of focus from the offense to its constituent elements, meant not only that different elements could have different mental states attached to them, but that now different elements also could have, or *not* have, a mental state attached to them. Strict liability, the *absence* of mens rea also became a characteristic of elements, rather than of offenses. Strictly speaking, therefore, in Code-speak there is no such thing as a "strict liability offense"; there are only strict liability elements.

So much for rules of interpretation. Here is a chart that shows them all (Chart 1):

---

76. See, e.g., Harmelin v. Michigan, 501 U.S. 957 (1991) (life without parole for simple possession); see generally Markus D. Dubber, Policing Possession: The War on Crime and the End of Criminal Law, 91 J. Crim. L. & Criminology 829 (2002).
77. N.Y. Penal Law § 15.15(2). The New York drafters dropped the Code's distinction between offenses defined in the Code and those defined elsewhere. They also changed Rule 1: the default mental state is negligence, not recklessness. Id. ("mental culpability" as default); § 15.00(6) ("culpable mental state" defined as requiring at least proof of "criminal negligence"). Only Rule 2 remained pretty much intact. Id. § 15.15(1).

Chart 1 RULES OF INTERPRETATION (MENS REA)
MODEL PENAL CODE

Rule 1	Recklessness Default (absence means presence I)
Rule 2	One-for-All (absence means presence II)
Rule 3	Strict Liability (absence means absence, for violations)

(D) Modes of Culpability

Let us assume we have managed to figure out, with the help of our three rules (and perhaps a bit of luck), what the offense definitions in our criminal code's special part look like, fully expanded, with gaps and ambiguities filled in as needed, keeping in mind that absence can, but need not, mean presence, at least when it comes to mens rea requirements. Now we can proceed to check whether the defendant's behavior matches the definition of an offense, or perhaps more than one. Or can we?

Not quite. For, as noted above, the Model Code drafters were not content to attach—or not attach—mental states to each and every element of an offense (as opposed to each offense as a whole). They also defined each mental state differently, depending on which type of element it accompanies. We are still at the preliminary, pre-matching, stage. But at least we are no longer just coloring in the outlines of offense definitions. We are now beginning to figure out what these offense definitions, or at least whatever mental state requirements they may contain, *mean*.

Chart 2 shows the definitions, arranged by type of offense element, taken from § 2.02(2).[78]

The Model Code drafters may have gotten a little carried away here in their drive for analytic precision. It is best not to get hung up on the fine points of the distinctions within the definition of a given mental

78. For a more detailed discussion of this topic and a more detailed chart, see Paul H. Robinson & Jane A. Grall, Element Analysis in Defining Criminal Liability, 35 Stan. L. Rev. 681, 697 (1983).

Chart 2 MODES OF CULPABILITY, BY OFFENSE ELEMENT
MODEL PENAL CODE[1]

	Conduct	Attendant Circumstance	Result
Purpose	conscious object	awareness, belief, hope	conscious object
Knowledge	awareness	awareness	awareness of practical certainty
Recklessness	[not defined]	conscious disregard of substantial & unjustifiable risk[2]	conscious disregard of substantial & unjustifiable risk
Negligence	[not defined]	failure to perceive substantial & unjustifiable risk[3]	failure to perceive substantial & unjustifiable risk

[1] § 2.02(2).
[2] The Code specifies that the "risk must be of such a nature and degree" that conscious disregard of the risk constitutes "a gross deviation from the standard of conduct that a law-abiding person would observe in the actor's situation." § 2.02(2)(c).
[3] The failure to perceive the risk must constitute "a gross deviation from the standard of care that a reasonable person would observe in the actor's situation." § 2.02(2)(d). On the (ir)relevance of the distinction between the Model Code's definition of the nature of the risk at stake in negligence and recklessness, see § 4.2(D)(iv) below.

state. (The drafters of criminal codes based on the MPC did not dwell on them either, as we will see shortly.[79]) The distinctions *among* the mental states are tough enough to keep track of.

One of the problems with taking the drafters too seriously here is that it is hard to classify the elements of living, breathing offenses by type. In the words of the drafters themselves: "[t]he distinction between conduct and attendant circumstance or result is not always a bright one...."[80] The distinction often is difficult to draw in the Model Code itself.[81] And it does not get any brighter when one moves into

79. See, e.g., N.Y. Penal Law § 15.05.
80. Commentaries § 2.02, at 240.
81. Try these questions: What is "conduct" in homicide (§ 210.1)? And "attendant circumstance"? And "result"? How about in causing suicide (§ 210.5(1))? In burglary (§ 221.1)?

real criminal law, bustling with awkward offense definitions that—
to put it mildly—were not put together by drafters eager to accommodate the Model Code's classification of offense element types.[82] But
these very distinctions of course take on crucial significance as soon as
the definition of a mental state varies with the type of offense element
it happens to accompany.

Still, the above chart was not included just for completeness's
sake. It is helpful to get a sense of what the Code drafters were after
when they set up their taxonomy of culpability. And with a little common sense, much of the chart turns out to make good sense. We will
use the simplified chart in the New York Penal Law for comparison
(Chart 3).[83] (At its best, the New York code is a less persnickety version
of the MPC.) Inevitably this will lead us to the more interesting topic,
the distinctions among the various mental states, rather than those
within each.[84]

(i) *Purpose.* Starting from the top, with purpose, it is easy to see that
what is distinctive about this mental state is the concept of "conscious
object" (or "objective," in the New York Penal Law). This point can be
obscured if one pays too much attention to the Model Code's definition
of purpose with respect to attendant circumstances. The Model Code
drafters themselves did not go out of their way to motivate the need for
this custom-made definition. (Perhaps not surprisingly, the New York
Penal Law eliminated it altogether.) The Model Code drafters, however, seemed more interested in pointing out that, when it came to
attendant circumstances rather than conduct or result, purpose did not
differ significantly from knowledge. In fact, early drafts simply defined

82. Here is the example used in the Commentaries, a relatively tame federal statute: "A
   person is guilty of an offense if, by fire or explosion, he (1) damages a public facility; or
   (2) damages substantially a building or a public structure." Commentaries § 2.02, at 240.
83. N.Y. Penal Law § 15.05. On the relationship between the Model Penal Code
   and the New York Penal Law, and New York criminal law in general, see Markus
   D. Dubber, New York Criminal Law: Cases & Materials (2008). For a (homicide) case
   showing the New York mens rea scheme in action, see People v. Baker, 4 A.D.3d 606,
   771 N.Y.S.2d 607 (2004).
84. For a common law precursor of the Code's culpability scheme, balanced precariously
   on the pin of "intention," see Regina v. Faulkner, 13 Cox Crim. Cas. 550, 557 (1877)
   (opinion of Fitzgerald, J.).

Chart 3 MODES OF CULPABILITY, BY OFFENSE ELEMENT
NEW YORK PENAL LAW[1]

	Conduct	Attendant Circumstance	Result
Purpose[2]	conscious objective	[not defined]	conscious objective
Knowledge	awareness	awareness	[not defined]
Recklessness	[not defined]	awareness & conscious disregard of substantial & unjustifiable risk[3]	awareness & conscious disregard of substantial & unjustifiable risk
Negligence	[not defined]	failure to perceive substantial & unjustifiable risk[4]	failure to perceive substantial & unjustifiable risk

[1] N.Y. Penal Law § 15.05.
[2] Actually, the New York Penal Law calls purpose "intention," and negligence "criminal negligence."
[3] The conscious disregard of the risk constitutes "a gross deviation from the standard of conduct that a reasonable person would observe in the situation."
[4] The failure to perceive the risk constitutes "a gross deviation from the standard of care that a reasonable person would observe in the situation."

purpose as to attendant circumstances as "know[ledge] of the existence of such circumstances."[85]

In fact, as we will see in just a moment, the Model Code drafters were refreshingly open about the limited significance of the distinction between the mental states of purpose and knowledge in general, even as they defined that very distinction in considerable detail.[86] In other words, whatever distinction one might draw between the definitions of purpose and knowledge as to attendant circumstances, it would be no more relevant than the difference between the definitions of purpose and knowledge as to any other offense element type.

85. Tentative Draft No. 4, § 2.02(2)(a)(2), at 12 (Apr. 25, 1955).
86. See Tentative Draft No. 4, at 124 (Apr. 25, 1955).

(ii) *Knowledge.* Knowledge is next. Here the watchword is *awareness.* This works well enough for conduct and attendant circumstances. I can be aware (or not) that I am doing something and that I am doing something under certain conditions, say when it is dark outside. Result is a little different. Assuming that I am not blessed (or cursed) with prescience, it makes no sense to say that I *know* that what I am doing will lead to a particular result. That is why the Model Code drafters defined knowledge regarding result not simply as awareness, but as awareness of a practical certainty, that is to say, the closest we ordinary mortals can come to knowing anything about the future. (Once again, the New York Penal Law drafters avoided this difficulty by not defining knowledge as to result at all.)

The distinction between purpose and knowledge, then, is that between conscious object(ive) and awareness. It is important to get this distinction straight. It is also important to realize that it makes little difference in the criminal law, generally speaking. As we saw earlier, the default mental state in the Model Code is recklessness. This means that the distinction between purpose and knowledge generally does not come up, as recklessness is enough for liability. What is more, most offenses that require more than recklessness with respect to any of their elements do not require purpose, but knowledge. For example, murder generally requires only proof of knowledge that one was causing the death of another person.[87]

Still there are some offenses that do require purpose, rather than "mere" knowledge.[88] The most frequently cited, and least frequent, example is treason, which requires the doing of something with the purpose of aiding the enemy.[89] Purpose also plays an important role

---

87. See § 210.1.
88. Note that the mental states in the Model Code are neatly stacked, so that proof of a "higher" mental state implies proof of any and all "lower" ones. In other words, proof of purpose implies proof of "mere" knowledge, recklessness, and negligence, and so on down the line. Needless to say, proof of any mental state, including negligence, implies proof of none whatever, that is, strict liability. The prosecution is always free to go beyond the call of duty and establish a "higher" mental state than is required by statute. § 2.02(5).
89. See Haupt v. United States, 330 U.S. 631, 641 (1947).

in the Model Penal Code's elaborate scheme of inchoate offenses.[90] By contrast, in the Code's convoluted provision on causation, the distinction between purpose and knowledge proved more difficult—or less important—to sustain.[91]

(iii) *Recklessness.* Considerably more significant than the distinction between purpose and knowledge is that between knowledge and recklessness. Unlike in the case of purpose or knowledge, the Model Code drafters provided only one definition of recklessness (as they did of negligence) for all types of offense elements. So one recklessness fits all—or nearly all, for the Code drafters did not provide a definition of recklessness (or negligence) for conduct. That is probably a good thing, not only because it makes it easy to see the gist of recklessness. It would also have been difficult to figure out just what it would mean to recklessly (or negligently) engage in conduct. Here mens rea bumps up against actus reus. As behavior is not conduct unless it is an act, and an act is not criminal unless it is voluntary, what would a voluntary yet reckless or negligent act look like? To pass the voluntariness prong of the act requirement, the defendant's behavior would have to be—or rather, under the Model Code's indirect approach to voluntariness as the absence of involuntariness, it would have not not to be—"a product of the effort or the determination of the actor, either conscious or habitual."[92] But how could someone engage in an act that is voluntary (or not involuntary) in this sense, and yet engage in it recklessly or negligently, as these mental states are defined in the Model Code? Recall that to act recklessly means to consciously disregard the risk that something is the case, and to act negligently is to fail to even perceive that risk. If all I am aware of is the risk that I *might be engaging* in some sort of conduct, it would be odd to classify that conduct as involving a voluntary act. And that goes double if I am unaware of even the possibility that I might be doing something, as in the case of negligence. In sum, if I am not actually aware of the fact (not the possibility) that I am engaging in one type of conduct, rather than another or none at all, it is

90. See § 5.2 below.
91. See § 2.03(2). See § 5.1 below.
92. § 2.01(2)(d).

hard to see how I can be said to engage in it voluntarily. Put differently, it would appear that nothing less than knowledge (as defined by the Code drafters) would do for conduct, as a matter of actus reus, rather than of mens rea.

The line between knowledge and recklessness is important for several reasons. Most obvious, it is the line that separates many more serious crimes from less serious ones. The prime example is, once again, homicide. In the Model Code scheme of things, the main line between murder and manslaughter is that between knowledge and recklessness. Murder is knowingly (or purposely) causing another's death; manslaughter is recklessly doing the same.[93]

The knowledge/recklessness distinction also tracks that between specific and general intent, which in turns affects the availability of certain defenses. Strictly speaking, the distinction between specific and general intent is as foreign to the world of the Model Penal Code as is the concept of intent itself. The point of the Code's taxonomy of mental states, after all, was to do away with confused mens rea concepts, intent chief among them (along with wilfulness, malice, scienter, and all the rest). But, despite the Code drafters' best efforts, talk of specific and general intent survives in American courtrooms and criminal codes (and criminal law classes), as does talk of intent and intention. And some of the substance of the distinction between the two types of intent persists even in the Code itself, as we will see

---

93. It is slightly more complicated than that. There is a reckless form of murder (though one that requires a certain elevated—"gross," "extreme," "aggravated," etc.—recklessness), § 210.2(1)(b); and there is an intentional (so-called "voluntary") form of manslaughter, § 210.3(1)(b). The former is the closest thing to the common law "felony murder" rule in the Code; the latter is the Code's version of the common law "provocation" defense to murder (see § 16 below). The felony murder rule, or at least one of its many versions, imposed murder liability on anyone who caused the death of another person in the course of a felony (e.g., a robbery), without requiring proof of any mental state with respect to the resulting death. See generally Guyora Binder, Felony Murder (2012). The Model Code drafters rejected this doctrine as a blatant violation of the Code's mens rea requirement, which limited strict liability to non-criminal offenses punishable at most by fine. See § 2.02(1) ("Except as provided in Section 2.05 [dealing with non-criminal offenses, or "violations"], a person is not guilty of an offense unless he acted purposely, knowingly, recklessly or negligently, as the law may require, with respect to each material element of the offense.").

when we get to the intoxication "defense." It turns out that the Code retains, in substance though not in form, the traditional—and somewhat counterintuitive—rule that intoxication is a defense only to specific intent crimes, but not to general intent (and generally *less* serious) ones—by allowing for evidence of intoxication to negative the mental elements of purpose and knowledge, but not recklessness or negligence.[94] Similarly, recall that the drafters insisted that their recklessness default rule of statutory interpretation (our Rule 1 above) not only fought definitional clutter, but also reflected the "general intent" requirement of the common law, such as it was, namely, as a sort of general presumption of mens rea, or intent, at least for common law crimes (i.e., those defined by the courts, rather than by statute) and in the absence of contrary legislative intent.[95]

As the distinction between specific and general intent, and the concept of intent that underlies it, continue to matter, even in the Code, it is useful to see how intent-talk maps onto Model-Penal-Code-talk. This diagram provides an overview of the relationship (Chart 4):

Chart 4 MODES OF CULPABILITY (MPC) VS. INTENT (COMMON LAW)

	Model Penal Code			
	Purpose	*Knowledge*	*Recklessness*	*Negligence*
Common Law 1[1]	Intent ⋯⋯⋯⋯⋯⋯⋯⋯⋯⋯⋯⋯⋯⋯⋯⋯⋯⋯⋯⋯⋯⋯			Criminal Negligence ⋯
	Specific ⋯	General	⋯⋯⋯⋯⋯⋯⋯⋯	
Common Law 2[2]	Intent ⋯⋯⋯⋯⋯⋯⋯⋯⋯⋯⋯⋯⋯⋯⋯⋯⋯⋯⋯⋯⋯⋯⋯⋯⋯⋯⋯⋯⋯			
	Specific ⋯⋯⋯⋯⋯⋯⋯⋯⋯⋯		General ⋯⋯⋯⋯⋯⋯⋯	

[1] Based on La. Crim. Code §§ 10–12 (1942) (pre-MPC codification).
[2] Based on State v. Cameron, 104 N.J. 42 (1986) (interpreting MPC-based provision).

94. See § 4.3(A) below.
95. § 4.2(C) above.

The Model Code drafters were right. Intent, specific and general, meant many things to many people—it still does. This chart makes no attempt to capture all, or even most, varieties of intent-talk. (For example, it ignores secondary intent offenses, such as assault with intent to kill, which are often called specific intent crimes as well.) It does show two of the more common, and recent, varieties: one based on the pre-MPC Louisiana criminal code, the other on a post-MPC New Jersey case.[96] The Model Code drafters of course would not have endorsed either, having sworn off intent-talk entirely. Still, if pressed, they might have acknowledged that both schemes were half right, or at least half not wrong. In differentiating between intent and negligence, the common law scheme no. 1 reflects the drafters' claim that their recklessness default rule codified the common law requirement of mens rea, that is to say, of intent, or scienter. By contrast, classifying negligence—which implies the *absence* of awareness—as a form of intent (or scienter), as in the second scheme, does not sound quite right. Common law scheme no. 2, however, has the advantage of drawing the line between specific and general intent at recklessness, rather than at knowledge. Although the common law certainly would provide support for limiting specific intent to purpose (as it would for a host of definitions of intent), expanding it to include knowledge fits better with the Model Code drafters' attempt to capture the common law's limitation of the intoxication defense to specific intent offenses. (Recall that intoxication under the Model Code may disprove knowledge (and purpose), but not recklessness (or negligence).)

Now that we have an idea of why the distinction between knowledge and recklessness matters—and how it may or may not relate to that between specific and general intent—let us see what that distinction is. Here we might differentiate between two axes of comparison, which I will call *attitude* and *probability*.[97] Knowledge and recklessness differ most clearly along the probabilistic axis. Knowledge requires certainty

96. For a recent case documenting and illustrating the continuing struggle to draw the distinction between general and specific intent, see United States v. Zunie, 444 F.3d 1230 (10th Cir. 2006).
97. If you like, you can also call them "subjective" and "objective," though these terms tend to come with a lot of excess baggage; plus probability also has a subjective aspect, if the actor's awareness of (or attitude toward) the risk in question makes a difference.

(or practical certainty, when it comes to result). Recklessness requires something less than 100 percent certainty, namely a substantial risk.[98] What is "substantial" the Code drafters did not say. They left this decision up to the jury[99] (or the judge, in a bench trial).[100] To illustrate, the difference between murder and (involuntary) manslaughter then is the difference between doing something one knows *will* cause the death of another person and doing something one knows *might* lead to that result.

It is clear enough why knowledge would result in greater criminal liability than recklessness, if one focuses on the issue of probability. It is worse (and more dangerous) to do something knowing it will result in some harm than doing the same thing thinking it might.

That is not to say, however, that culpability (or dangerousness) is directly proportional to probability. Take purpose, for example. Purpose is the "highest" mode of culpability—purposeful action is more culpable and punished more severely than any other type of action, including knowing action. Yet along the probabilistic axis, knowledge lies far ahead of purpose; purpose, when it comes to conduct and result, is defined without respect to probability.[101] What matters is whether the actor had the "conscious object(ive)" of acting in a certain way or bringing about a certain result. It does not matter how likely it is that he will

98. The Model Code also requires that the risk be "unjustifiable." That issue, however, may be treated in the context of justification defenses generally. See Chapter 2 below (necessity, consent). The drafters had in mind typical justification situations such as a surgeon taking a chance on a dangerous operation when the alternative is almost certain death. Commentaries § 2.02, at 237.

99. Commentaries § 2.02, at 237. Every reference to the jury in the Commentaries, and in this text as in any discussion of American criminal law, should be treated with caution. The jury in American criminal law today is more a symbol than an institution, and its significance more hypothetical than actual, as the overwhelming majority of criminal cases are disposed of by the juryless process of plea bargaining.

100. This is one instance of the Code drafters, in a Legal Process vein, explicitly ascribing discretion to process participants, and particularly the jury, in the interpretation and application of norms that the drafters felt could not profitably be defined with greater precision by the legislature. In other words, jurors in this case were the process participants best suited to exercise the requisite discretion in the process of making and applying law. For another similar instance, see the discussion of causation, § 5.1 below. On Legal Process and the Model Penal Code, see § 2 above.

101. The definition of purpose as to an attendant circumstance mentions, but does not require, awareness. Belief or hope will do.

succeed in realizing his conscious object(ive).[102] In the case of treason, for instance, it does not matter whether the traitor purposely turning over top secret documents is sure to succeed in "aiding the enemy," or whether there is merely a chance that he might. Treason is all purpose, and all attitude. Probability of success is irrelevant.[103]

Let us now turn to the attitudinal axis. There, knowledge and, recklessness look similar enough. Both imply awareness, of a fact in one case, and of a substantial risk in the other. But recklessness requires more than awareness, namely conscious disregard. The New York Penal Law makes this point explicit, by defining recklessness as awareness *plus* conscious disregard of a risk.[104] Arguably, there is a difference between simply being aware of a risk, say that one's behavior might result in someone's death, and consciously disregarding it.

To see this issue more clearly, let us take a look at it from another perspective, that of German criminal law. German criminal law distinguishes sharply between a case in which the actor *hopes* that her behavior will not result in the proscribed harm, or perhaps even that she will be able to *avoid* that result, and a case in which she has no similar qualms and is happy to take her chances, and thus *accepts* the harmful result, should it occur. Even though the risk of harm I am aware of is the same in both cases, German criminal law treats only the second case as an instance of intentional conduct.[105]

---

102. Cf. People v. Steinberg, 79 N.Y.2d 673 (1992) (intention regardless of awareness of risk); United States v. U.S. Gypsum Co., 438 U.S. 422, 445 (1978) (quoting Wayne R. LaFave & Austin W. Scott, Jr., Criminal Law 196 (1972)) (purpose regardless of likelihood of success).

103. We will talk about impossible attempts later on. The Model Code, by the way, does not recognize an impossibility defense in attempts. See § 5.2(A) below.

104. See chart 3 above.

105. German criminal law draws a basic distinction between intention (*Vorsatz*, or *dolus*) and a mode of culpability less than intention (*Fahrlässigkeit*, or *culpa*). Criminal liability requires *Vorsatz* unless otherwise provided by statute. *Vorsatz* comes in several varieties, and so does *Fahrlässigkeit*. In the example above, the second case exemplifies *bedingter Vorsatz*, or *dolus eventualis*—as opposed to purpose (*Absicht*), or knowledge (*Wissentlichkeit*, or *dolus directus*). The first case illustrates *bewußte Fahrlässigkeit*, or *culpa* with awareness—as opposed to nonconscious *culpa*, which does not require awareness of a risk and in this regard resembles negligence. For a more detailed comparative analysis, see Markus D. Dubber & Tatjana Hörnle, Criminal Law: A Comparative Approach ch. 8.A (2014).

Example: let us say I am eager to try out my new high-powered rifle. I drive to a large abandoned lot across town and take aim at the windows of a dilapidated burnt-out building some distance away. I end up shooting and seriously wounding a homeless person asleep in the building. I was aware all along that this might happen, though I was not sure it would. In one case, though, I sincerely hope that the building is unoccupied and that, even if it is not, I will not end up hitting whoever is in it. In the other, I could not care less if someone gets hurt—what was the victim doing trespassing anyway?

Now, under German criminal law, I would have acted intentionally in the second case (with *dolus eventualis*), but not in the first.[106] The question is whether the Model Penal Code could—or should—differentiate between these cases in a similar way. I clearly did not act knowingly with respect to the proscribed result—I was not certain enough that it would come about. Was I reckless? Clearly I was reckless in the second case. I was aware of the risk and then consciously disregarded it. Whether the first case also qualifies as recklessness turns on our reading of "conscious disregard." If conscious disregard adds nothing to the awareness of the risk, then I was reckless in both cases. If conscious disregard, however, requires more, in particular an *acceptance* of the risk actually manifesting itself, that is to say, of the homeless man actually dying, then case one does not qualify as an instance of recklessness.[107]

---

106. The Model Code instead attempts to differentiate between cases of this sort by adding a sui generis, mens rea-type, element, "circumstances manifesting extreme indifference to the value of human life." § 211.1(2)(a); see also § 210.2(1)(b). The precise status of this clause remains in doubt. See, e.g., People v. Register, 60 N.Y.2d 270, 276 (1983) ("neither the mens rea nor the actus reus"; "not an element in the traditional sense"), rev'd, People v. Feingold, 7 N.Y.3d 288 (2006). Moreover, it applies by definition only to result offenses involving threats to "human life." Finally, differentiating recklessness from "gross" recklessness still would not allow the Code to distinguish recklessness with conscious disregard from recklessness with mere awareness.

107. See generally Alan Michaels, Acceptance: The Missing Mental State, 71 S. Cal. L. Rev. 953 (1998); David M. Treiman, Recklessness and the Model Penal Code, 9 Am. J. Crim. L. 281 (1981); see also Kenneth W. Simons, Should the Model Penal Code's Mens Rea Provisions Be Amended?, 1 Ohio St. J. Crim. L. 179, 197 (2003) (citing People v. Reagan, 723 N.E.2d 55, 56 (N.Y. 1999)); Stephen P. Garvey, What's Wrong with Involuntary Manslaughter?, 85 Tex. L. Rev. 333, 342 (2006).

The point of this comparative analysis is not to suggest either that the Model Penal Code could not differentiate between these cases or that it should. Likewise, it is not to suggest that German law doctrine in particular is right to draw the mentioned distinction, in this particular way or in any other, or to insist that drawing it is a matter of great consequence. In fact, the difficulty of drawing the all-important line that separates *Vorsatz* from *Fahrlässigkeit* has long vexed German law doctrine and helps explain why the Model Penal Code scheme may seem attractively straightforward by comparison.[108]

From the Model Penal Code's treatmentist perspective, it is not difficult to suggest that someone who not only recognizes a substantial risk, but also accepts the resulting harm should the risk manifest itself, displays a higher level of criminal dangerousness than someone who does not. Whether the difference in degrees of dangerousness is significant—or reliably determinable—enough to support a distinction between one mental state and another, particularly one as momentous as that between recklessness and negligence, is another question.

(iv) *Negligence.* Arguably, the line between recklessness and negligence is even more significant than that separating knowledge from recklessness. As a general rule (often broken), criminal liability ends where recklessness ends, and negligence begins. Recklessness is the default mental state in the Model Penal Code and, at least in the reading of the Model Code drafters, marks the lower limit of the common law's requirement of mens rea (or intent, or scienter). That is not to say that there are no crimes that require nothing more than negligence, only that there are not many. The special part of the Model Code, for example, includes three: negligent homicide, assault (with a deadly weapon), and criminal mischief (with dangerous means).[109] (The New York Penal Law has four: negligent homicide, assault (with a deadly weapon), vehicular assault, and vehicular manslaughter.[110])

108. See, e.g., Thomas Weigend, Zwischen Vorsatz und Fahrlässigkeit, 93 ZStW 657 (1981); Bernd Schünemann, Geleitwort, in Markus D. Dubber, Einführung in das US-amerikanische Strafrecht vii (2005); see generally Markus D. Dubber & Tatjana Hörnle, Criminal Law: A Comparative Approach ch. 8.A (2014).
109. §§ 210.4, 211.1(b), 220.3.
110. N.Y. Penal Law §§ 120.00(3), 120.03(1), 125.10, 125.12.

Along the probabilistic axis, negligence occupies the same spot as recklessness; a substantial risk, rather than practical certainty, is enough. The difference between negligence and recklessness is entirely a matter of attitude. Recklessness implies a conscious disregard of the risk (see above); negligence requires neither awareness, nor disregard, of the risk. It is instead the very failure to be aware of the risk that the Model Code calls negligence.[111] I should have been aware, but was not. And that is why I am culpable (and dangerous), and need penal treatment. (Negligence thus is a sort of omission mens rea, the *failure* to have a mental state rather than having one.)

Actually, in the fine print of the Model Code lies buried another distinction between recklessness and negligence. The points of comparison differ. In the case of recklessness, the factfinder is to consider whether the risk was substantial and unjustifiable enough to warrant penal treatment by asking herself whether the defendant's behavior "involves a gross deviation from the standard of conduct that a law-abiding person would observe in the actor's situation." In the case of negligence, the same standard applies, except that now the point of comparison is not "a law-abiding person," but "a reasonable person."[112] Not much rides on this distinction; it was ignored by many MPC-based criminal codes, including the New York Penal Law (which uses the reasonableness standard in both cases[113]). Instead of pondering the distinction between a law-abiding and a reasonable person, it is good to keep in mind the point of these clauses. They were not meant to settle deep questions of criminal law, but to provide some guidance to jurors (or factfinders more generally) faced with the difficult task of applying the Code's admittedly amorphous definitions of recklessness and negligence.[114]

At this point let us pause to review the various ways in which the Code's modes of culpability differ—or do not differ—from one another. This diagram tries to do just that (Chart 5):

---

111. See People v. Strong, 37 N.Y.2d 568 (1975) (manslaughter versus negligent homicide).
112. "Reasonable" plays a central role in the Code's approach to the excuse defenses of duress and provocation. See §§ 13, 16 below.
113. N.Y. Penal Law § 15.05(3) & (4).
114. Commentaries § 2.02, at 237, 241. Presumably the requirement of a "gross" deviation, rather than a plain deviation, also represents an attempt to differentiate criminal

Chart 5 MODES OF CULPABILITY

	Purpose	*Knowledge*	*Recklessness*	*Negligence*
CONDUCT				
attitude	conscious object	awareness	[not defined]	[not defined]
probability	irrelevant	100%	[not defined]	[not defined]
CIRCUMSTANCE				
attitude	awareness, belief, hope	awareness	conscious disregard	none
probability	irrelevant	100%	substantial risk	substantial risk
RESULT				
attitude	conscious object	awareness	conscious disregard	none
probability	irrelevant	practical certainty	substantial risk	substantial risk

(v) *Strict Liability.* The above chart gives a decent overview of the various mental states, as defined by the Code. It may be misleading, however, in that it suggests that there is no criminal liability beyond negligence. But negligence is not the end of the line. There is still strict liability to be contended with, even if strict liability is only an option for the Code's sui generis civil offenses, the "violations." This means our line-drawing work is still not done. Fortunately, the line between negligence and strict liability is relatively bright. Negligence implies the

negligence from civil negligence in tort law. Traditionally, American criminal law has sidestepped this issue in various ways, by simply labeling criminal negligence "*criminal* negligence" (as in the New York Penal Law) or by explaining, no more helpfully, that criminal negligence is "that degree of negligence that is more than the negligence required to impose tort liability." Commentaries § 2.02, at 242 (quoting Jerome Hall, General Principles of Criminal Law 124 (2d ed. 1960)). Note, in light of the previous discussion of recklessness and *dolus eventualis*, that German criminal law does not differentiate between criminal and civil negligence. Markus D. Dubber & Tatjana Hörnle, Criminal Law: A Comparative Approach ch. 8.A (2014).

culpable failure to perceive a risk one should have recognized. Strict liability implies neither a mental state (such as perception), nor its absence. It is a mode of culpability that imposes criminal liability without regard to mental states (or to put it more sharply, it is a mental state that makes no mention of a mental state). For strict liability, your attitude toward a result, for example, is as irrelevant as the likelihood of the result actually coming about. Strict liability does not show up on either of the axes defining the other four modes of culpability. Chart 6 provides a complete overview of modes of liability (as opposed to mental states).

(E) Matching Conduct to Offense

Now, finally, the matching can begin. We started our analysis of criminal liability, in the previous section (§ 4.1), by checking whether the defendant passes the general act requirement—whether his behavior qualifies as an actus, so to speak. If he does not pass, our inquiry ends: the defendant is not liable.

If he does pass, we move on to the next step—to determine whether his actus was also reus, that is, whether his behavior qualified not only as conduct but as *criminal* conduct. This we do by inquiring whether his behavior matches any of the offenses defined and categorized in the special part of a given criminal code. As we saw, each offense may consist of elements of various types—thus capturing a particular actus reus. Each of these elements in turn may, or may not, have a mental state attached to it—thus adding the mens rea ingredient and completing the definition of the crime.

Much of criminal law in action is occupied with this matching exercise: Does the defendant's conduct match the definition of an offense? This legal question should not be confused with the factual question of whether the state can *prove* that the defendant's conduct matches the definition of the offense as charged.[115]

This matching procedure is, by and large, a matter for the *special part* of criminal law. In fact, that is what the special part is all about: specifying

---

115. Notice that questions of provability usually do not come up in criminal law exams. Ordinarily, you will be asked to assume certain facts and then run them through the analysis of criminal liability.

Chart 6 MODES OF CULPABILITY (INCLUDING STRICT LIABILITY)

	Purpose	Knowledge	Recklessness	Negligence	Strict Liability
CONDUCT					
attitude	conscious object	awareness	[not defined]	[not defined]	irrelevant
probability	irrelevant	100%	[not defined]	[not defined]	irrelevant
CIRCUMSTANCE					
attitude	awareness, belief, hope	awareness	conscious disregard	none	irrelevant
probability	irrelevant	100%	substantial risk	substantial risk	irrelevant
RESULT					
attitude	conscious object	awareness	conscious disregard	none	irrelevant
probability	irrelevant	practical certainty	substantial risk	substantial risk	irrelevant

which forms of behavior are criminalized. In the special part you will find discussions of just what it means, in the abstract, to murder, assault, steal, embezzle, and annoy. And once you have figured this out, you can investigate whether a particular behavior, engaged in by a particular person at a particular time in a particular place, matches the ideal type of crimes called murder, assault, theft, embezzlement, and public nuisance.[116]

So much for the actus reus. Questions of mens rea, by contrast, have been largely extracted from the special part and moved into the general part. This is one way of looking at what the Model Code drafters did when they overhauled the law of intent. They replaced a cornucopia of intents that varied from offense to offense (and not only from judge to judge) with four modes of culpability. Although there were never as many mentes reae as there were actus rei, there certainly was considerable variety among the mental elements attached to the mass of criminal offenses that has cropped up in the common law over the centuries. After the Model Code, there were only four left. Colorful mental states such as "malice aforethought" (murder) and "*animus furandi*" or "*lucri causa*" (larceny) gave way to the generic quartet of purpose, knowledge, recklessness, and negligence.

So instead of defining mental states in the special part, the Model Code drafters defined them in the general part, once and for all. To illustrate this division of labor: the special part specifies the elements of manslaughter, including the requisite mental state (recklessly causing the death of another human being), and the general part defines the mental state (recklessness).

Mens-rea-matching thus is a matter of the general part, and therefore, it is a matter for us. Now the Model Code does not just define all modes of culpability in the general part, laying out the abstract concepts against which messy life is to be matched. It also highlights two

---

116. There *are* a very few offense definitions that appear in the Model Code's general part. I am thinking here of the inchoate offenses (attempt, solicitation, conspiracy, possession). Except for possession, however, these are not really freestanding offenses. Instead, they establish a type of criminal liability, and as such, attach to existing offense definitions in the special part. In this sense there is no crime of attempt; there is only attempted murder, attempted rape, and so on. These we will take up a little later on, in § 5.2 below. (Possession we have already dealt with, in § 4.1 above.)

scenarios that might preclude such a match: intoxication and mistake. To these we now turn.

§ 4.3 Intoxication and Mistake

The first thing to notice about the Model Penal Code's provisions on intoxication and mistake is that they are largely superfluous.[117] They mainly serve to illustrate two, particularly common, situations in which the defendant lacks the mens rea required for criminal liability. It is confusing to refer to intoxication and mistake, in this sense, as "defenses," unless you think of a defense as the absence of an offense. If we must call them defenses, we might think of them as "failure-of-proof"[118] or "element-negating" defenses or, following our tripartite analysis of criminality, *level one* defenses.

As their titles suggest, the intoxication and mistake provisions spell out the circumstances under which a defendant may lack the requisite mental state because she was intoxicated or because she was mistaken about some matter of relevance. Neither provision is *entirely* superfluous, but for slightly different reasons.[119] The intoxication section actually does the opposite of what it appears to be doing; rather than establish a defense of intoxication, it sets up what amounts to an intoxication exception to the general rule that criminal liability requires a match between behavior and offense definition.[120] In other words, the intoxication provision *contracts* the scope of intoxication as a level one defense.

---

117. The Model Code's provision on *consent* (§ 2.11(1)) is also largely superfluous, but for a different reason. The consent provision is redundant insofar as it clarifies that the presence of consent precludes conviction of an offense that includes the absence of consent as one of its elements. By contrast, the provisions on intoxication and mistake are redundant insofar as they clarify that the absence of a mode of culpability—say, knowledge—precludes conviction for an offense the definition of which includes that mode of culpability. Cf. § 11 below.

118. See Paul H. Robinson, Criminal Law Defenses: A Systematic Analysis, 82 Colum. L. Rev. 199, 204–08 (1982).

119. Similarly, the Code provision on *consent*, another level one "defense," is also largely redundant—though not completely, because consent may also be a level *two* defense (i.e., a justification). See § 11 below.

120. § 2.08(2).

At the same time, the intoxication provision *expands* the scope of the intoxication defense, by recognizing intoxication as a *level three* defense, an excuse.[121] The Code drafters made it clear that, as a general matter, intoxication, no matter how severe, could not amount to an excuse in and of itself. *Involuntary* intoxication, however, could qualify as an excuse if it was severe enough to amount to criminal insanity (or rather the inability characteristic of insanity, without the underlying mental defect—a sort of "insanity" without insanity).[122]

And mistake too, it turns out, can be an excuse. In certain strictly limited circumstances, *ignorance of law* is a defense (notwithstanding the old saw that *ignorantia legis non excusat*). But let us take a look at intoxication first.

(A) Intoxication

The Model Code explains that intoxication precludes criminal liability if the defendant lacked the requisite mental state because he was drunk (or high). (Actually, it observes—with a characteristic double negative—that intoxication is *not* a defense *unless* it "negatives an element of the offense," that is to say, it disproves a mental state requirement.[123]) Nothing out of the ordinary so far. But the Model Penal Code then goes on to exempt from this general, self-explanatory rule any offense that requires a mental state below knowledge in the Model Penal Code's hierarchy of mental states (purpose/knowledge/recklessness/negligence). The drafters established what they recognized as a "special rule for drunkenness":[124] "When recklessness establishes an element of the offense, if the actor, due to self-induced intoxication, is unaware of a risk of which he would have been aware had he been sober, such unawareness is immaterial."[125]

---

121. Excuses are discussed in Chapter 3 below.
122. § 2.08(4). Insanity is discussed in § 17 below.
123. To put this in terms of "negativing" (or "negating") instead of "disproving" an offense element makes room for "defenses"—such as intoxication—that do not place the burden of proof on the defendant.
124. Tentative Draft No. 9, at 8 (May 8, 1959).
125. § 2.08(2).

Negligence too is not negatived by intoxication. Negligence actually implies unawareness; so saying that you were unaware of a risk because you were drunk does not prove that you were not negligent; it explains *why* you *were* negligent.[126] (You are inculpating, not exculpating, yourself here.)

That intoxication does not preclude negligence traditionally has gone without saying, and, in fact, it continues to go without saying in the Model Code. Recklessness is the sticking point, and it is an important one as so many crimes require recklessness—it is the default mental state, after all. To say that intoxication is irrelevant as to recklessness is to say it is irrelevant for most of criminal law. Here the Code showed somewhat uncharacteristic deference to traditional—and underrationalized—criminal law doctrine and simply followed the old common law saw that intoxication can serve to disprove only "crimes of specific intent." Under this rule, a drunk defendant would avoid a murder conviction (which required a showing of "specific intent"), but he would still be liable for manslaughter (which required only "general intent").

The hostility toward the intoxication defense in the common law ran deep and wide. Intoxication, after all, was a crime in public and a sin, at least, in private.[127] That hostility persists to this day, as evidenced by a Montana statute providing that voluntary intoxication "may not be taken into consideration in determining the existence of a mental state which is

---

126. As it is awareness that matters, intoxication does preclude knowledge and purpose, at least to the extent that they imply awareness. That is obviously the case for knowledge. As we saw earlier on, to know something means to be aware of it, or to be practically certain that it will come about. Purpose is not so clear. Recall that the Model Code does not define purpose in terms of awareness. If attached to conduct or result, purpose means conscious object—where consciousness may be said to imply awareness (as in the case of recklessness, which requires a "conscious disregard"), not of the conduct or the result (as that would imply knowledge), but of one's object, or aim, to engage in that conduct or to bring about that result. Purpose as to an *attendant circumstance*, however, may—but need not—involve awareness; recall that belief or hope that an attendant circumstance exists is enough. See § 4.2(D)(i) above.

127. Cf. the "public" intoxication statute at issue in Powell v. Texas, 392 U.S. 514 (1968): "Whoever shall get drunk or be found in a state of intoxication in any public place, *or at any private house except his own*, shall be fined not exceeding one hundred dollars." Id. at 517 (quoting Texas Penal Code art. 477 (1952)) (emphasis added).

an element of [a criminal] offense."[128] In upholding this statute, the U.S. Supreme Court could quote from an 1820 opinion by Justice Story:

> This is the first time, that I ever remember it to have been contended, that the commission of one crime was an excuse for another. Drunkenness is a gross vice, and in the contemplation of some of our laws is a crime; and I learned in my earlier studies, that so far from its being in law an excuse for murder, it is rather an aggravation of its malignity.[129]

The Model Code adopted the common law rule, merely substituting "knowledge or purpose" for "specific intent" and "recklessness" for "general intent."[130] In the drafters' view, the lack of awareness at the time of the offense, which ordinarily would preclude recklessness, is irrelevant if caused by intoxication because the original act of excessive drinking "has no affirmative social value to counterbalance the potential danger."[131] And it is in this very act that the actor's culpability—and abnormal dangerousness—lies.[132] It makes no difference that this act is not itself criminal, and does not form part of the definition of the subsequent offense committed while intoxicated.[133]

---

128. Mont. Code Ann. § 45–2–203 (upheld in Montana v. Egelhoff, 518 U.S. 37 (1996)).
129. Montana v. Egelhoff, 518 U.S. 37, 44 (1996) (quoting United States v. Cornell, 25 F. Cas. 650, 657–58 (No. 14,868) (C.C.R.I. 1820)); see also 4 William Blackstone, Commentaries on the Laws of England 26 (1769) ("the law of England, considering how easy it is to counterfeit this excuse, and how weak an excuse it is, (though real) will not suffer any man thus to privilege one crime by another").
130. See State v. Cameron, 104 N.J. 42 (1986).
131. Tentative Draft No. 9, at 9 (May 8, 1959).
132. Commentaries § 2.08, at 359.
133. It is manslaughter, not "manslaughter after getting drunk," or even "getting drunk with the purpose of committing homicide." In German criminal law, the significance of intoxication turns on the actor's mode of culpability when she got drunk. So, in Model Code terms, if she got drunk with the purpose of committing a crime, say to get up her courage, she is guilty of crimes that require purpose. Analogously, if she got drunk knowing full well that she would commit a crime under the influence, she would be liable for crimes requiring knowledge, and so on down through recklessness (awareness of a good chance that she would do it) and negligence (culpable unawareness of that chance). See Claus Roxin, Strafrecht Allgemeiner Teil 781–90 (3d ed. 1997) ("actio libera in causa").

In sum, voluntary—or what the Code calls "self-induced"—intoxication matters only to the extent that it negatives knowledge or purpose. It is irrelevant for crimes that require recklessness or negligence. Having adopted a narrow view of voluntary intoxication as a level one, or failure-of-proof, defense, the drafters also failed to recognize it as an excuse, or level three, defense. Under the Code, voluntary intoxication cannot amount to an irresponsibility defense, even if it is so severe as to render the person incapable of telling right from wrong or of controlling her behavior, that is to say, so severe as to reduce her to criminal insanity.[134]

The Code is more forgiving, and more consistent, when it comes to what used to be called involuntary intoxication—intoxication that is not self-induced or "pathological."[135] Flexibility on involuntary intoxication comes cheap, however. Cases of involuntary intoxication are extremely rare, and certainly incomparably rarer than cases of voluntary intoxication. The drafters, in fact, could not find a single case in which the defense of involuntary intoxication had succeeded.[136]

Even so, the drafters provided for involuntary intoxication not as a level one, element-negating "defense," but as an affirmative excuse, or level three, defense.[137] Unlike its voluntary cousin, involuntary intoxication is an excuse if it is so severe as to cause an incapacity to tell right from wrong

---

134. § 2.08(3). German criminal law does recognize an excuse of irresponsibility through intoxication, voluntary or not, under the same provision that also addresses cases of insanity. § 20 StGB [German Criminal Code] (total incapacity); see also § 21 StGB (diminished capacity). Those who qualify for this excuse, however, do not necessarily escape criminal liability altogether. In the case of voluntary intoxication, they are liable for a separate offense, gross intoxication (Vollrausch). § 323a StGB. See generally Brian Foley, Same Problem, Same Solution?: The Treatment of the Voluntarily Intoxicated Offender in England and Germany, 4 Trinity Coll. L. Rev. 119 (2001); see also Markus D. Dubber & Tatjana Hörnle, Criminal Law: A Comparative Approach ch. 8.D (2014).

135. It may be misleading to speak of involuntary and voluntary intoxication because talk of voluntariness is, in Model Penal Code language, limited to the act requirement. Involuntary intoxication, however, does not imply an involuntary act, at least in the Code's scheme of things. Whether intoxication, voluntary or not, might be so severe as to preclude voluntary action is another question. The Code here deals only with intoxication's (limited) relevance to mens rea, not to actus reus.

136. Tentative Draft No. 9, at 10 n.25 (May 8, 1959).

137. Without more, an affirmative defense in the Model Penal Code places the burden of production, though not that or persuasion, on the defendant. § 1.12(2).

73

or to keep oneself from doing something one knows to be wrong. Here involuntary intoxication takes the place of a mental disease or defect in the classic excuse defense of insanity. In the case of insanity, as we will see in greater detail in Chapter 3, the same types of incapacity are caused not by intoxication but by some mental disease or defect.

Of the two kinds of involuntary intoxication the Code recognizes, one is more obvious than the other. Most clearly, intoxication is involuntary in the strict sense of "not self-induced" if it is *other*-induced, as when someone forces me to become intoxicated (e.g., by injecting me with heroin while I am sleeping, or while I am tied to a chair) or gets me to intoxicate myself without knowing it (e.g., by slipping alcohol into a high school reunion punch). Intoxication can also be involuntary without being other-induced, as when I mistake cocaine for powdered sugar, without anyone having misled me.

But the Code recognizes another form of involuntary intoxication besides intoxication that is "not self-induced," or other-induced. "Pathological" intoxication is supposed to deal with cases in which a person is abnormally sensitive to the effects of an intoxicant she consumes voluntarily.[138] Pathological intoxication "means," to quote the Code, "intoxication grossly excessive in degree, given the amount of the intoxicant, to which the actor does not know he is susceptible." In this case, not only is the consumption of the intoxicant voluntary, as in the case of involuntary self-induced intoxication, so is the intoxication itself. What is involuntary, in other words, is not the intoxication so much as its degree.

(B) Mistake

As a level one defense, mistake operates much like intoxication.[139] Unlike intoxication, however, the Code does not place external—"public policy"—limitations on the scope of mistake as a level one defense. Like *involuntary* intoxication, mistake is a defense if it negatives any mode of culpability identified in the offense definition. So under a statute proscribing the sale of liquor to anyone under twenty-one, if I thought my customer was twenty-one, I did not "know" he was nineteen. If the

---

138. See State v. Sette, 259 N.J. Super. 156 (1992) (not self-induced versus pathological intoxication).

139. See, e.g., People v. Gudz, 18 A.D.3d 11, 793 N.Y.S.2d 556 (2005).

statute requires "knowledge" with respect to the attendant circumstance of the purchaser's age, then my mistake regarding his age would constitute a level one, or failure of proof, defense.

What if a different mental state were required? How about recklessness? My mistake would not do me any good as long as I was aware not of *the fact* that he was underage, but of a substantial chance that he was. Similarly, in the case of negligence, my mistake would not help me if I was not, but should have been, aware of that substantial chance.

If no mental state is required—as is likely in our liquor-selling example—then even a non-negligent mistake would be of no use. Even if there is nothing that did, or should have, tipped me off about my customer's age, I would have committed the offense as defined. As in all level one "defenses," mistake is no defense against strict liability; you cannot negative mens rea if there is no mens rea to be negatived.

For that reason, questions of the relevance of mistake as a level one defense often arise in strict liability cases. A defendant argues that he did not commit some crime because he made a mistake, generally about some attendant circumstance, and often about a specific attendant circumstance: age. The easiest way to dismiss this argument is to hold that the element about which the defendant claims to have been mistaken is a strict liability element.

That is what happened in the most famous mistake/strict liability case of them all, *Regina v. Prince*.[140] Prince was convicted under a statute that made it a misdemeanor to "unlawfully take…any unmarried girl, being under the age of sixteen years, out of the possession and against the will of her father or mother, or of any person having the lawful care or charge of her." In his defense, Prince argued that "the girl Annie Phillips, though proved by her father to be fourteen years old on April 6, 1875, looked very much older than sixteen, and the jury found upon reasonable evidence that before the defendant took her away she had told him that she was eighteen, that the defendant bona fide believed that statement, and that such belief was reasonable."[141]

The initial question in *Prince* was whether "being under the age of sixteen years" was a strict liability element, or, in traditional common law

140. (1875) L.R. 2 C.C.R. 154.
141. Id.

terms, whether scienter was required with respect to it, where scienter was roughly equivalent to purpose-or-knowledge-or-recklessness-but-probably-not-negligence-unless-it-is-gross. In Model Code terms, if it is a strict liability element, then mistake makes no difference. Is it?

Applying our trusted rules of interpretation, and assuming that the statute appeared as quoted in the Model Code, without more, the answer would be no. For under Rule 1, recklessness is the default mental state "[w]hen the culpability sufficient to establish a material element of an offense is not prescribed by law." (Rule 2 does not apply because no mode of culpability appears anywhere in the definition of the offense, so that none could be applied from one element to all.[142] Rule 3 does not apply because the offense appears in the Code itself and is a misdemeanor, which carries a possible sentence of incarceration.) If recklessness applies, then a reckless mistake would not be a defense. Merely mistaking the girl for eighteen would not be enough, provided I thought there was a good chance she might be under sixteen. (If negligence applied instead, being wrong would not help as long as I *should* have thought there was such a chance, and so on.)

But everyone agreed that Prince's mistake was "reasonable," that is to say, it was not reckless, or even negligent, in Model Code language.[143] The reason he still lost was that the court decided, in Model Penal Code terms, that the element about which he was reasonably mistaken— "being under the age of sixteen years"—was a strict liability element, rendering his mistake irrelevant.

---

142. Actually, Prince argued that "unlawfully" was just such a mental state. Not so under the Model Code. Cf. §§ 2.02(9) (illegality of conduct not offense element), 3.11(1) (defining unlawful force). Unlawfully is more commonly taken to refer, albeit redundantly, to the absence of justifications. See Regina v. Prince, (1875) L.R. 2 C.C.R. 154 (opinion of Bramwell, B.) ("The word 'unlawfully' means 'not lawfully,' 'otherwise than lawfully,' 'without lawful cause'—such as would exist for instance on a taking by a police officer on a charge of felony or a taking by a father of his child from her school."). Note that "unlawfully" also appears as an attendant circumstance, which may—or may not—have a mental state attached to it. See, e.g., §§ 212.1 (kidnapping) ("unlawfully"), 221.2(2) (trespass) ("not licensed or privileged," "in a manner prescribed by law"), 223.2. (theft by unlawful taking or disposition), 224.3 (fraudulent destruction, removal or concealment of recordable instruments) ("writing for which the law provides public recording").
143. § 1.13(16).

Given that Prince was charged with a criminal offense, a misdemeanor, rather than a non-criminal violation, this reading of the age element would have been inconsistent with the Model Penal Code's mens rea requirement (§ 2.02(1)). Note, however, that the Code carves out a related exception to this requirement: the age element of any sex offense is strict liability if the "critical age" is ten (as in rape, defined as a "male ha[ving] sexual intercourse with a female" who is "less than 10 years old"[144]). If it is an age other—meaning higher—than ten, then it is up to the defendant "to prove by a preponderance of the evidence that he reasonably believed the child to be above the critical age."[145]

This narrow exception to the Code's general mens rea rule goes beyond the other two exceptions to the mens rea requirement that we encountered earlier on—permitting strict liability for "violations" as well as for offenses defined outside the criminal code proper.[146] Note that rape under the Code is a serious felony, as it is in all other American criminal codes. The exception may be narrow, but it also has real bite.

There are of course, really, two exceptions here. One is clear-cut. If the critical age is ten, then age is a strict liability element—no mens rea needed. But what is supposed to happen if the critical age is over ten is not so clear. As only a "reasonable" mistake about the victim's age counts as a defense—and the Code elsewhere defines a "reasonable" mistake as one that is neither reckless nor negligent—we could read at least negligence back into the age element, so that the actor must have been at least negligently wrong regarding the victim's age for the offense to be made out.

Now we indeed would have a mental state element, and thus would have brought the statute back into line with the Code's commitment to mens rea, even if only a watered-down version thereof—as we would require negligence and not quite the ordinary default of recklessness.

The problem is, though, that the statute now bumps into another Code requirement—since constitutionalized in *In re Winship*[147]—that

---

144. § 213.1(1)(d).
145. § 213.6(1).
146. § 2.05.
147. 397 U.S. 358, 364 (1970) ("every fact necessary to constitute the crime with which [the defendant] is charged").

ite bear the burden of proving, beyond a reasonable doubt, every element of an offense, including mens rea.[148] So how can the Code shift the burden of proof onto the defendant?

The easy, and not particularly helpful, answer is that the Code here transforms mistake about age into an "affirmative defense," procedurally speaking.[149] But surely the Code, simply by transforming the absence of an *offense* element into a *defense*, could not avoid the constraints of *Winship*.[150]

Note also that, even under the Code itself, an affirmative defense ordinarily does not place the burden of proof on the defendant. Instead, the defendant only bears the burden *of production* (of "adduc[ing] supporting evidence"), while the burden *of persuasion* (the other half of the burden of proof) remains on the state.[151] Mistake about age thus would be a kind of super-affirmative defense, which shifts the entire burden of proof onto the defendant—like ignorance of law, for instance (as we will see in a moment).[152] And what exactly would be the theory of excuse that could give rise to an affirmative defense of mistake of age—unavoidability, lack of self-control, irresponsibility?[153]

Let us assume, however, that we are dealing neither with a strict liability offense nor with the exceptional offense definition that establishes a burden-of-proof-shifting affirmative defense. Let us assume, in other words, that we are dealing with a perfectly ordinary offense and that the

---

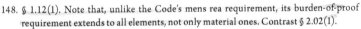

148. § 1.12(1). Note that, unlike the Code's mens rea requirement, its burden-of-proof requirement extends to all elements, not only material ones. Contrast § 2.02(1).

149. Substantively speaking, mistake about age presumably would function as an excuse (i.e., a level three defense), on the assumption that no one would characterize a mistake about the victim's age as *justifying* facially criminal conduct (i.e., functioning as a level two defense). See § 7 below.

150. Actually, it probably could. See Patterson v. New York, 432 U.S. 197 (1977) (provocation); Martin v. Ohio, 480 U.S. 228 (1987) (self-defense).

151. § 1.12(2). Even the burden of production falls on the defendant only if the state does not introduce evidence of the defense as part of its case. As long as "there is evidence supporting [the] defense," there is no need for the defendant to produce any. § 1.12(2)(a).

152. § 2.04(4); see also §§ 2.07(5) (due diligence), 2.13(2) (entrapment), 5.07 (temporary possession).

153. The Code's approach to excuses is discussed in § 12 below.

Code's normal, and normally redundant, mistake provision applies—
that any mistake negativing an offense element precludes criminal liability, just as any other level one ("failure-of-proof") defense would.

It is worth noting, even in run-of-the-mill cases, that not just any
mistake will negative any mental state element. For instance, a *reckless*
mistake with respect to an offense element will preclude conviction on
an offense that requires knowledge (i.e., an accurate belief, or awareness) with respect to that element. (An unreasonable mistake is still
a mistake.) But it will not stand in the way of criminal liability for an
offense that requires recklessness with respect to the element in question. (A reckless mistake is still reckless.) In other words, a mistake may
amount only to a partial "defense," and mitigate liability from a more
serious offense (for instance, one requiring knowledge or purpose) to a
less serious one (one requiring recklessness or negligence), rather than
precluding criminal liability altogether.

What is more, the Code provides that, even if my mistake
"defense" does succeed with respect to a given offense, I may not
escape criminal liability altogether. Rather I will be punished (or subject to peno-correctional treatment) for whatever offense I thought—
mistakenly—I was committing, rather than for the one I actually did
commit:

> Although, ignorance or mistake would otherwise afford a defense
> to the offense charged, the defense is not available if the defen-
> dant would be guilty of another offense had the situation been
> as he supposed. In such case, however, the ignorance or mistake
> of the defendant shall reduce the grade and degree of the offense
> of which he may be convicted to those of the offense of which he
> would be guilty had the situation been as he supposed.[154]

To see how the drafters might have come up with this odd-sounding rule,
let us return to the chestnut of *Regina v. Prince*.[155] The opinions in that

154. § 2.04(2).
155. (1875) L.R. 2 C.C.R. 154.

AN INTRODUCTION TO THE MODEL PENAL CODE

case laid out various ways of analyzing a mistake claim. We have already discussed one—rejecting the claim as irrelevant to a strict liability element, here the age of the unmarried girl taken out of her father's possession. The others involve the same sort of thought experiment embodied in the Code passage quoted above. Each requires comparing the defendant's imaginary world (the world of fiction), that is the world as he thought it—mistakenly—to be, with the world of fact. The opinions differ in the question each asks about the world of fiction ("had the situation been as he supposed"). In one, the mistake claim would be irrelevant if the defendant, in the world of fiction, had committed a *wrong* (wrongfulness test).[156] In another, the mistake does not matter if, in the world of fiction, he had committed an *unlawful* act, that is to say, an act in violation of civil or criminal law (illegality test).[157] In yet another, even a wrongful unlawful act in the world of fiction would not preclude the defendant from relying on a mistake:[158] his mistake claim would fall on deaf ears only if he had committed a crime, rather than a civilly illegal act (such as a breach of contract or a tort), in the world of fiction—though obviously not the one he stands accused of in the world of fact (criminality test).

The Model Code takes one step further down this progression from hypothetical wrongfulness to illegality to criminality, with each being a subset of the other. It too disallows a mistake defense *to the crime charged* if the defendant would have committed a crime even in the world of fiction. But the Code does not stop here, at the criminality test familiar from *Prince*. Conviction of the crime charged, it turns out, does not necessarily mean punishment for the crime charged. Instead, the defendant is prescribed peno-correctional treatment on the basis of the crime he thought he had committed, in the world of fiction. So, let us say selling liquor to a fifteen-year-old is a misdemeanor, and selling it to a sixteen-year-old a violation. I am charged with the misdemeanor because the buyer is in fact fifteen, but I mount a successful defense of mistake of fact, that I thought she was sixteen. In that case, the Code

156. See id. (opinion of Bramwell, B.).
157. See id. (opinion of Brett, J.).
158. See id.

would convict me of selling liquor to a fifteen-year-old, but then "reduce the grade and degree of the offense of which [I] may be convicted to those of the offense of which [I] would be guilty had the situation been as [I] supposed," that is to say, reclassify the offense of conviction as a violation, and punish (or rather treat) me accordingly.

The correctional regimen thus is matched to the penological diagnosis of the offender's specific criminal disposition, rather than to the abstract offense she actually committed, once again reconfirming that offense definitions in the Code serve as rough indicators of criminal disposition, which, in certain circumstances, may be disregarded. That is how someone can be convicted of one crime (in fact), but treated as though she had committed another crime (in fiction).

Not surprisingly, holding someone liable for an offense she did not in fact commit, but only thought she did, is not that easy, doctrinally speaking. The most obvious way of dealing with this problem would have been to convict the defendant of an *attempt* to commit the offense she thought she was committing, rather than of the one she did commit.[159] Another would have been to convict of the lesser—though fictional—offense, rather than convicting of the more serious—and factual—offense, and then punishing for the lesser one. It was for procedural reasons[160] that the drafters instead opted for the, considerably less elegant, conviction-for-one and punishment-at-the-grade-and-degree-of-the-other solution.

What if the factual offense is *less serious* than the fictional one? What if the defendant, under the circumstances as she supposed them to be, had committed a felony, but it turns out that her conduct amounted to a misdemeanor instead? It would seem that, under the Code, she would be criminally liable for (or at least punishable at the grade and degree of) the more serious, fictional, offense. The Model Code's approach to

159. This would result in pretty much the same punishment—or penal treatment—as conviction of the consummated offense, because the Code punishes attempts on par with consummated offenses, except if the attempted offense is a first degree felony, in which case the attempt is punished as a second degree felony. See § 5.05(1).

160. Mostly, that it would be unfair to convict a defendant of an offense not charged in the indictment, particularly in cases where there is no lesser included offense of which the defendant would have been guilty had she not been mistaken. See Commentaries § 2.04, at 273–74.

the mistake issue after all rests on the proposition that a person should be treated according to the offense she thought she committed, rather than to the one she did commit. That is not so, however, according to the Code drafters. Mistakes are supposed to mitigate liability, not to aggravate it, even if the world of fiction was worse (or more dangerous) than the world of fact. Mistakes serve only to *"reduce the grade and degree of the offense of which he may be convicted to those of the offense of which he would be guilty had the situation been as he supposed."*[161] As the Commentaries explain, "an actor should not be held liable for more serious consequences than those for which he had the requisite culpability, *nor should he be held liable for a more serious consummated offense if no such offense has occurred.*"[162] But why?[163]

We cannot leave the topic of mistake without at least mentioning the distinction between mistakes of fact and mistakes of law. This distinction, illustrated with varying degrees of success in scores of common law opinions, plays no role in the Model Code's approach to mistake. Under the Code, it makes no difference how a mistake is classified; the only thing that matters is whether or not it negatives an element of the offense. (Hence, § 2.04 speaks of "[i]gnorance or mistake as to a matter of *fact or law*.") Under the common law, classification made all the difference, as is so often the case.[164] Mistakes of fact mattered, mistakes of law did not.[165] As one might suspect, the problem was telling the two apart. What looked like law from one angle looked like fact from another (are not laws facts as well, in a sense?), and what about mistakes in the application of law to fact, and was interpretation law, or was it fact? The distinction between law and fact has never been able to hold much water—just look at the Sisyphean efforts to distinguish between

---

161. § 2.04(2) (emphasis added).

162. Commentaries § 2.04, at 274 (emphasis added).

163. A similar question will arise in the context of the Code's treatment of the impossibility defense in inchoate offense cases. See § 5.2 below.

164. Recall, for instance, the key role in the law of intoxication of the "obscure, unanalyzed distinction between specific and general intent." Tentative Draft No. 9, at 4 (May 8, 1959); see § 4.3(A) above.

165. Many codes based on the Model Code have retained the traditional limitation to mistakes of fact. See, e.g., N.Y. Penal Law § 15.20(1) ("mistaken belief of fact"); cf. § 15.20(2) (ignorance of law as excuse).

the tasks of jury and judge in the modem criminal trial (in the United States and elsewhere[166]), not to mention the attempt to differentiate legally impossible from factually impossible attempts.[167]

And yet, in effect, if not in doctrine, the distinction between mistakes of fact and mistakes of law persists even in the Model Code. So the bulk of mistakes negativing an offense element—of mistakes as a level one (of failure-of-proof) defense—will be mistakes of fact. So the mistake about the girl's age in *Prince* is a mistake of fact that negatives the mens rea, if any, attaching to the age element of the offense. (It turned out, of course, that there was no mental state to be negatived.) By contrast, a mistake regarding another attendant circumstance element, that the girl was in her father's "possession," for instance, might qualify as a mistake of law, or at least as a hybrid mistake of "legal fact" (or the application of law to a set of facts), if it is based on a misunderstanding of the concept of possession in the domestic law of the time.

At the same time, the paradigmatic mistake as a level three defense— an excuse—under the Model Penal Code is a mistake of law. In the common law, of course, there was no mistake of law; the maxim *ignorantia legis non excusat* was considered an indispensable bulwark against criminal chaos—who after all would not claim not to have known that murder is a crime? This anxiety accounted for much of the hostility toward mistake of law. Holding the line separating mistake of fact and mistake of law thus became essential to maintaining the king's peace—or public order, later on.

The Model Code drafters were willing to make room for mistake of law in some cases. We have already seen that the Code does not categorically preclude mistake of law as a level one defense—as long as the mistake negatives an element of the offense.[168] What is more, the Code

---

166. Cf. Albert W. Alschuler & Andrew G. Deiss, A Brief History of the Criminal Jury in the United States, 61 U. Chi. L. Rev. 867 (1994); Markus D. Dubber, The German Jury and the Metaphysical *Volk:* From Romantic Idealism to Nazi Ideology, 43 Am. J. Comp. L. 227 (1995).

167. Impossibility is discussed in § 5.2 below.

168. Most obviously in offenses that include "unlawfully" as an attendant circumstance. See supra n.142; see also Liparota v. United States, 471 U.S. 419 (1985) ("not authorized").

provides for a separate level three mistake of law defense. In certain, limited, circumstances, ignorance of the law does excuse after all. We will discuss this excuse in greater detail later on;[169] for now, let us see how it differs from mistake as a level one "defense."

Ignorance of law is a defense, properly speaking; knowledge of the law is not an element of the offense, so that ignorance of it would negative it. Ignorance of the law is an affirmative defense that the defendant must prove by a preponderance of the evidence.[170]

As a level three defense, ignorance of the law should be a defense to all offenses, including strict liability ones. This is so because, unlike a level one mistake, it does not negative the mens rea attached to a particular offense element, such as age.

That is not to say that ignorance of law may not also be a level one defense, but only if the definition of the offense in fact includes awareness of law as one of its elements. That is how some courts have interpreted the very un-MPC mens rea of "wilfulness." As wilfulness does not exactly fit any of the Model Penal Code mental states, courts in MPC jurisdictions have tried to squeeze it into the Model Code quartet of mental states as best they can—ignoring, by and large, what the Code itself says about wilfulness (that it is synonymous with knowledge).[171] In New York, for instance, wilfulness is knowledge plus non-ignorance of law, though not of the specific criminal statute in question, but of the governing law generally speaking. In other words, the defendant acts wilfully as long as she acts knowingly and is aware of the illegality (or unlawfulness), if not the criminality, of her action.[172]

---

169. § 15 below.

170. § 2.04(4). In fact it is a super-affirmative defense in that it places the entire burden of proof on the defendant, rather than merely the burden of production. For another such defense, as to the age of the victim in certain sex offenses, see § 4.3(B) above.

171. § 2.02(8). The Code does not use wilfulness in the definition of offenses, by design. At the 1955 ALI meeting, Herbert Wechsler responded to Judge Learned Hand's remark that wilfully is an "awful word": "I agree with Judge Hand, and I promise you unequivocally that the word will never be used in the definition of any offense in the Code. But because it is such a dreadful word and so common in the regulatory statutes, it seemed to me useful to superimpose some norm of meaning on it." ALI Proceedings 160 (1955).

172. People v. Coe, 71 N.Y.2d 852 (1988); see also Ratzlaf v. United States, 510 U.S. 135 (1994); Bryan v. United States, 524 U.S. 184 (1998); see generally Sharon L. Davies,

§ 4.4 Liability for Another's Conduct

To complete our discussion of the "conduct" that, according to § 1.02, may constitute a crime, let us take a look at how the Model Penal Code handles cases in which one person's conduct becomes that of another.[173] When is one person's conduct—which matches the definition of some crime—treated as though it were also another person's conduct? When does one person's actual conduct become another's constructive conduct? When may one person's conduct be *imputed* to another?

The Model Code provides two answers to this question:

(1) when "acting with the kind of culpability that is sufficient for the commission of the offense, he causes an innocent or irresponsible person to engage in such conduct," or

(2) "he is an accomplice of such other person in the commission of the offense."[174]

Answer (2) tends to attract the lion's share of doctrinal attention. That makes sense, both because it is more complex than answer (1) (what after all is an accomplice?) and because it applies to more cases. But the law of complicity makes a lot more sense if one sees it in its doctrinal context, that is, as but one way in which, as the Code puts it, "a person is legally accountable for the conduct of another person."[175] Keeping in mind that complicity is about conduct may also make distinguishing it from conspiracy a little easier. Complicity is a theory of imputation. Conspiracy is a crime. Complicity is about conduct. Conspiracy is about an agreement. But we are getting ahead of ourselves.[176]

The Jurisprudence of Willfulness: An Evolving Theory of Excusable Ignorance, 48 Duke L.J. 341 (1998).

173. For a useful discussion of the common law of complicity, including its historical development, see Francis B. Sayre, Criminal Responsibility for the Acts of Another, 43 Harv. L. Rev. 689 (1930).

174. § 2.06(2). That section also contains another answer: whenever the Code says so. § 2.06(2)(b). One example is the crime of "aiding suicide." § 210.5(2).

175. § 2.06(2).

176. Cf. § 5.2(B) below.

(A) Instruments

The basic idea underlying answer (1) is that the criminal law will treat another person's conduct as my own if I use him as a mere means to my criminal ends. The same principle precludes criminal liability in cases where one person is tossed by another into the path of a third, and thus is used as the means to commit an assault. In that case, the tossee is not liable because she has not committed a voluntary act. By contrast, the tosser—and only the tosser—is liable because he—and only he—has.

Now, the Code's imputation provision deals with situations in which the tool has engaged in a voluntary act, and in this sense engaged in "conduct"—thus raising the question of whether her conduct can be imputed to another. According to the Code, this imputation is permissible under two conditions—causation, and innocence or irresponsibility.

From the point of view of causation, the imputation provision is redundant. It says, in effect, that one person is liable for criminal conduct if she caused it. And whether she caused it or not will then be decided according to the law of causation.[177] The difficulty here is, of course, that what is being caused is not some resulting harm—such as death—but another person's conduct. That other person, however, presumably is perfectly capable of making up her own mind about whether she wants to go ahead and let her conduct be "caused" by another person or not.

Presumably, yes, but only presumably. That presumption does not hold in cases where the person whose conduct is being caused is "innocent or irresponsible." I cannot make up my own mind about some criminal conduct if I do not even know I am engaging in that conduct. So if you hand me what I think is cold medicine, which I then feed to my sick child, but which actually turns out—as you well know—to be poison, then I might "technically" have been the one who engaged in the conduct that fits the definition of homicide—causing the death of another person—but you were the one who caused me to cause the death.

"Innocence" is not necessarily limited to cluelessness, though.[178] Suppose I knew full well that you gave me a poison pill, but you

---

177. Discussed in § 5.1 below.
178. The concept of "innocence" does not quite fit into a criminal code, or so it would seem. Not even the law of criminal procedure recognizes it—instead speaking in

held a gun to my head, forcing me to feed it to my coughing eight-year-old. In that case, should not my conduct be imputed to you as well, as your threat transformed me into a mere means to your criminal ends?

Then again, perhaps this would be a case of using an "irresponsible" person, rather than an innocent one. Depending on one's view of the duress defense—in particular whether it applies to murder—I may be able to excuse my conduct. Under the Model Code—which does permit the defense in murder cases—I would have a decent argument that you subjected me to a threat so grave that I could not be held responsible for my failure to ignore it, and instead do what you ordered me to do.[179]

What about other excuses? Military orders? Entrapment? Ignorance of law? If one takes a broad view of responsibility, and regards all excuses as addressing the question whether a particular actor in a particular setting could be held responsible for his concededly unlawful actions, then any person who places another person in a position that would excuse that person of criminal liability would be legally accountable for that other person's facially criminally conduct.

The Model Code, however, appears to take a narrower view of responsibility—and therefore of irresponsibility as well. In devotes an entire article of its general part to "responsibility" (art. 4), but deals there with only two defenses against criminal liability, insanity and infancy. What we can say with confidence then is that anyone who uses a "madman" or a "child"[180] to commit criminal conduct will be accountable "as if the conduct were his own."[181] Just who counts as a madman or a child presumably is to be determined in reference to the Code's treatment of insanity and infancy in article 4.

terms of guilt ("guilty") or its absence ("not guilty"). Cf. § 14 below (predisposition in entrapment).

179. See § 2.09. Then again, perhaps that elusive "person of reasonable firmness in [my] situation would have been unable to resist" the threat, given that the victim is someone to whom I owe a duty of care.

180. Commentaries § 2.06, at 302; see, e.g., Johnson v. State, 38 So. 182 (Ala. 1905).

181. Commentaries § 2.06 at 300; see generally Commonwealth v. Tavares, 382 Pa. Super. 317 (1989).

(B) Complicity

Innocent or irresponsible human instruments are one thing. In fact, they are the exception. The presumption, and the rule, is that the person who actually engages in the facially criminally conduct is neither innocent nor irresponsible. How can that person's conduct be imputed to me? How can *my* criminal liability "derive" from *his* criminal conduct?[182]

This is the challenge of the law of complicity. There is no doubt that the person who commits the act defined in the criminal statute has committed a crime. This person is the principal. The question is whether criminal liability can be extended to someone else, the would-be accomplice. Who is an accomplice, then?

That, at any rate, is the question under the Model Code scheme of things. This scheme considerably simplified the doctrine of complicity (of "parties to crime," or "accessorial liability") under the common law.[183] The common law set up an intricate set of distinctions so as to capture the various degrees of participation of various parties to a crime. Here is the Supreme Court's pithy summary:

> In felony cases, parties to a crime were divided into four distinct categories: (1) principals in the first degree who actually perpetrated the offense; (2) principals in the second degree who were actually or constructively present at the scene of the crime and aided or abetted its commission; (3) accessories before the fact who aided or abetted the crime, but were not present at its commission; and (4) accessories after the fact who rendered assistance after the crime was complete.[184]

182. That is how assisted suicide differs from complicity—and solicitation. Suicide is not a crime (anymore), so that aiding or soliciting suicide cannot make me an accomplice. Hence the need to create "Aiding or Soliciting Suicide as an Independent Offense." § 210.5(2); but see People v. Duffy, 79 N.Y.2d 611 (1992) (causing suicide as homicide).

183. Note, once again, that this differentiation among various participants in a course of criminal conduct is not merely a relic of the old common law. German criminal law recognizes a similar taxonomy of participation, and of culpability.

184. Standefer v. United States, 447 U.S. 10, 15 (1980); see also 4 William Blackstone, Commentaries on the Laws of England 34–35 (1769). In misdemeanors, no such fine distinctions were drawn; everyone was a principal.

As so often, the Model Code replaced this elaborate set of rules with a single, flexible standard, to be applied by a process participant exercising her discretion as guided by the Code.[185] The challenge no longer was to figure out who counts as what kind of principal or accessory, but to get right to the heart of the matter—who counts as an accomplice? And the answer is:

> A person is an accomplice of another person in the commission of an offense if...with the purpose of promoting or facilitating the commission of the offense, he
>
> (i) solicits such other person to commit it; or
> (ii) aids or agrees or attempts to aid such other person in planning or committing it.[186]

The Model Code thus retained the substantive core of common law complicity. What the common law had called aiding or abetting, the Model Code called aiding or soliciting. At the same time, the Code drafters tried to improve on the common law in various ways. Most important, they sought to focus doctrinal attention on what they considered the core issue, the relationship between the accomplice's and the principal's conduct, rather than on formal distinctions among categories of principals and accessories. In addition to spelling out the obvious (but not necessarily the common law), namely, that omission can constitute complicity, the drafters also tried to put some meat on the bare bones of the elusive concept of "abetting."[187] And so, in its solicitation section, the Code defined soliciting as "with the purpose of promoting or facilitating its commission...command[ing], encourag[ing] or

---

185. See § 2 above (Model Code's Legal Process approach).
186. § 2.06(3). Subsection (iii), on complicity by omission, is discussed below. Note how the various subsections of § 2.06 hang together. Subsection (1) provides that you can be "legally accountable" for another's conduct. Subsection (2) next explains what "legally accountable" means, including being an "accomplice." And subsection (3) then lays out who counts as an "accomplice."
187. According to Merriam-Webster, derived from Anglo-French abeter: a- (from Latin ad-) + beter, to bait.

request[ing] another person to engage in specific conduct which would constitute such crime or an attempt to commit such crime."[188]

Moreover, the Code clarified—and arguably expanded—the scope of "aiding," that other form of common law complicity, by extending accomplice liability to mere attempts to aid. The common law did not require but-for (sine qua non) causation for accomplice liability;[189] rather than limiting accomplice liability to cases in which the principal would not have been able to commit the offense without her accomplice's assistance, the common law required merely that the accomplice's assistance was a contributing factor, that it made some difference, rather than *the* difference.[190] The Code, by contrast, extended accomplice liability even to those cases where the would-be accomplice was of no use to the principal whatsoever. From the perspective of penal treatment, the penological diagnosis of dangerousness is the same regardless of whether an actor succeeds in crime, or merely does everything she can to succeed, but then fails in the end, for one reason or another; as we will see shortly, this approach drives the Model Code's approach to inchoate liability in general, and to the law of accomplice liability in particular.[191]

At the same time, the Code rejected what had come to be known as the *Pinkerton* rule, according to which conspiracy, by itself, implies complicity. Under *Pinkerton v. United States*,[192] every member of a conspiracy automatically was criminally liable, as an accomplice, for any act of a co-conspirator committed in furtherance of the conspiracy. No additional proof of aiding or abetting was required. The conspiracy itself, without more, satisfied the conditions of complicity, even if there was no evidence that the purported accomplice did anything—or tried

---

188. § 5.02(1). The original draft of the complicity provision referred not to solicitation, but spelled out what soliciting meant: "command[ing], request[ing], encourag[ing] or provok[ing]." Tentative Draft No. 1, § 2.04(3), at 11 (May 1, 1953).
189. On the general doctrine of causation, which requires both but-for (or factual) and proximate (or legal) causation, see § 5.1 below.
190. See, e.g., State v. Tally, 15 So. 722, 738–39 (Ala. 1894).
191. See § 5.2 below.
192. 328 U.S. 640 (1946).

to do anything—to aid or abet, or even knew about, the specific offense committed by her co-conspirator.

As the liability of an accomplice is parasitic on the principal's conduct, through imputing the latter's conduct to the former and treating the accomplice as *if* she herself had engaged in it, the proper focus of inquiry under the Code is on the principal's conduct in committing the offense, rather than on some prior agreement between the principal and another. The question is whether the would-be accomplice in fact solicited the would-be principal to commit the specific offense, or in fact aided, or attempted to aid, her in committing it. Conspiracy—an agreement to engage in certain criminal conduct—may be sufficient to establish "aiding or abetting," but it need not be. On the issue of complicity, conspiracy thus is of evidentiary significance. It does not establish complicity as a matter of law.

The Code drafters regarded the rejection of the *Pinkerton* rule—which remains in force in many jurisdictions, including federal criminal law—as "[t]he most important point at which the Model Code formulation diverges from [the common law]."[193] Whether it is of more than doctrinal significance, however, is another question.[194] The practical effect of transforming a legal rule into an evidentiary standard is to give the factfinder (in theory the jury, in practice the judge, or rather the plea bargaining prosecutor) more wiggle room. Whether the process participants in question will use that discretion to reach a different result—in this case to find no complicity where *Pinkerton* would have found it as a matter of law—is another question. (The same question arises with respect to the Code drafters' decision to "reject" another categorically harsh common law rule—felony murder—by transforming it into an evidentiary standard.[195]) At least in theory, and in good Legal Process

193. Commentaries § 2.06, at 307.
194. For a case in which it apparently made a difference, see People v. McGee, 49 N.Y.2d 48 (1979); see also State v. Stein, 27 P.3d 184 (Wash. 2001).
195. See § 210.2(1)(b), defining a type of murder based on a presumption of recklessness and "extreme indifference to the value of human life," which arises from the commission of certain predicate felonies. Unlike in traditional felony murder, the state retains the burden of proving the requisite mens rea for murder, namely, in this case, recklessness and indifference. On the question of whether indifference is a mental

fashion, they would exercise the "discretionary powers conferred by the Code...in accordance with the criteria stated in the Code and, insofar as such criteria are not decisive, to further the general purposes stated in [§ 1.02]."[196]

In the present context, suffice it to note that the drafters went out of their way to compensate for contracting the scope of complicity resulting from their abandonment of *Pinkerton* by broadening the definition of complicity itself. How else could one explain a linguistic monstrosity such as "aids or agrees or attempts to aid such other person in planning or committing" an offense? Perhaps the Model Code drafters felt the need to reassure legislators, judges, and prosecutors throughout the land that nothing much had changed and that anyone who was reached by *Pinkerton* would be covered by the Code's complicity provision as well, when they deemed it appropriate.

So much for the Code's treatment of the so-called actus reus of complicity. On the subject of its mens rea, what the Code almost did is more interesting than what it did. This was one of the few issues on which the Code did not adopt the view of its principal drafter, Herbert Wechsler. Wechsler favored knowledge as the mens rea for complicity.[197] Judge Learned Hand, however, preferred purpose. Hand won.[198] A clause that would have based complicity on mere knowledge that one's conduct was

state here, see People v. Register, 60 N.Y.2d 270 (1983). For a comprehensive study of the state of the felony murder rule after its "abolition" in the Model Code, see Guyora Binder, Felony Murder and Mens Rea Default Rules: A Study in Statutory Interpretation, 4 Buff. Crim. L. Rev. 399 (2000); see generally Guyora Binder, Felony Murder (2012).

196. § 1.02(3).

197. Knowledge remains sufficient in other jurisdictions (which generally operate with a general concept of intent that encompasses both purpose and knowledge, and often many things besides, such as *dolus eventualis*). See, e.g., R. v. Hibbert, [1995] 2 S.C.R. 973 (Can.) (purpose requirement leads to "perverse consequences"); see generally Markus D. Dubber & Tatjana Hörnle, Criminal Law: A Comparative Approach ch. 10 (2014). On *dolus eventualis* as a form of intent bordering on recklessness, see § 4.2(D) above.

198. Commentaries § 2.06, at 318–19. Contrast United States v. Peoni, 100 F.2d 401 (2d Cir. 1938) (Hand, J.), with Backun v. United States, 112 F.2d 635 (4th Cir. 1940) (Parker, J.).

aiding another person's commission of an offense was struck from the original draft of the Code's complicity section.[199]

So it is purpose, then, that is needed for complicity under the Code.[200] The line between knowledge and purpose, however, may not be so hard to cross. The law has long recognized various ways in which purpose can be inferred from knowledge in general, and in cases of complicity in particular.[201] And the Model Penal Code drafters themselves acknowledged that the line between the two mental states was "narrow" to begin with.[202]

That knowing assistance does not qualify for complicity—for the imputation of one person's conduct to another—does not mean that it will not be punished. Unlike the Model Code itself, some of the criminal code revisions it inspired inserted a separate offense of facilitation, which essentially criminalizes the type of conduct captured by the deleted knowledge clause in the Model Code's original complicity provision.[203]

---

199. Here is what it would have said: "A person is an accomplice of another in commission of a crime if…acting with knowledge that such other person was committing or had the purpose of committing the crime, substantially facilitated its commission." Tentative Draft No. 1, § 2.04(3), at 11 (May 1, 1953). An alternate version would have read: "acting with knowledge that such other person was committing or had the purpose of committing the crime, he knowingly provided means or opportunity for the commission of the crime, substantially facilitating its commission." Id.

200. Though that is not entirely true. Although purpose is required for the imputation of a principal's conduct to her accomplice, it is not required for the imputation of an *instrument's* conduct to her user under § 2.06(2)(a). Commentaries § 2.06, at 302–03. Innocent or irresponsible persons, in this sense, are treated like inanimate objects— such as a hammer, or a remote control robot—that somehow are capable of voluntary acts, and therefore, conduct. Their user's criminal liability will depend entirely on the mens rea of the offense, if any. To say that he was reckless in causing his human instrument to engage in criminal conduct is just another way of saying that he was reckless in committing the criminal act, and therefore is liable for any offense with a mens rea of recklessness. In the Commentaries' stark example, "[o]ne who recklessly leaves his car keys with an irresponsible agent known to have a penchant for mad driving should…be accountable for a homicide due to such driving if the irresponsible agent uses the car in that way." Id. at 302.

201. See, e.g., People v. Lauria, 59 Cal. Rptr. 628 (Cal. App. 1967).

202. Tentative Draft No. 4, at 124 (Apr. 25, 1955).

203. See, e.g., N.Y. Penal Law § 115.00: "A person is guilty of criminal facilitation in the fourth degree when, believing it probable that he is rendering aid…to a person

In sum, then, complicity under the Model Code consists of purposely aiding or abetting ("soliciting") the commission of an offense by another person. In that case, that other person becomes my principal and I her accomplice, which means that her conduct will be imputed to me, or that I will be "legally accountable" for her conduct.

Given this basic concept of complicity, the rest of the Code's complicity section pretty much falls into place. As complicity is imputation of conduct, and conduct may consist of omission or commission, it is no surprise that omission in the face of a duty to act may amount to complicity.[204]

Similarly redundant is the Code's provision dealing with result offenses, that is to say, with offenses that contain a result element.[205] Being an accomplice means being held legally accountable for another person's conduct, not necessarily for the results of that person's conduct. Complicity puts me in the shoes of another person, treating his conduct as my own; I still have to walk in them. In other words, it means that my behavior satisfies one of the elements of the offense, namely the conduct element. Whether it also satisfies another, the result element, is another question.[206]

If the result element requires some sort of mens rea, including a mens rea other than purpose, then my liability for that result will depend on whether I had the requisite mens rea with respect to the result. And the answer to that question has nothing to do with the answer to the question of whether the principal had the requisite mens rea or not. This means also that the principal and I may face different criminal liability—that we have committed different result offenses—if these offenses differ in the mens rea they require with respect to their result element. So, to pick everyone's

who intends to commit a crime, he engages in conduct which provides such person with means or opportunity for the commission thereof and which in fact aids such person to commit a felony." Note that the New York statute requires less than knowledge, but a belief in the probability of assistance. At the same time, it limits facilitation to felonies. See, e.g., People v. Adams, 307 A.D.2d 475, 763 N.Y.S.2d 347 (2003). Although it is categorized as an inchoate—or incomplete—offense, it betrays its origin in the law of complicity by requiring the actual commission of the facilitated offense. For a discussion of inchoate offenses, see § 5.2 below.

204. § 2.06(3)(iii).
205. § 2.06(4).
206. See Riley v. State, 60 P.3d 204 (Alaska App. 2002).

favorite result offense, accomplice and principal may have committed different types of homicides. If the principal acted with the conscious objective of causing death, then he is guilty of murder. If his accomplice acted only with recklessness toward the possibility of death, then she is guilty of manslaughter.

To say that the mens rea of complicity is purpose, then, really is to say that the mens rea of complicity *with respect to conduct* is purpose. With respect to result, it is whatever it is in the definition of the offense. That leaves attendant circumstances, the third, and last, type of element recognized in the Model Code. What complicity's mens rea requirement is here—whether it is purpose (like conduct) or whether it is determined by the definition of the offense (like result)—the Code does not say.[207] That is just as well, as where conduct ends and attendant circumstance begins is not always easy to tell, as we already know from our discussion of offense element types; plus, recall that acting purposely with respect to attendant circumstances is defined as "being aware of the existence of such circumstances" (which is identical to the definition of knowledge) or "believ[ing] or hop[ing] that they exist"[208] (which is getting close to recklessness, insofar as belief is awareness of a risk smaller than practical certainty).

But let us assume that one can differentiate between conduct and attendant circumstance in a particular offense and that there is a significant difference between recklessness, and certainly negligence, and purpose with respect to an attendant circumstance. In that case it would seem that the Model Code should treat attendant circumstances as it does result, so that the mens rea attaching to any attendant circumstance would be that specified in the offense, rather than purpose. That way, the only difference between the analysis of the criminal liability of the principal and of the accomplice would be in the mens rea regarding conduct (unless of course the offense itself requires purpose with respect to conduct, in which case here too accomplice and principal would be treated alike). Conduct is different because, as we have seen, conduct is the nexus between principal

---

207. Commentaries § 2.06, at 311 n.37. See also Commentaries § 5.03, at 408–14 (conspiracy).
208. § 2.02(2)(a)(ii).

and accomplice, the conduit through which liability passes from one to the other. Once that nexus is established, each faces the liability to the extent that his mental state fits the requirements of a given criminal statute.[209]

As complicity imputes the principal's conduct to the accomplice, thus putting the accomplice in the principal's shoes, it also makes sense to impose accomplice liability on a person who is incapable of committing the offense herself.[210] So I can be guilty of receiving a bribe as an accomplice, even if I am not a public official, and therefore could not have been guilty of that offense as a principal. My liability is parasitic on the principal's conduct, and so if she committed the crime, so did I.

But what if *paying* a bribe is also a crime? If my assistance to the bribe recipient consisted in my payment of the bribe, then I would be liable both for receiving the bribe (under an accomplice theory) and for paying it (as a principal).[211] (In fact, if the public official solicited the bribe, she would be liable twice as well, once as principal in her bribe reception and once as accomplice to my bribe payment.) To deal with this situation,[212] the Code provides that accomplice liability does

209. For this reason, it is possible under the Code to be an accomplice to a principal who commits a crime that requires less than purpose with respect to one or all of its elements. See, e.g., People v. Flayhart, 72 N.Y.2d 737 (1988) (negligent homicide). Although the accomplice's mental state with respect to *her* conduct must be purpose, the principal's mental state with respect to the elements of the offense *he* committed is irrelevant for determining the accomplice's liability (though it is of course very relevant for figuring out his own liability). The significance of the principal for purposes of the accomplice's liability is only as a stand-in whose actual conduct can be attributed to the accomplice as constructive conduct. That principal and accomplice hang together only by the thread of conduct, and therefore could face different liability, was not so clear under the common law, given its talk of "shared intent" between accomplice and principal (or rather among the various types of accessories and principals). See, e.g., Maiorino v. Scully, 746 F. Supp. 331 (S.D.N.Y.1990) (murder and attempted murder for one, manslaughter and assault for the other).
210. § 2.06(5).
211. See, e.g., Standefer v. United States, 447 U.S. 10 (1980). For another example, the relation between seller and buyer (or rather distributor and possessor), of particular importance to drug criminal law, see People v. Manini, 79 N.Y.2d 561 (1992).
212. But not only with this sort of double-dipping. The Code drafters were also concerned about cases in which a legislature may not want to criminalize accomplice conduct, even if that conduct is not covered by some other offense that would generate principal liability, as in the case of bribe paying and bribe receiving. The drafters cited

not extend to conduct "inevitably incident" to the commission of the offense, unless the legislature provides otherwise.[213] Note, however, that the Code drafters did not think of this limitation as integral to their approach to complicity (or as required by the double-jeopardy proscription[214]): legislatures remain free to criminalize inevitably incident conduct as complicity; they just have to say that they are doing so.

Now, since complicity liability flows from one person (the principal) to another (the accomplice), can the accomplice stop the flow? If so, how? By "terminat[ing] his complicity prior to the commission of the offense."[215] This provision is the analog to the abandonment (or renunciation) provision in the law of attempt (and other inchoate offenses), except that here it is the accomplice who changes his mind, rather than the (would-be) principal.[216] Now, while "renunciation of purpose" is enough to avoid attempt liability, something more is required if I am the accomplice. If it is just me, or if I am the principal, changing my mind about committing the crime means that the crime will not be committed. By contrast, if I am an accomplice, I can abandon my criminal scheme and the crime might still be committed, by the principal. So the law of complicity requires not only that I stop doing what I am doing—that I stop aiding or abetting—but that I undo what I have done. According to the Model Code, this does not mean that I must succeed in preventing the commission of the crime, or that I do everything possible to prevent it. It instead requires that I "deprive [my complicity] of effectiveness in the commission of the offense," which is another way of saying that I eliminate it as a contributing cause. Just how I might do this depends on the nature of my assistance. If I supplied

---

"ambivalence in public attitudes" toward extending accomplice liability in cases such as that of a woman in a criminal late-term abortion prosecution against a doctor: "if liability is pressed to its logical extent, public support may be wholly lost." Commentaries § 2.06, at 325.

213. § 2.06(6). The Code also specifically provides that the conduct of "victims" cannot generate liability in their own victimization. § 2.06(6)(a).

214. Double jeopardy is not supposed to be a problem because the Fifth Amendment provides that no one may "be subject for the same offense to be twice put in jeopardy of life or limb," and reciprocal offenses are not "the same."

215. § 2.06(6)(c).

216. See § 5.2(D) below.

the means for committing the crime (e.g., weapons or burglary tools), I have to take them back. If all I did was encourage, then discouragement may be enough. Alternatively, I can "make proper efforts to prevent the commission of the offense," perhaps by alerting the police, or the victim, or in some other way, though, once again, these efforts need not be successful.

The renunciation—or "termination"—provision in essence provides for exceptional cases in which purposely aiding or abetting another person to commit an offense does not render me legally accountable for that person's criminal conduct. If I renounce my criminal purpose and make "proper efforts" to prevent the crime, then the principal's conduct will not be imputed to me after all. This is an exception that proves the rule of imputation by assistance. Put differently, renunciation rebuts the presumption of criminal dangerousness triggered by conduct sufficient to warrant derivative liability.

The provision in the Model Code's complicity section that fits least comfortably with the Code's general approach to complicity as derivative liability is the very last one, according to which an acquittal of the purported principal does not bar conviction of the purported accomplice. But without a principal, how can there be an accomplice, if the accomplice's liability derives from the principal's?[217]

The short answer, according to the Code drafters, is: the jury. Juries, alas, have been known to reach inconsistent verdicts. And one wrong acquittal, that of the principal, is enough. Why compound one error by another? In the words of the Commentaries, "[w]hile inconsistent verdicts of this kind present a difficulty, they appear to be a lesser evil than granting immunity to the accomplice because justice has miscarried in the charge against the person who committed the offense."[218] But how would we know which is the miscarriage of justice, the acquittal of the principal, or the conviction of the accomplice? Not to worry, though, because—as the Commentaries stress—the commission of the offense must still be proved for accomplice liability (even if the person who is

217. See, e.g., People v. Taylor, 12 Cal. 3d 686 (1974) ("collateral estoppel" bars conviction of accomplice after acquittal of principal).
218. Commentaries § 2.06, at 328; see also Standefer v. United States, 447 U.S. 10 (1980).

supposed to have committed it is acquitted),[219] and this is, at any rate, "a matter of procedure that need not be resolved in the substantive criminal code,"[220] for whatever that hedge is worth.[221]

(C) Corporations

Before we move on, we need to touch briefly on another corner of criminal law doctrine in which the conduct of one person is imputed to that of another, or even to a "corporate" entity other than a natural person.[222] In the latter case, the Code holds a corporation (or unincorporated association) legally accountable for the conduct of certain persons, its "agents," who act on its behalf. Corporate liability thus resembles complicity in that it requires the imputation of conduct. It differs from complicity in that the target of the imputation is not another person, but a nonpersonal entity (or, in Model Penal Code lingo, not a "natural person" but a nonnatural one[223]). That constructive person, the corporation, is incapable of conduct and so the conduct of its agent cannot, strictly speaking,

---

219. But see § 5.01(3) (attempt liability for aiding crime not committed).

220. Id.

221. Still, some substantive questions remain. What if the principal is acquitted not because she did not engage in the offense (i.e., because she did not satisfy level one of the analysis of criminal liability), but because she had a valid defense, either a justification or an excuse? If she is justified, it would seem that her accomplice would not be held criminally liable either, but not because he was not an accomplice, but because he too could avail himself of the justification defense—placing him in her shoes. In the case of an excuse, would the instrument theory of imputation apply (see above), or could he still be an accomplice (i.e., an aider or abettor), even if the principal is excused? Without jumping the gun too much (see § 7 below) one common—if not particularly precise—way of capturing the distinction between a justification and an excuse is to say that the former is about the act, and the latter about the actor. A justification renders the act not unlawful, whereas an excuse renders the actor not responsible for her act (however unlawful). As a characteristic of the act, a justification is imputed from principal to accomplice along with the act; as a characteristic of the actor, an excuse is not. See, e.g., United States v. Lopez, 662 F. Supp. 1083 (N.D. Cal. 1987); State v. Montanez, 894 A.2d 928 (Conn. 2006).

222. § 2.07.

223. The Model Penal Code was not alone in resolving the long-standing dispute about the personhood of corporations by codificatory fiat. It defines "person" to include "any natural person and, where relevant, a corporation or an unincorporated association." § 1.13(8).

be imputed to it at all. (It cannot be placed into the principal's shoes because it does not have legs, or if it does, it cannot walk.[224]) Instead, the corporation's accountability must rest on another basis, the aforementioned *agency*.[225]

While the Code thus permits the imputation of a person's conduct to a corporation, it does not provide for interpersonal vicarious liability, that is, for the imputation of one person's conduct to another person within the corporation, such as from a lower level employee to his supervisor. A manager may, of course, be liable as an accomplice for the conduct of her subordinate, provided that she aided or abetted his conduct as specified in the law of complicity. But the mere relationship between the two within the corporation—or between an employer and her employee—does not generate criminal liability of one for the conduct of the other. Under the Model Code, *respondeat superior* does not apply to criminal liability, not even in the corporate context.[226]

§ 5 "...THAT INFLICTS OR THREATENS..."

So far, we have covered the first—and traditionally the single most important—component of the definition of crime laid out in § 1.02 of the Model Penal Code: conduct. Recall that this section defines crime

---

224. One might conclude that these and similar difficulties, or idiosyncracies, of corporate criminal liability are reasons to reject the possibility of corporate criminal liability altogether. The Model Penal Code does not seriously consider this option; after all, the Supreme Court long ago had blessed corporate criminal liability, albeit in a hasty opinion that treated the result as a foregone conclusion, N.Y. Central & Hudson River R.R. Co. v. United States, 212 U.S. 481 (1909). German criminal law continues to reject corporate criminal liability, at least de jure, if not de facto. See Thomas Weigend, Societas delinquere non potest? A German Perspective, 6 J. Int'l Crim. J. 927 (2008); see generally Markus D. Dubber & Tatjana Hörnle, Criminal Law: A Comparative Approach ch. 11 (2014).

225. This theory of imputation applies to any conduct of a corporate agent, no matter what the crime. See, e.g., Commonwealth v. Penn Valley Resorts, 343 Pa. Super. 387 (1985) (homicide); People v. Warner-Lambert, 51 N.Y.2d 295 (1980) (same).

226. But see United States v. Dotterweich, 320 U.S. 277 (1943) (recognizing vicarious criminal liability); Commonwealth v. Koczwara, 397 Pa. 575 (1959) (same except "in cases involving true crimes").

as "conduct that inflicts or threatens substantial harm to individual or public interests."

Traditional Anglo-American criminal law concerned itself largely with the two general elements of any crime: actus reus and mens rea. We saw how the Model Code differentiated these two concepts into a taxonomy of offense elements and modes of culpability, complete with rules of statutory interpretation and theories of imputing one person's conduct to another. Let us now take a closer look at the relation between conduct as defined in a criminal statute and the harm it might—or might not—inflict. In the next, and final, section of the current chapter, we will consider the nature of that harm, rather than its relation to conduct.[227]

§ 5.1 Causation

The doctrinal locus for questions of the connection between conduct and harm, or more specifically the conduct and the result elements of an offense, is the law of causation—the "causal relationship between conduct and result."[228] The first thing to note about causation is that it is only an issue in result offenses, that is to say, in offenses that contain a result element. The prime example of these is homicide, which is all result, as the Model Code's definition makes plain: "A person is guilty of criminal homicide if he purposely, knowingly, recklessly or negligently causes the death of another human being."[229] Under this definition, it matters not how the person causes the death of another, just *that* he does. For purposes of homicide liability, poisoning, tripping, stabbing, shooting, pushing, and running over are all the same. Conduct is required to be sure—even if by omission—but it is the connection between the conduct, unspecified in the definition of the offense, and the death that makes all the difference. Causation is not an issue in conduct offenses, such as driving while intoxicated or adultery, or status offenses, such as

---

227. See § 6 below.
228. § 2.03. See David J. Karp, Note, Causation in the Model Penal Code, 78 Colum. L. Rev. 1249 (1978).
229. § 210.1(1).

drug possession or vagrancy, which are criminalized regardless of whatever harmful consequences they may have.

The next thing to note about causation is that it consists of two components. First, there is factual (or but-for) cause. For conduct to cause a result for purposes of the criminal law, it must be a *conditio sine qua non* of the result. Next, there is legal (or proximate) cause. For an antecedent to be a cause, it must be both, factual and legal. Perhaps the best way to think of legal cause is as whatever the law of causation requires beyond factual cause for conduct to count as a cause, no matter how circular that may sound.[230] The Model Code makes this point straightforwardly at the very outset of its causation section:

(1) Conduct is the cause of a result when:
    (a) it is an antecedent but for which the result in question would not have occurred; and the relationship between the conduct and result satisfies any additional causal requirements imposed by the Code or by the law defining the offense.[231]

Perhaps not surprisingly, most of the law of causation is about legal cause. In fact, the rest of the Code section on causation is about these very "additional causal requirements imposed by the Code." It turns out that these additional causal requirements differ depending on the mode of culpability, if any, that attaches to the result element of the offense in question.

But let us briefly deal with factual cause first, before tackling the intricacies of the amorphous concept of legal cause. The Model Code did not add anything to traditional factual cause analysis, and did not find new solutions to old factual cause problems. These problems tend

230. The concept of "legal cause" in tort law is no less tautological. See Restatement (Second) of Torts § 9 ("the causal sequence by which the actor's tortious conduct has resulted in an invasion of some legally protected interest of another...such that the law holds the actor responsible for such harm unless there is some defense to liability").
231. § 2.03(1).

to arise in cases with two potential but-for causes. If two actions constitute sufficient concurrent causes of a result, that is to say, if either of them would have been sufficient to cause the result, then neither of them is the result's but-for cause. Suppose two people, acting independently, each fire one fatal shot at a third. Neither shot is the but-for cause of the victim's death because the victim would have died even if it had not been fired. The only way the victim would not be dead is if neither shot had been fired. And yet, the law of causation treats both shots as but-for causes. How? By stressing that the ~~causation inquiry focuses on the particular harm inflicted at a particular time in a particular way, rather than on the abstract category of harm captured in the statute~~ ("death of another human being"). And the particular harm inflicted at a particular time in a particular way was in fact caused by the two shots. Plus, although each individual shot does not make for a but-for cause, they do constitute a single, cumulative, but-for cause. But for *one or the other* being fired, the victim's death would not have occurred.

But-for cause does not sound like much. To see that it has some bite, compare it with the type of causal connection required for accomplice liability. Recall that for assistance to count as complicity, it is not necessary that it be the *conditio sine qua* the principal could not have committed the offense.[232] Here the Model Code follows traditional analysis, as exemplified in this passage from the well-known case *of State v. Tally*:[233]

> The assistance given…need not contribute to the criminal result in the sense that but for it the result would not have ensued. It is quite sufficient if it facilitated a result that would have transpired without it. It is quite enough if the aid merely rendered it easier for the principal actor to accomplish the end intended by him and the aider and abettor, though in all human probability the end would have been attained without it.

---

232. Tort law, too, requires less than but-for cause. Being "a substantial factor in bringing about the harm" is enough. Restatement (Second) of Torts § 431(a).
233. 15 So. 722, 738–39 (Ala. 1894).

Not every antecedent is a contributing cause, not every contributing cause is a but-for cause, and—most important—not every but-for cause is a proximate, or legal, cause. Most of the criminal law of causation concerns itself with this third, and final, filter applied to the myriad of antecedents to a particular harm, the infliction of which is proscribed in a criminal statute.

The law of causation in this sense resembles the law of complicity. Both are about attribution, or imputation. The law of complicity sets out the conditions under which one person's conduct can be imputed to another. The law of causation determines when a particular harm—the "result"—can be attributed to a person's conduct.

There is of course a fairly straightforward way of making the necessary connection between result and conduct, and thereby enabling the imputation of the one to whoever committed the other: one might decide that factual cause, or cause strictly speaking, is enough.[234]

The Model Code, however, does not stop there. It makes explicit the normative component of the apparently factual inquiry of traditional common law causation analysis. Rather than speaking in terms of "chains of causations" that are "broken" by intervening causes, as the common law did, the Model Code instead frames the legal cause analysis openly in terms of culpability and fair attribution. The question is not whether some conduct is the cause of some result. The question instead is whether some result ought to be attributed to the person engaging in that conduct.

Once again, the Code drafters can be seen as replacing common law rules about how to handle particular clusters of causation issues with a general, flexible standard, the application of which is left to the guided discretion of process participants (in particular the jury).[235] Note, however, that the drafters did not go quite as far in the direction of flexibility and normativity as they might have gone. In the end, they shied away from specifically instructing the factfinder—the hypothetical jury—to disregard a result "too remote or accidental in its occurrence to have

---

234. Arguably this is true of the law of torts. See Restatement (Second) of Torts § 435 (foreseeability irrelevant).
235. See § 2 above (Legal Process and the Model Penal Code).

a just bearing on the actor's liability or on the gravity of his offense." The open invitation to considerations of justice was instead relegated to noncommittal brackets.[236]

As it is about attribution, Model Code causation resembles complicity. Another way to think about causation in the Code, however, is to place it alongside two other related doctrinal questions: mens rea and attempt. As in the case of complicity, so too in the law of causation, attribution is largely a matter of culpability—and mental states in particular. That is not to say that causation and mens rea are one and the same thing. Think of mens rea as a first cut at the question of culpability at an abstract level—the level of the definition of the offense. If there is no mens rea, then the question of causation does not even come up.

Causation takes the culpability inquiry to a lower, factual, level—the level of what actually happened. Assuming the connection among an actor, the defendant, and a general *type* of result as defined in a statute—say, death—has been established, we next ask ourselves whether a similar connection exists between the actor's particular conduct and the particular way in which the abstract result—death—came about: by stabbing, by firing a gun, by punching, in the head or in the stomach, once, twice or three times, by aiming at one person, but hitting another instead, who dies within three minutes or five days or two years, after having been run over by a drunk driver, receiving improper medical care, committing suicide in despair over her injuries, and so on. None of these details appears on the face of the criminal statute—in this case, as in the vast majority of causation cases, homicide—and yet it is these details that determine whether a particular result can be attributed, causally, to the particular conduct of a particular person.

And so the Model Code's causation test looks like a particularized, and simplified, version of the Code's mens rea test. The type of result defined in the statute—death—is run through the complex mens rea test; now the specific result that actually occurred—death by

236. § 2.03(2)(b) & (3)(b) ("too remote or accidental in its occurrence to have a [just] bearing on the actor's liability or on the gravity of his offense"); see Commentaries § 2.03, at 261. For other uses of this drafting technique, see §§ 4.01(1) (insanity), 210.6 (capital sentencing factors).

strangulation through the use of an electric cord in the dark—is run through the streamlined causation test.

There are five modes of culpability—counting strict liability.[237] There are three causation tests. One for purpose and knowledge (or, more precisely, for offenses in which purpose or knowledge are attached to the result element; murder would be an example). One for recklessness and negligence (e.g., manslaughter and negligent homicide, respectively). And one for strict liability.

The basic idea is straightforward. If purpose or knowledge is required with respect to the abstract offense element (death), then "purpose" or "contemplation" is required with respect to the specific result (e.g., death by strangulation). If recklessness or negligence is the result mens rea, then the actual result need not have been within the actor's purpose or her contemplation; instead, it must have merely been "within the risk of which the actor is aware" for recklessness (which, you will recall, is defined as awareness and disregard of a risk), and within the risk of which she "should be aware" for negligence (defined in the Code's mens rea provision, § 2.02, as constructive, but not actual, awareness of a risk).

Most interesting causation cases are not covered by these background rules. They are about the exceptions. The Code specifically deals with two particularly common ones: (1) different victim, and (2) different harm. Differences in the identity of the victim are irrelevant. If the actual result differs from the one contemplated[238] only in that it affected a different victim (a person or piece of property), that result is still causally attributed to the actor. Let us say I aim at Karl's head and pull the trigger, fully contemplating that I will hit and kill him. Karl ducks at the last moment and I hit and kill Melinda instead, who had been standing behind Karl. According to the Code's causation analysis, Melinda's death will be attributed to my conduct (aiming and pulling the trigger), even though the only result I had contemplated was Karl's death.

---

237. See § 4.2 above.

238. Or whatever the requisite mental state might be—for example, if recklessness is in the statute, rather than purpose or knowledge, then contemplation is not required, but awareness of the risk that the actual result might come about is.

Differences between actual and contemplated harm may or may not be relevant, depending on whether the actual harm is more or less serious than the contemplated harm. If I thought I would inflict *greater* harm than I actually managed to inflict, then the actual harm will nonetheless be attributed to my conduct. Not so if, by contrast, I planned to do less harm than I ended up inflicting. Suppose I aim a gun at Richard's stomach and pull the trigger with the intent to kill him. If he survives, I will still be liable for (aggravated) assault, even though—strictly speaking—the particular harm that actually occurred was not within my contemplation (I had hoped to kill him, after all, not just to inflict (serious) bodily injury).[239] If, conversely, I try merely to hurt him, but end up killing him instead, I will not be liable for murder. That does not mean that I will not be liable for another type of homicide, though. Even if I did not intend to kill him, I may have been reckless or negligent with respect to his death, if I knew—or should have known—there was a good chance that he would die from a shot in the stomach.

And so the Code uses causation analysis to dispose of two irksome problems of criminal liability. Or rather, it takes care to explain that strict causation analysis does not stand in the way of assigning criminal liability in certain, supposedly unobjectionable, cases despite differences between the actual and the contemplated result.

More difficult are cases of a mismatch between actual and contemplated result that do not fall into either category (different victim or contemplated harm more serious than actual harm). What are we to do in cases where the actual harm bears a sufficient resemblance to the harm contemplated (say death), but is "remote or accidental" nonetheless? How, in other words, are we to handle the causation issues most likely to appear in a law school exam (and least likely to appear in real life)? What if I hit my unsuspecting neighbor over the head with a snow shovel in retaliation for the inconsiderate use of his supercharged snowblower in subzero degree weather after a solid week of heavy snowfall, fully intending to kill him? Assume further that, having snapped out of my homicidal rage, I remorsefully drag the lightly bleeding, but

---

239. § 211.1(2).

still conscious, man into my car and, over snowbanks and through unplowed sidestreets, rush him to the hospital, where he falls into the hands of the inevitably incompetent surgeon/intern/nurse, who naturally misdiagnoses him as suffering from appendicitis, mistakenly removes his left lung, and then, accidentally drops three dollars in small change into his opened chest cavity before sewing him back up. Add, if you like, that he, upon awakening—miraculously—the next morning, rips out the "tubes inserted into his nasal passages and trachea in order to maintain the breathing process"[240] and, for some additional remoteness, that his chance of recovery upon proper treatment would have been 100 percent.

It is here that the Code drafters threw up their hands and placed the issue squarely in the jury's lap. For the Code explains simply that "remote or accidental" harms are attributable to an actor only if they are not "too remote or accidental." How is the jury to tell the difference between remote and too remote? By asking itself whether the harm still has "a [just] bearing on the actor's liability or on the gravity of his offense." In other words, "remote" harms are imputable to a person if they are [justly] imputable to her, in which case they are not "too remote."

Apart from its circularity, the problem with this approach to the most vexing causation problems in the criminal law is that it does not provide the factfinder with much guidance to speak of. (It is a standard, not a rule, after all.) The drafters jettisoned the panoply of more or less rigid rules developed by common law judges, which turned on such factors as "intervening or concurrent clauses, natural or human; unexpected physical conditions; distinctions between mortal and non-mortal wounds,"[241] and, perhaps most significant, the foreseeability, actual or constructive, of the result.[242] An alternative formulation would have incorporated the latter factor into the causation analysis by asking whether the result "occurs in a manner which the actor knows or should

240. United States v. Hamilton, 182 F. Supp. 548, 549 (D.D.C. 1960).
241. Commentaries § 2.03, at 261.
242. We might also add the most straightforward, and least attractive, of these rules, the "year-and-a-day rule," which barred the attribution of deaths occurring more than a year after the act in question. Cf. Rogers v. Tennessee, 532 U.S. 451 (2001).

know is rendered substantially more probable by his conduct."[243] Note, however, that the Code's flexible standard does not render the traditional causation factors irrelevant. It merely transforms them from dispositive rules into guidelines for the application of a less artificial standard that exposes the underlying issue of imputation for all the world to see, no matter how uncomfortably vague it might be. And so (actual) foresight and (constructive) foreseeability are alive and well in contemporary causation law, even in MPC jurisdictions such as New York,[244] as are the other familiar analytic tools such as "supervening causes."[245]

But what about strict liability? If you conceive of causation in terms of attribution, and therefore of culpability, then strict liability crimes (more precisely, crimes with a strict liability result element) will pose a problem. If you are criminally liable even if you lacked mens rea with respect to the abstract result element in the statute, then surely you are criminally liable even if you lacked mens rea with respect to the specific harm that actually occurred.

Causation, in other words, would be reduced to factual, but-for, causation. That is how it stood in the original draft of the causation provision.[246] And that is exactly what some courts concluded, even (or perhaps especially) in the most serious of all strict liability crimes, felony murder—which does without mens rea with respect to the result element of "murder," though it may require all manner of mens rea with respect to any or all elements of its other half, the (predicate) "felony."[247]

Not so according to the final version of the Code. Even for strict liability crimes, there is now a legal cause requirement beyond factual cause: *probability*, objectively speaking—that is, without any

---

243. Commentaries § 2.03, at 261 n.17 (quoting Tentative Draft No. 4, at 16 (Apr. 25, 1955)).

244. See, e.g., People v. Kibbe, 35 N.Y.2d 407 (1974); People v. Warner-Lambert, 51 N.Y.2d 295 (1980). New York did not codify causation. For a similar result in an MPC jurisdiction that did, see Commonwealth v. Rementer, 410 Pa. Super. 9 (1991).

245. See, e.g., People v. Griffin, 80 N.Y.2d 723 (1993) (medical malpractice). This also means that Hart & Honoré's well-known study of causation in (criminal) law, which emphasized the significance of intervention by an autonomous agent, has lost little of its relevance. See H.L.A. Hart & A.M. Honoré, Causation in the Law (1959).

246. Commentaries § 2.03, at 264 n.21.

247. See, e.g., People v. Stamp, 82 Cal. Rptr. 598 (Cal. App. 1969).

requirement that the actor be—or should be—aware of, or contemplate, that result or even the risk that it might come about. Anything else would be, as the Commentaries explain, unjust.[248] But then so is strict liability.

So causation is like complicity in that it is about attribution, though of a particular result to one's conduct, rather than of another's (the principal's) conduct. Like complicity, it is also about mens rea. Attribution for purposes of culpability turns, among other things, upon one's attitude toward the result (or, in the case of complicity, the other person's conduct).

What happens if the "causal relationship between conduct and result"[249] is not such as to permit attributing one to the other, and therefore to me, the actor? If criminal liability (for result offenses) requires causation, does the absence of causation imply absence of criminal liability? No, because there is always *attempt*.

§ 5.2 Inchoate Offenses

Attempt is one of the Model Code's "inchoate offenses."[250] The others are, in order of appearance, conspiracy, solicitation, and possession.[251] To say that inchoate offenses are inchoate[252] (or "incomplete,"[253] "anticipatory,"[254] or "preparatory"[255]) is a polite way of saying that they are not offenses at all, at least insofar as a criminal offense is conduct (including

---

248. Commentaries § 2.03, at 264.

249. § 2.03.

250. See generally Herbert Wechsler et al., The Treatment of Inchoate Crimes in the Model Penal Code of the ALI: Attempt, Solicitation, and Conspiracy, 61 Colum. L. Rev. 571 (1961).

251. The Model Code does not contain a provision on facilitation, which appears among the inchoate offenses in some criminal codes based on the Code. See, e.g., N.Y. Penal Law § 115.00. As it requires the commission of the offense, facilitation, however, is best thought of not as an inchoate offense, but as a sort of mini complicity—aiding with less than purpose. See § 4.4(B) above.

252. "1. In an initial or early stage; incipient. 2. Imperfectly formed or developed." American Heritage Dictionary of the English Language: Fourth Edition (2000).

253. See, e.g., Chisler v. State, 553 So. 2d 654 (Ala. Crim. App. 1989) (quoting Ala. Code § 13A–2–23 cmt. at 40).

254. See, e.g., N.Y. Penal Law tit. G ("Anticipatory Offenses").

255. See, e.g., Texas Penal Code ch. 15 ("Preparatory Offenses"). "Preparatory" is problematic as "preparation" short of an "attempt" is not punishable.

nonconduct, namely an omission) that matches the statutory definition of a criminal offense. So whatever attempted murder is, it is *not* murder. But in criminal law—at least in modern criminal law—if you get close enough to the actual commission of a criminal offense, you will be punished (or subjected to peno-correctional treatment) even if you came up short.

Inchoate offenses, then, are not offenses at all, but lay out ways in which criminal law holds someone liable even if she did not actually commit a criminal offense. So we do not convict people of "attempt," but of "attempted murder," not of "conspiracy," but of "conspiracy to distribute drugs," and so on. Inchoate liability, in other words, is parasitic on "choate" liability[256]—in theory, at least, as the crime was never actually completed.

Note, however, that the Model Code, as does American criminal law generally, also treats inchoate offenses as "offenses of general applicability."[257] Attempting—or conspiring or soliciting another—to commit *any* offense, no matter how minor, is criminal. Inchoacy, in other words, is truly a general mode of criminal liability, rather than a doctrinal tool for expanding the reach of particular offense definitions.[258]

---

256. "Choate" being, according to the Oxford English Dictionary, "[a]n erroneous word, framed to mean 'finished,' 'complete,' as if the *in-* of *inchoate* were the L. negative."

257. This is the title of the chapter on inchoate offenses in the Proposed New Federal Criminal Code of 1971. Prop. New Fed. Crim. Code ch. 10 (1971). In German criminal law, an attempt to commit a felony is always punishable, an attempt to commit a misdemeanor only if the statute specifically so provides. § 23 StGB. For a comparative analysis, see Markus D. Dubber & Tatjana Hörnle, Criminal Law: A Comparative Approach ch. 12 (2014).

258. That is not to say that the Code does not *also* recognize a host of specific attempt offenses in its special part. For *attempts*, see, e.g., §§ 211.1 (assault), 221.1(2)(a) (burglary), 224.7(3) (deceptive business practices), 241.6(1) (witness tampering); for *solicitations*, see, e.g., §§ 210.5(2) (aiding suicide), 224.8 (commercial bribery), 224.9(2) (rigging publicly exhibited contest), 240.1 (official bribery), 240.3 (compensation for past official action), 240.5 (gifts to public servants), 240.7 (selling political endorsement), 241.6(3) (witness tampering), 251.2(2)(d) & (h) (prostitution), 251.3 (loitering to solicit deviate sexual relations); for *conspiracies*, see, e.g., §§ 224.8 (commercial bribery), 224.9(2) (rigging publicly exhibited contest), 240.1 (official bribery), 240.3 (compensation for past official action), 240.5 (gifts to public servants), 240.6(2) (compensating public servant for assisting private interests), 240.7 (selling political endorsement), 241.6(3) (witness tampering), 251.2(2)(h) (prostitution), 251.4(2) (obscenity).

Despite their derivative status, and their fairly recent introduction into Anglo-American criminal law, inchoate offenses lie at the very core of the Model Code.[259] The drafters lavished considerable attention on this topic, and so will we. It is here that the Code's treatmentism emerges most clearly. An attempt is punished because—and insofar as—it reveals a person's abnormal criminal disposition. The same goes for the other inchoate offenses. As criminal disposition is key, there is no reason to retain the old common law rule that attempts should be punished less severely than consummated offenses.[260] A consummated offense and its inchoate version provide the same evidence of criminal disposition. If we were to catch the criminal earlier, rather than later, there is no reason we should punish him any less than we would have otherwise. His penological diagnosis is the same, so is his need for penal treatment, and so should be his punishment (which is but an outmoded word for treatment).[261] Likewise, impossible attempts (even legally impossible ones) are punishable,[262] along with unilateral "conspiracies"[263] and uncommunicated "solicitations."[264]

(A) Attempt

One way behavior might fall short of a complete offense is by failing to bring about the *result* specified in the criminal statute. If I set out to kill my roommate by thrusting a steak knife into his rib cage, but succeed

---

259. The origin of modern attempt law is generally traced back to the 1784 English case of Rex v. Scofield, Cald. 397 (1784). See generally Francis B. Sayre, Criminal Attempts, 41 Harv. L. Rev. 821 (1928). Attempts to commit particular offenses, particularly robbery, were punished long before then. 4 William Blackstone, Commentaries on the Laws of England 241 (1769).
260. See § 5.05(1).
261. Equal treatment for equal diagnosis also meant doing away with other (common law) rules, (1) that an inchoate offense could be punished *more* harshly than its consummated version, and (2) that the inchoate version—specifically conspiracy—and the consummated version of a single crime could be punished cumulatively. See, e.g., Pinkerton v. United States, 328 U.S. 640 (1946); Callanan v. United States, 364 U.S. 587 (1961).
262. See § 5.01 ("conduct which would constitute the crime *if the attendant circumstances were as he believes them to be*") (emphasis added); Commentaries § 5.01, at 307–20.
263. See § 5.04.
264. See § 5.02(2).

only in hurting him, then my behavior matches the definition of murder (purposely or knowingly causing the death of another human being) in every element except the result. He is a human being. He is another human being. I acted with purpose. But I did not cause the result I intended, namely his death. As I set out to engage in behavior that would match the definition of the criminal offense of murder in every respect, but failed to do so, I am not liable for murder, but for attempted murder.

Note the distinction between attempt and causation here. This case does not raise a causation question because the abstract result element laid out in the statute (death) did not in fact occur. As my roommate survived, my behavior cannot be described as causing the death of another human being—or anyone else, for that matter. Without that result element—without a dead person—the question whether that result could be attributed to me does not arise. Hence no causation question.

Now assume that my roommate did die, but only after a sequence of intervening causes and unforeseeable turns of events that would make his death "too remote" to be fairly attributable to me. In other words, let us assume my act of stabbing him does not qualify as a legal cause of his death. In that case, I would escape murder liability because even though most of the elements of murder are satisfied (purpose, death, another human being), one is not: causation. Although this time there is a dead person, there is no causal connection between my act and the corpus delicti. Nonetheless, as I did my best to satisfy all of the elements, including causation, I am still liable for attempted murder.[265]

Unlike causation, the question of attempt does not arise only in result offenses. An attempt can fall short in as many ways as there are building blocks of criminal liability (offense element types).[266] Failing to bring about an intended *result* is only one. Consider, for example, the lobbyist who slips an envelope stuffed with cash to a tourist whom she mistakes for a powerful legislator. Here the missing element is an *attendant circumstance*: the bribe recipient being a "public servant."[267] Or take

265. Cf. People v. Dlugash, 41 N.Y.2d 725 (1977).
266. Cf. Francis B. Sayre, Criminal Attempts, 41 Harv. L. Rev. 821 (1928).
267. § 240.1(1).

the case of the ex-husband whose plan to burn down his gasoline-soaked former family home fails only because he cannot get any of the soggy matches in his pocket to strike a flame. Here there is no *conduct* element (assuming arson requires one to "start a fire"[268]).

By attempting to commit a crime, but failing for one reason or another, I have revealed myself as a person in need of peno-correctional treatment. In the words of the New York Court of Appeals, "[t]he ultimate issue is whether an individual's intentions and actions, though failing to achieve a manifest and malevolent criminal purpose, constitute a danger to organized society of sufficient magnitude to warrant the imposition of criminal sanctions."[269] Or, in the language of the Code Commentaries, "the primary purpose of punishing attempts is to neutralize dangerous individuals."[270] And so attempt law is about diagnosing these human dangers, about detecting the all-important "indication that the actor is disposed toward [criminal] activity, not alone on this occasion but on others."[271]

In thinking about attempts, it is useful to distinguish incomplete from complete attempts. Incomplete attempts cover cases in which the defendant has not done everything she thought was necessary to consummate the offense. In the case of a complete attempt, she has done all she planned to do, but her efforts fell short nonetheless.

Let us start with *incomplete attempts.* In attempts that fall short on conduct (§ 5.01(1)(c)), dangerousness is indicated if two symptoms are present: a "substantial step" (the actus reus of attempt) and purpose (the mens rea of attempt). The first symptom, however, collapses into the second as the point of the substantial step requirement is merely evidentiary—a step is substantial if it is "strongly corroborative of

268. § 220.1(1).
269. People v. Dlugash, 41 N.Y.2d 725, 726 (1977).
270. Commentaries § 5.01, at 323.
271. Commentaries art. 5, at 294 (introduction). The point of criminal attempt law is *not* that even an unsuccessful attempt at committing a crime can inflict harm upon the intended victim (who, for instance, might have escaped death by the skin of her teeth). Unlike in tort law, there is no requirement that the intended victim even be aware of the attempt on her physical or psychological integrity. See Restatement (Second) of Torts § 22.

the actor's criminal purpose."[272] Purpose, however, is just a stand in for extreme dangerousness. As we saw in our discussion of the Code's taxonomy of mental states, purpose stands atop the hierarchy of modes of culpability and, as such, calls for the most intensive form of peno-correctional intervention. Purposeful criminal actors, in other words, are as dangerous as they come. And it is those human dangers that attempt law seeks to identify and eliminate.

Once again, the Code drafters identify a basic question—the diagnosis of abnormal criminal dangerousness manifesting itself as "purpose"—and then adopt a flexible standard ("substantial step") in the place of a cornucopia of time-honored rules developed by common law courts to carve up nebulous doctrinal territory (the distinction between (nonpunishable) "preparation" and (punishable) "attempt"). These rules are then reclassified as evidentiary factors to be taken into account when addressing the basic question. Unlike in other pockets of doctrine, however, in the case of attempts, the Code drafters actually listed many of the traditional rules for locating the *locus poenitentiae* by differentiating mere "preparation" from "attempt," and—now—differentiating a mere step from that all-important "substantial step:"[273]

(a) lying in wait, searching for or following the contemplated victim of the crime;

(b) enticing or seeking to entice the contemplated victim of the crime to go to the place contemplated for its commission;

(c) reconnoitering the place contemplated for the commission of the crime;

(d) unlawful entry of a structure, vehicle or enclosure in which it is contemplated that the crime will be committed;

(e) possession of materials to be employed in the commission of the crime, which are specially designed for such unlawful use

---

272. § 5.01(2). Well, actually, the double-negative-happy Model Code provides that a step *cannot* be substantial *unless* it is evidence of purpose.

273. More precisely, it lists not the rules themselves ("last proximate act," "physical proximity," "dangerous proximity," "indispensable element," "probable desistance," "abnormal step," and of course "*res ipsa loquitur*"), but the factual scenarios driving their application. Cf. Commentaries § 5.01, at 321–29.

or which can serve no lawful purpose of the actor under the circumstances;

(f) possession, collection or fabrication of materials to be employed in the commission of the crime, at or near the place contemplated for its commission, where such possession, collection or fabrication serves no lawful purpose of the actor under the circumstances;

(g) soliciting an innocent agent to engage in conduct constituting an element of the crime.[274]

It is often said that the Code's approach to the actus reus in (incomplete) attempts focuses not on what the actor has not done, but on what she has done instead.[275] It is a "substantial step" that turns preparation into attempt, not the "last proximate act" before the commission of the target offense. That makes perfect sense, of course, as the Code does not punish attempt because it is almost a consummated offense. An attempt does not just *approximate* a real offense; it is just as good for purposes of the Code's treatmentism. What matters is the actor's abnormal dangerousness, no matter how it might manifest itself.

While keeping the magical line between preparation and attempt firmly in mind, it is worth reminding ourselves that there is one type of inchoate offense that is even more inchoate than preparation: possession.[276] Possession, unlike the other inchoate offenses in the Code, actually is a self-standing offense. The Code contains two broad possession offenses, which permit the state to identify dangerous persons long before they have engaged in an act that amounts to a preparation, never mind an attempt to commit a specific crime. It is a misdemeanor both to possess "any instrument of crime" and to possess "any offensive weapon."[277]

---

274. § 5.01(2)(a)–(g).
275. Commentaries § 5.01, at 329; see, e.g., Commonwealth v. Donton, 439 Pa. Super. 406 (1995).
276. See § 4.1(D) above. Not only is possession not quite an attempt, the attempt to possess is itself criminal. People v. Ryan, 82 N.Y.2d 497 (1993).
277. §§ 5.06 & .07.

Possession of a criminal instrument requires "purpose to employ it criminally." Possession of an offensive weapon does not. Criminal purpose, however, is easily found, thanks to a litany of presumptions attaching to the possession of "a firearm or other weapon on or about his person, in a vehicle occupied by him, or otherwise readily available for use." Establishing that possession, which gives rise to the presumption of criminal purpose, is simplified in turn by its very own set of "Presumptions as to Possession of Criminal Instruments in Automobiles."

There is no need to show criminal purpose if the item possessed qualifies as an offensive weapon, rather than merely as an instrument of crime. The definition of offensive weapon, however, is rather generous, including "any bomb, machine gun, sawed-off shotgun, firearm specially made or specially adapted for concealment or silent discharge, any blackjack, sandbag, metal knuckles, dagger, or other implement for the infliction of serious bodily injury which serves no common lawful purpose." Should the item possessed not fit into this broad category of commonly possessed items, it has a yet greater chance of qualifying as an instrument of crime, which includes "(a) anything specially made or specially adapted for criminal use; or (b) anything commonly used for criminal purposes and possessed by the actor under circumstances which do not negative unlawful purpose."

We have already seen, in our discussion of the act requirement, how tenuous my relationship to an object may be to count as "possession." If we add this flexible concept of possession to the broad range of items the possession of which is criminal, we end up with an offense of remarkable scope. The key, as in all inchoate offenses, is purpose, as a placeholder for criminal dangerousness. Possession is criminal because—and only insofar as—it manifests criminal purpose.[278] Possession is presumptive evidence of that purpose, and will result in a diagnosis of criminal dangerousness with a prescription of peno-correctional treatment unless I can rebut that presumption, or "negative" that purpose.[279]

---

278. Even more remotely, *proximity* to an item is criminal, as presumptive evidence of possession, unless I can rebut the presumption. See, e.g., § 5.06(3).

279. See §§ 5.06(1)(b) & 5.07.

Let us now move on to *complete attempts*. In the first type of case, covered in § 5.01(1)(a), the actor does everything she planned on doing, but nonetheless does not quite manage to commit the crime because things are not what they seemed. Take Lady Eldon, for instance. In Francis Wharton's classic hypothetical, Lady Eldon does her best to smuggle French lace into England. Her attempt proves futile, however, because—unbeknownst to her—the lace in question turns out to be not French, but English (the bad news), hence cheap and, more important, not subject to duty (the good news).[280] The really bad news for Lady Eldon, however, is that she qualifies for attempt liability under the Model Penal Code; she did everything she thought was necessary, with the requisite purpose, to commit the offense of smuggling and would have succeeded, had "the attendant circumstances [been] as [s]he believe[d] them to be," that is, had the lace been French.

Now, interestingly, Lady Eldon's hypothetical is usually cited not as an example of an attempt but as an illustration of a non-attempt, that is, of a case that would qualify as an attempt were it not for the so-called impossibility defense, and the defense of legal impossibility in particular. The idea is that it was impossible for Lady Eldon to consummate the crime she intended to commit and that therefore she should not be held liable for trying to commit an uncommittable offense. Courts attempted to draw a line between legal impossibility (which was a defense) and factual impossibility (which was not), without, however, ever getting much beyond listing instances of each category of impossibility instead of formulating a workable test for distinguishing one from the other. (The classic illustration of a supposed instance of factual—and therefore irrelevant—impossibility was the pickpocket *manqué* who tries to pick an empty pocket.[281])

---

280. The classic American case on legal impossibility is *People v. Jaffe*, the first in a string of decisions struggling with the question of whether I can attempt to "receive stolen property" when the property was not in fact stolen, although I thought it was. 185 N.Y. 497 (1906) (no); Booth v. State, 398 P.2d 863 (Ct. Crim. App. Okla. 1964) (no; recommending adoption of MPC attempt provision); Commonwealth v. Henley, 504 Pa. 408 (1984) (yes; applying MPC attempt provision).

281. See, e.g., Booth v. State, 398 P.2d 863, 870 (Ct. Crim. App. Okla. 1964); see also People v. Dlugash, 41 N.Y.2d 725 (1977).

The Code makes a point of rejecting the impossibility defense in all its permutations.[282] It does so in the very definition of the type of complete attempt under consideration; impossible or not, attempt liability applies if the defendant would have succeeded in consummating the offense "if the attendant circumstances were as he believe[d] them to be." From the Code's treatmentist perspective, it makes no difference whether the actor's attempt was impossible, as what counts is not the likelihood of success (or the proximity to consummation), but the actor's dangerousness. And an impossible attempt provides the same evidence of dangerousness as a possible one (or, for that matter, a successful one): "the actor's criminal purpose has been clearly demonstrated; he went as far as he could in implementing that purpose; and, as a result, his 'dangerousness' is plainly manifested."[283] Simply put, using "impossibility as a guide to dangerousness of personality presents serious difficulties," and therefore should be disregarded by any system of criminal law designed to provide accurate diagnoses of criminal dangerousness.[284]

Finally, let us take a look at the other *complete attempt* scenario spelled out in the Code, in § 5.01(1)(b). Here the actor failed to bring about the proscribed *result*; she engaged in her conduct as planned, but it

---

282. See Commentaries art. 5, at 295.

283. Commentaries § 5.01, at 309. Still, the Code recognizes a limited exception to the general rule that impossibility is not a defense to an attempt. As the mistaken belief that there is *no* criminal statute covering my conduct may—in limited circumstances, discussed in § 15 below—excuse my violation of that statute, so the mistaken belief that there *is* a criminal statute where there is none will shield me from being punished for attempting to violate it. Commentaries § 5.01, at 318; see Commonwealth v. Henley, 504 Pa. 408, 416 (1984) ("fisherman believes he is committing an offense in fishing on a certain lake without a license when a fishing license is, in fact, not required in the subject jurisdiction"). What, after all, would I be charged with if the crime I tried my best to commit does not exist? Under the Code, attempting to commit a noncrime is no more criminal than conspiring to commit it. Cf. § 5.2(B) below (Code's rejection of common law conspiracy to commit "corrupt, dishonest, fraudulent, or immoral" act).

284. In extreme cases, where the actor's conduct is "so inherently unlikely to result or culminate in the commission of a crime that neither such conduct nor the actor presents a public danger," the Code authorizes judges to reduce the punishment or even to dismiss the prosecution altogether. § 5.05(2). In these exceptional cases, the actor's attempt to commit a crime, and her criminal purpose, were not symptomatic of criminal dangerousness, present or future.

did not have the desired effect. To take everyone's favorite result crime, murder, I load my gun, aim, pull the trigger, fire the bullet, and still miss. There is nothing particularly interesting or innovative about the Model Code's treatment of this run-of-the mill type of attempt.

Note, however, that the Code here does not in fact require purpose for attempt liability. Although purpose to bring about the result that did not happen is certainly enough, "the belief that [the act] will cause such result" will do just as well.[285] Here the purely evidentiary significance of the general purpose requirement (the "mens rea" of attempt) becomes clear, or clearer still. Purpose as to the result is not required for attempt liability because if an actor merely believes that her conduct will bring about a certain proscribed result "the manifestation of the actor's dangerousness is just as great—or very nearly as great—as in the case of purposive conduct."[286]

In fact, it turns out that under the Model Code's approach to attempt, purpose is also not required with respect to attendant circumstances. For attendant circumstances, attempt requires nothing more—or less—than whatever the object crime requires. This means that, for example, if the object offense requires no mens rea whatsoever regarding a particular attendant circumstance—say, the victim's age in statutory rape—then neither does attempt. If an attendant circumstance is a strict liability element in the object offense, then it is one in the attempt to commit the offense as well.[287]

The often-mentioned "purpose" requirement for attempt, that is, the claim that purpose is "the mens rea" of attempt, sweeps not quite as broadly as it might appear at first glance. How, then, would the Model Penal Code handle the issue of attempting nonintentional crimes? To

285. "Purpose or belief" really means "intent," as a general concept encompassing purpose and knowledge. See Commentaries § 5.01, at 305. In the context of attempt, the Code drafters thus could not get around invoking the concept of intent, which they otherwise did so much to avoid.

286. Commentaries § 5.01, at 305. This assumes that a mens rea *less* than purpose—knowledge or less—would suffice for conviction of the object offense, which is almost always the case. Otherwise the person would not have been "acting with the kind of culpability otherwise required for commission of the crime." § 5.01(1).

287. Commentaries § 5.01, at 301–02.

begin with, we would need to translate this question into Model Penal Code lingo. Reformulated, the question might be whether it is possible to attempt an offense that features a mental state other than purpose. The answer is clearly yes. We have already seen that the Model Penal Code retains the object offense's mental state requirements with respect to any attendant circumstance elements. The question, however, arises most frequently in cases of homicide, and reckless or negligent homicide in particular. The real issue, then, would be whether it is possible to attempt an offense that contains a result element with a "nonintentional" mental state.

If we set aside the Model Code drafter's distaste for the concept of "intent"—as is only fair and proper in this case as they did so themselves[288]—the Code has a straightforward answer to our question: no. As we just learned, to attempt a crime, "when causing a particular result is an element of the crime" (as death is in homicide), I would have to do (or omit to do) something "with the purpose of causing or with the belief that it will cause" that result.[289] In other words, the mens rea of attempt (here purpose or belief [read "knowledge"])—as opposed to the mens rea of the object offense (here, recklessness or negligence)—determines the mens rea attaching to the result. An attempt to commit reckless or negligent homicide under the Code thus would actually amount to an attempt to commit murder (which requires purpose or knowledge regarding the result, death).[290] Or, put another way, I cannot be held liable for "attempted manslaughter" or "attempted negligent homicide," at least insofar as that would imply that I acted only with recklessness or negligence regarding the risk of death. For attempt, I would need purpose or knowledge regarding the result, and that would qualify me for

---

288. See Commentaries § 5.01, at 305.

289. Why belief, rather than knowledge? Because knowledge is an accurate belief. If my belief about the occurrence of the result would have been accurate, however, I would have succeeded in bringing it about and thus actually committing the offense, rather than trying but failing. Purpose, defined as "conscious object," does not require a similar adjustment as it applies both to successful and to failed attempts—it does not matter whether I achieved my object or not.

290. See J.C. Smith, Two Problems in Criminal Attempts, 70 Harv. L. Rev. 422, 434 (1957).

murder liability—or rather *attempted* murder liability as, after all, I did not succeed in actually causing the death of another human being.

That is not to say, however, that someone who engages in some conduct while recklessly disregarding a good chance of fatal harm to another—say, by shooting "at a pickup truck carrying three teenage girls"[291]—but is lucky enough not to inflict that harm would escape criminal liability altogether. For these cases of "nonintentional attempts,"[292] the drafters inserted a broadsweeping new crime, reckless endangering, which criminalizes any conduct "which places or may place another person in danger of death or serious bodily injury."[293] Reckless endangering, however, does not quite fill the hole left by the omission of reckless or negligent attempts. For one, it does not cover negligent endangering. Plus, it is only a misdemeanor, a designation that is consistent with its considerable scope (including only potentially dangerous conduct, such as threats of threats of harm) but does not quite fit with the Code's treatmentist approach to attempt law. After all, the reckless endangerer who escapes manslaughter charges by the skin of her teeth because her errant bullet barely misses its target has displayed a significant criminal disposition calling for peno-correctional treatment—in fact, a dangerousness indistinguishable from that found in another person who was not so lucky and is marked, and treated, as a manslaughterer instead, and therefore as a felon, rather than as a mere misdemeanant.

Also note that the drafters' decision to do away with attempts to commit nonintentional result crimes—such as involuntary manslaughter—was not based on considerations of logical impossibility, conceptual essence, etymological origin, or even linguistic awkwardness, all of which have been invoked in common law opinions, and in scholarly commentary.[294] The problem is not that it is "impossible" to attempt

---

291. See, e.g., State v. Lyerla, 424 N.W.2d 908 (S.D. 1988).
292. They are *nonintentional* in that the actor lacks purpose (or belief) regarding the result; they are *attempts* in that the result did not occur.
293. § 211.2.
294. Under the Code, it is "impossible" to attempt a reckless or negligent result offense only in the sense that, given the purpose or belief requirement for attempt with respect to result, any attempt to commit a reckless or negligent result offense would automatically be an attempt to commit a purposeful or knowing result offense.

to bring about results nonintentionally because attempt "implies" or "requires" intent, logically or in any other way.[295] Instead, it is that "the scope of the criminal law would be *unduly extended* if one could be liable for an attempt whenever he recklessly or negligently created a risk of any result whose actual occurrence would lead to criminal responsibility."[296] From the drafters' treatmentist perspective, this exception for result offenses does not quite make sense, however. Once again, the lucky almost-manslaughterer has displayed the very same dangerousness as the unlucky consummated one, and therefore requires the very same peno-correctional treatment. And, as we know, attempt law is all about the identification, and diagnosis, of the criminally disposed.

(B) Conspiracy
American courts have long marveled, in horror, at the unique danger inherent in the very idea of conspiracy. Here is one example taken from a 1961 opinion by Justice Felix Frankfurter:

> [C]ollective criminal agreement—partnership in crime—presents a greater potential threat to the public than individual delicts. Concerted action both increases the likelihood that the criminal object will be successfully attained and decreases the probability that the individuals involved will depart from their path of criminality. Group association for criminal purposes often, if not normally, makes possible the attainment of ends more complex than those which one criminal could accomplish.

---

295. Contrast People v. Campbell, 72 N.Y.2d 602, 605 (1988) ("Because the very essence of a criminal attempt is the defendant's intention to cause the proscribed result, it follows that there can be no attempt to commit a crime which makes the causing of a certain result criminal even though wholly unintended.").

296. Commentaries § 5.01, at 304 (emphasis added). The drafters had no similar qualms about extending attempt liability to offenses that required less than purpose with respect to elements other than the result. For instance, they specifically noted that reckless endangerment—the very crime they had designed to capture conduct that would otherwise qualify as an attempt to commit reckless or negligent result offenses—could be attempted, even though it required less than purpose. Reckless endangerment, they explained, "aimed at the prohibition of particular reckless *behavior*, rather than the prohibition of a particular *result*." Id. n.16 (emphasis added).

Nor is the danger of a conspiratorial group limited to the particular end toward which it has embarked. Combination in crime makes more likely the commission of crimes unrelated to the original purpose for which the group was formed. In sum, the danger which a conspiracy generates is not confined to the substantive offense which is the immediate aim of the enterprise.[297]

It is no surprise, then, that the treatmentist Model Code would find a prominent place for this traditional crime of exceptional human dangerousness:

> There is little doubt…that as a basis for preventive intervention by the agencies of law enforcement and for the corrective treatment of persons who reveal that they are disposed to criminality, a penal code properly provides that conspiracy to commit crime is itself a criminal offense.[298]

As in the common law, the core of conspiracy under the Code is an agreement.[299] It is this agreement that gives rise to criminal liability, by transforming a lonely criminal thought hatched in the mind of a single, powerless individual into a criminal plan. By entering into an agreement with another person, I reveal myself as one of those persons who suffer from an abnormal disposition to engage in *criminal* conduct, by distinguishing myself from those untold millions who harbor criminal thoughts, but never share them with others, never mind act on them in any way. But my decision to seek out likeminded protocriminals, and to join hands with them, in the pursuit of a common criminal goal is not only symptomatic of my extraordinary dangerousness; by combining forces with another similarly dangerous person, I multiply my already considerable dangerousness through the synergy of cooperation.

---

297. Callanan v. United States, 364 U.S. 587, 593–94 (1961).
298. Commentaries § 5.03, at 388.
299. Id. at 421 (§ 5.03 "rests on the primordial conception of agreement as the core of the conspiracy idea").

So much for what courts like to call the gravamen of conspiracy. If this basic idea is kept in mind, the Model Code's approach to conspiracy falls into place fairly readily. As in the case of attempt, the "actus reus" and "mens rea" of conspiracy amount to a list of factors relevant to a diagnosis of dangerousness. The actus reus is the agreement. What an agreement is the Code does not say. Presumably, any meeting of the minds will do, with no requirement that the agreement take any particular form, written or otherwise. This is nothing new, except that under the Model Code even an *apparent* meeting of the minds will do. The Code adopts what its drafters call the "unilateral" theory of conspiracy, that is to say, of a one-sided agreement.[300] This criminal law version of a tango for one—or, if you prefer, the sound of one hand clapping—makes perfect sense, of course, if the point of conspiracy law is to identify and eliminate dangerous people. From the treatmentist perspective, the person who thinks she is doing something is indistinguishable from the person who actually does it. There were no impossible attempts in the previous section, and there are no impossible conspiracies now. Even if a particular "conspiracy," say between me and a police informant, poses no danger whatsoever, the Code steps in to assign me the indicated peno-correctional treatment.[301] The "incapacity, irresponsibility, or immunity" of my purported partner in crime is simply irrelevant for purposes of coming up with an individualized assessment of my dangerousness.[302]

Common law traditionally required another act for conspiracy liability: some "overt" act "in furtherance of" the first, central, and alarmingly covert, act of agreement. The Model Code retains the overt act requirement, except in cases of serious conspiracy, that is to say, conspiracies to commit a felony.[303] Agreements to commit serious crimes apparently are by themselves sufficiently indicative of exceptional criminal

---

300. See People v. Berkowitz, 50 N.Y.2d 333 (1980) (acquittal of co-conspirator); see also People v. Washington, 8 N.Y.3d 565, 869 N.E.2d 641 (2007).
301. See People v. Schwimmer, 66 A.D.2d 91, 411 N.Y.S.2d 922 (1978) (undercover officer and confidential informer).
302. This much we know from the law of complicity. See § 2.06(7).
303. § 5.03(5).

dangerousness to warrant peno-correctional treatment, even without further evidence of criminal purpose in the form of an additional act designed to put them into action.

As in the case of attempt, the actus reus in conspiracy reveals itself as purely instrumental. The law of conspiracy requires whatever actus reus is necessary to firm up a diagnosis of mens rea, that is to say, of criminal dangerousness. As in the case of attempt, that mens rea is purpose. Only purpose, the "highest" of the Code's modes of culpability, warrants state interference already at the point of inchoacy, even before an offense defined in the Code's special part has been committed. Judge Learned Hand's view that only purpose would do for *complicity*, and knowledge would not, won out in conspiracy as well. As the Commentaries point out, "the Institute at its 1953 meeting adopted Learned Hand's view as to complicity," and "[t]he case for this position seems an even stronger one with respect to the inchoate crime."[304]

Note that the Code here means what it says. Conspiracy requires purpose with respect not only to conduct, but also with respect to result.[305] Recall that a look at the fine print reveals that in the case of attempt, the purpose requirement applies in full force only to conduct. In the case of result (the all-important element in homicide), attempt liability would attach even to those who merely believed in the success of their criminal efforts, that is, those who acted with the closest thing to knowledge one could have with respect to future events, but not with purpose.[306]

Having figured out that purpose is the mens rea of conspiracy, it is time briefly to see how the Code handles conspiracies to commit non-purpose crimes. If the object of the conspiracy is a *result offense* (such as homicide) and the mental state with respect to that result (death) is recklessness or negligence (as in manslaughter and negligent

304. Commentaries § 5.03, at 406.
305. As to attendant circumstances, attempt requires whatever mental state the definition of the consummated offense requires. Whether this is enough for conspiracy—or if purpose is required for that element type as well—was a question the drafters left open, as they had done in their treatment of complicity. Id. at 413.
306. See § 5.2(A) above.

homicide, respectively), then the Code's approach is the same as in the case of attempt.[307] Under the Code, I cannot attempt to recklessly or negligently cause harm, nor can I conspire to do so. Also, as in attempt, *conduct offenses* are a different story; there is no problem, in the drafters' eyes, with imposing criminal liability on me for conspiring—or attempting—to commit a conduct offense that requires less than purpose, as long as I engage in purposeful conduct myself in doing the conspiring, or the attempting. In the case of "a crime defined in terms of conduct that creates a risk of harm, such as reckless driving or driving above a certain speed limit," or reckless endangering, we might add, from our discussion of attempt, "it would suffice for guilt of conspiracy that the actor's purpose was to promote or facilitate such conduct—for example, if he urged the driver of the car to go faster and faster."[308]

The Code's focus on individual dangerousness may be difficult to bring into line with the concept of conspiracy as an agreement. It is preferable, however, to an alternative approach to conspiracy that regards it not as an agreement, but as a *group* (a syndicate, an organization, a gang, a cabala—or a union, or a party). Throughout its relatively brief history as a general inchoate crime, conspiracy has been used to ferret out and destroy "conspiracies" that for one reason or another were considered dangerous by those wielding the power to apply the criminal law.[309] Given its history, and the conceptual ambiguity at its heart, conspiracy law threatens to circumvent one of the vaunted principles of American criminal law: that guilt is personal.[310] Not only does it impose criminal liability on a group, the "conspiracy," from which the liability of its members is then derived; in addition to *group liability*, it makes room

---

307. Unlike in the case of attempt, however, the answer would also be no if the object offense requires knowledge as to result. For unlike attempt, conspiracy requires purpose (and not just purpose or knowledge) as to the result. If we stick with homicide, a conspiracy to commit murder (which requires purpose or knowledge as to result) would be possible, but only if the state proves purpose as to the result (death).

308. Commentaries § 5.03, at 408.

309. The history of modern American conspiracy law thus is to a large extent a history of its abuse, perhaps most famously against labor unions. See generally Francis B. Sayre, Criminal Conspiracy, 35 Harv. L. Rev. 393 (1922).

310. See, e.g., People v. McGee, 49 N.Y.2d 48, 60 (1979).

for *vicarious liability*, that is, one person's liability for the behavior of another. It does not help matters that conspiracy as thus understood, by imposing *status liability* on the basis of one's being a conspirator, flaunts another basic principle of American criminal jurisprudence: the act requirement.

The Model Code tries to clean up conspiracy's act in various ways. By limiting conspiracy liability to agreements to commit *crimes*, rather than to engage in any act that qualifies as "corrupt, dishonest, fraudulent, or immoral, and in that sense illegal,"[311] the drafters made conspiracy less broad and less vague, at the same time.[312] By stressing the individual dangerousness of each "conspirator" (an unfortunate term, given that it defines the person in terms of her membership in the conspiracy, considered as a group), the Code narrowed the focus of conspiracy from the group to the individual. Even the Code's fiction of a unilateral agreement can be seen in this light. So focused is the Code's conspiracy analysis on the individual that it denies the inherent bilateralism of an agreement.

What is more, the Code rejects the so-called *Pinkerton* doctrine, a particularly blatant manifestation of the view that conspiracy liability is unconstrained by the principle of personal guilt. As we noted in our discussion of complicity, this doctrine, which survives in federal law and the law of several states, holds every conspirator liable—as an accomplice—for any criminal offense committed by any co-conspirator "in furtherance" of the conspiracy. *Pinkerton* collapses the distinction between conspiracy and complicity, treating one as a sufficient ground for the other, and thus turning every conspirator into her co-conspirator's accomplice. This approach makes perfect sense if one thinks of conspiracy as a criminal group whose members are vicariously liable for each other's actions as members. The basis of *Pinkerton* conspiracy liability is not the person's connection with the substantive crime, but the connection of the substantive crime with the conspiracy ("furtherance").

---

311. State v. Kemp, 126 Conn. 60, 78 (1939) (quoting State v. Parker, 114 Conn. 354, 360 (1932)).

312. They did not, however, take the additional step of further limiting objects of conspiracy from only crimes to only *some* crimes. In the Code, conspiracy remains an inchoate crime of general application. See Commentaries § 5.03, at 391–93.

Assuming the requisite connection between the crime and the criminal enterprise, liability of each partner in the enterprise follows from her own connection to the enterprise (membership). The conspiracy thus quite literally is at the center of the analysis of criminal liability.

The Model Code instead attempts to differentiate conspiracy from complicity. It insists that conspirators are just like other people, and that therefore the liability of each party to a conspiratorial agreement must be assessed individually. The question is not whether the offense can be functionally connected to the enterprise (furtherance), but whether my conduct in perpetrating the offense can be imputed to another party to the agreement. And we already know how imputation works:

> A person is an accomplice of another person in the commission of an offense if
> (a) with the purpose of promoting or facilitating the commission of the offense, he
>   (i) solicits such other person to commit it; or
>   (ii) aids or agrees or attempts to aid such other person in planning or committing it.[313]

As the second clause makes explicit, an agreement or a common plan may well make out accomplice liability. Conspiracy thus may well imply complicity. One follows from the other, however, only if the agreement is specific enough to count as an agreement entered into "with the purpose of promoting or facilitating" the particular criminal conduct actually committed, rather than some general plan to create criminal mischief, or to form a criminal organization. In other words, the particular scope of the agreement, rather than its mere existence, determines the scope of accomplice liability to which it gives rise.

In many, perhaps most, cases, the Model Code's analysis will reach the same results as the *Pinkerton* doctrine, particularly if "reasonable foreseeability" is recognized as a meaningful limitation on the extension of *Pinkerton* liability among co-conspirators.[314] The analysis, however,

313. § 2.06(3).
314. See Pinkerton v. United States, 328 U.S. 640, 648 (1946).

remains clearly distinct. In its individualized approach, the Code does its best to contain a notorious uncontainable offense, a crime "so vague that it almost defies definition."[315] Rather than abandon conspiracy altogether, the drafters did their best to tame it, by abandoning *Pinkerton* instead.[316]

Doing away with conspiracy as a general inchoate offense, after all, would have meant disregarding a convenient doctrinal locus for the assessment of the all-important criminal dangerousness. In fact, what initially looks like conspiracy's oppressive weakness is transformed into its penological strength. Its very flexibility makes room for the sort of penological diagnosis that lies at the heart of the Code's theory of inchoacy.

Once evinced, the abnormal criminal disposition of the conspirator called for appropriate peno-correctional treatment. And as the dangerousness of the conspirator was identical to that of the perpetrator of the conspiracy's object, the Code provided for identical peno-correctional treatment of both, consistent with its general approach to inchoate offenses. The conspiracy and its object are punished the same. In the law of attempt, treating inchoate and consummated offenses in the same way meant increasing the punishment for attempt, which traditionally had been less—often significantly less—than that for the substantive offense. In the law of conspiracy, it also meant putting a stop to the practice of punishing conspiracies *more harshly* than, and *in addition to*, their objectives, on the ground that they by themselves posed a danger independent of and beyond that posed by the commission of their object offense.[317]

315. Krulewitch v. United States, 336 U.S. 440, 446 (1949) (Jackson, J., concurring) (quoted in Commentaries § 5.03, at 402).
316. Commentaries § 2.06, at 307 ("The reason for [abandoning *Pinkerton*] is that there appears to be no other or no better way to confine within reasonable limits the scope of liability to which conspiracy may theoretically give rise.").
317. As each of the inchoate offenses is but a tool for diagnosing a single condition, abnormal dangerousness, it also makes no sense to permit convictions of more than one inchoate offense per unconsummated crime. § 5.05(3). Any of the inchoate offenses will do for diagnostic purposes. It is the condition that rails for peno-correctional treatment, not its symptom, or symptoms, with the specific degree and nature of dangerousness being determined by the object crime.

Under the Model Penal Code, the dangerousness of one planning an offense was determined by the dangerousness of the one actually committing it. The danger of conspiring to do X was nothing more—and nothing less—than doing X. Conspiring to commit murder evinced the same quantity and quality of criminal dangerousness as committing murder—or attempting to commit it, for that matter (or soliciting it, as we will see shortly).

At the same time, the Code modified another rule found in the common law, which merged the conspiracy into the completed crime. Although it made no sense to punish conspiracies more harshly than their objects, cumulative punishment remained appropriate if the conspiracy encompassed offenses other than the one actually committed. A conspiracy to commit murder thus merged into murder. A conspiracy to commit murder and theft did not. The defendant, after all, had evinced the degree and type of dangerousness associated with murder as well as that associated with theft.[318]

(C) Solicitation

We have already seen that a unilateral agreement can make a conspiracy. From the Code's treatmentist perspective, the person who *thinks* she is conspiring with another to commit a crime is indistinguishable from the person who actually manages to form a conspiracy. In other words, as the inchoate crime is indistinguishable from the consummated crime, so is the inchoate version of the inchoate crime from the inchoate crime itself—problems of infinite regress notwithstanding.

What is more, it turns out that the Code actually recognizes, as a separate offense, just such an inchoate inchoate crime: solicitation, which, as the Commentaries explain, "may, indeed, be thought of as an attempt to conspire."[319] Treatmentism demands nothing less:

> There should be no doubt on this issue. Purposeful solicitation presents dangers calling for preventive intervention and is

---

318. Commentaries § 5.06, at 390.
319. Commentaries § 5.02, at 365–66; see also State v. Jenson, 195 P.3d 512 (Wash. 2008).

sufficiently indicative of a disposition towards criminal activity to call for liability.[320]

Solicitation is meant to provide for the peno-correctional treatment of those abnormally dangerous persons who managed to slip through the already finely woven net of the two main inchoate offenses, attempt and conspiracy—which it combines into a single inchoate inchoate crime, thus extending the sphere of state intervention to reach conduct that would not quite qualify for either.

The most remarkable thing about solicitation in the Code may be its existence, which is testimony to the strength of the drafters' commitment to treatmentism in general, and to the prosecution of inchoate offenses in particular. A close second, however, would be its scope, which is remarkable even for an inchoate offense under the Code. As we know, unilateral conspiracies, or agreements with myself, are just as criminal as actual conspiracies. We also know that solicitation punishes the attempt to form a one-sided agreement. What is more, attempts to solicit—"uncommunicated solicitations"—are treated the same as successful solicitations, that is to say, attempts to enter into a criminal agreement, uni- or multilateral.[321]

Assuming the all-important "purpose," a letter offering $1,000 to an undercover police officer for murdering my ex-husband which I mistakenly slip into the return slot at my local public library, rather than the mailbox right next to it, will make me criminally liable for solicitation—not for attempted solicitation, but solicitation. It would make no difference to my liability, and my exposure to peno-correctional treatment, whether the letter actually reached its intended reader, whether that reader had any intention of taking me up on my offer, or even of pretending to take me up on it, or even whether there ever was a possibility that she might (agree or pretend to agree, that is);[322] and, if we

---

320. Commentaries § 5.02, at 366.

321. § 5.02(2); cf. People v. Lubow, 29 N.Y.2d 58, 62 (1971) (exploring the scope of this "new kind of offense, simpler in structure than an attempt or a conspiracy, and resting *solely* on communication without need for any resulting action").

322. As an attempt to conspire, it is no surprise that impossibility is not a defense to solicitation, subject to the utter impossibility (pins in voodoo doll) exception also familiar from the law of attempt. Commentaries § 5.02, at 370 (citing § 5.05(2)).

are dealing with anything other than a first-degree felony, then it would not even make a difference whether she actually went ahead and put that agreement into action, or at least tried to do so. The only thread that holds these widely different scenarios together is my purpose, which we long ago have come to recognize as a proxy for abnormal dangerousness. "The crucial manifestation of dangerousness lies in the endeavor to communicate the incriminating message to another person, it being wholly fortuitous whether the message was actually received."[323]

Solicitation, however, is not just an attempt to conspire—a double inchoacy. It is also a familiar foundation for accomplice liability. One way of having another person's conduct imputed to me is by "soliciting" her to engage in it.[324] Imputation of another person's conduct to me, however, presumes that the conduct actually took place. Solicitation, by contrast, does not. And so solicitation turns out to be not only attempted conspiracy, but attempted complicity as well.[325]

(D) Renunciation
Each of the inchoate offenses in the Code—attempt, conspiracy, and solicitation—provide for an affirmative defense of renunciation.[326] The

---

323. Commentaries § 5.02, at 381.
324. § 2.06(3).
325. Attempted complicity (i.e., conduct that would qualify as complicity but for the substantive offense not taking place, thus preventing the imputation of the would-be principal's conduct to the would-be accomplice) is also dealt with in the attempt provision. § 5.01(3) treats as an attempt "conduct designed to aid another to commit a crime that would establish his complicity...if the crime were committed," on the by now familiar ground that "the actor who attempts to aid...manifests the same *dangerousness of character* as the actor who himself attempts to commit the offense." Commentaries § 5.01, at 356 (emphasis added). Solicitation covers failed attempts to *solicit*, rather than to *aid*, the commission of the crime. See § 2.06(3)(i) (soliciting) & (ii) (aiding). So the crooked but hapless police officer who, belatedly, tries to tip off gamblers about a police raid after the raid has occurred (see Commonwealth v. Haines, 147 Pa. Super. 165 (1942)) would be guilty of attempt, under § 5.01(3), rather than of solicitation, under § 5.02. Whether differential treatment of these cases is necessary—in fact, whether we need a crime of solicitation if we have an expansive crime of attempt—is, of course, another question.
326. §§ 5.01(4), 5.02(3), 5.03(6). Recall that an affirmative defense under the Model Code imposes not the burden of proof, but only the burden of production, on the defendant.

renunciation has to be "complete and voluntary," two conditions the Code drafters defined with characteristic indirectness:

> [R]enunciation of criminal purpose is not voluntary if it is moti-
> vated, in whole or in part, by circumstances, not present or apparent
> at the inception of the actor's course of conduct, which increase the
> probability of detection or apprehension or which make more dif-
> ficult the accomplishment of the criminal purpose. Renunciation
> is not complete if it is motivated by a decision to postpone the
> criminal conduct until a more advantageous time or to transfer the
> criminal effort to another but similar objective or victim.[327]

So interrupting a gas station holdup just because the police have arrived does not amount to renunciation.[328]

As inchoate crimes are about dangerousness, so is the defense of renunciation. According to the Commentaries, renunciation "signifi-cantly negatives dangerousness of character."[329] Assuming the actor's preparatory conduct evinces criminal purpose, a diagnosis of abnormal dangerousness follows, except if contrary evidence indicates otherwise. Renunciation is that contrary evidence that can rebut the presumption of dangerousness:

> In cases where the actor has gone beyond the line drawn for
> defining preparation, indicating prima facie sufficient firmness

---

§ 1.12(3). There is no renunciation provision for the remaining inchoate offense codi-fied in the Code's general part, possession—whatever such a provision might look like. It is possible, of course, to discontinue possession of an object or to rebut a pre-sumption of possessing it with a "criminal purpose," thus avoiding a diagnostic infer-ence of dangerousness. There is also an affirmative defense allowing a "defendant to prove by a preponderance of evidence that he possessed or dealt with [an 'offensive weapon'] solely as a curio or in a dramatic performance, or that he possessed it briefly in consequence of having found it or taken it from an aggressor, or under circum-stances similarly negating any purpose." § 5.07.

327. § 5.01(4).
328. E.g., Stewart v. State, 85 Nev. 388 (1969).
329. Commentaries § 5.01, at 360. The drafters also mention another rationale for the renunciation defense: to give actors an incentive to abandon their criminal plan even

of purpose, he should be allowed to rebut such a conclusion by showing that he has plainly demonstrated his lack of firm purpose by completely renouncing his purpose to commit the crime.[330]

The versions of the renunciation defense do not differ significantly among the various inchoate offenses in the Code.[331] In attempt, renunciation requires that the actor "abandoned his effort to commit the crime or otherwise prevented its commission,"[332] in solicitation that he "persuaded" the solicitee not to commit the crime "or otherwise prevented the commission of the crime,"[333] and in conspiracy that he "thwarted the success of the conspiracy."[334] Each time, however, what matters is whether the renunciation occurred "under circumstances manifesting a complete and voluntary renunciation of his criminal purpose."

§ 6 "... SUBSTANTIAL HARM TO INDIVIDUAL OR PUBLIC INTERESTS"

We have almost come to the end of our discussion of the first level of the analysis of criminal liability, the question of whether a crime has been committed in the formal sense of conduct fitting the definition of a criminal offense. So far, we have teased out what the Code means by "conduct" that "inflicts or threatens" something. We now briefly turn to that something, namely "substantial harm to individual or public interests." We will not spend much time on this aspect of criminal law, not because it is not important, but because it is beyond our scope. The taxonomy of criminal harm is by and large a matter for the special part of criminal

---

at the last minute, that is, even after evidence of dangerousness has become conclusive. Id. at 359–60.

330. Id. at 359.

331. Cf. § 4.4(B) above, discussing the analogous termination "defense" in complicity. § 2.06(6)(c). Unlike renunciation, termination is not an affirmative defense under the Code.

332. § 5.01(4).

333. § 5.02(3).

334. § 5.03(6).

law, rather than for the general part, which deals with the principles of criminal liability that apply to the entire cornucopia of crimes.

§ 6.1 Substantial Harm

There is one provision in the general part that does address if not the object (or objects) of criminal harm, then its extent. Section 2.12 assigns to the trial judge extensive authority to dismiss prosecutions even if they allege criminal conduct, that is, conduct that matches an offense definition and is neither justified nor excused.[335] Traditionally, the task of weeding out what the Code calls "de minimis infractions" has been left to the discretion of prosecutors. The Model Penal Code provision sets up a judicial check in cases where this traditional filter has failed for one reason or another, including excessive prosecutorial zeal or perhaps even vindictiveness.

Most interesting, for our purposes, is the drafters' attempt to guide the discretion to disregard "merely technical violations of law."[336] Traditionally, the discretion to bring to bear the state's machinery of law enforcement in a particular case has been entirely unconstrained by law. American criminal law accepts applicatory discretion as a fact of life, trusting in "the good sense of prosecutors."[337] Continental criminal law, by contrast, has adopted the principle of compulsory prosecution to protect defendants from the bad sense of prosecutors, and other state officials. Prohibiting prosecutorial discretion, however, is not the same as eliminating it. In fact, more recently, civil law countries have recognized the "opportunity principle" as a counterbalance to compulsory prosecution, allowing dismissal in cases that meet certain criteria, including the seriousness of the crime, the public interest in a criminal prosecution, and the degree of culpability.[338] The Model Code's de minimis provision tries to set out criteria of this sort.

335. See Stanislaw Pomorski, On Multiculturalism, Concepts of Crime, and the "De Minimis" Defense, 1997 B.Y.U. L. Rev. 51.
336. Commentaries § 5.12, at 399.
337. United States v. Dotterweich, 320 U.S. 277, 285 (1943).
338. See, e.g., §§ 153, 153a, 153b, 257c StPO [German Code of Criminal Procedure]. These provisions have become a common basis for plea bargaining, or its continental

Two of the three grounds for dismissal are miniature replicas of a justification and an excuse defense. This makes sense. Even de minimis infractions, after all, remain infractions, and "technical violations of law" are still violations. There would be no need for an extraordinary dismissal if the conduct charged did not match the definition of some offense. One ground for dismissal covers cases of implied consent (a justification) that fall "within a customary license or tolerance, [not] expressly negatived by the person whose interest was infringed."[339] Another, and potentially the broadest,[340] rationale sounds more like a general excuse defense of unavoidability for exceptional and unanticipated cases, involving conduct that "presents such other extenuations that it cannot reasonably be regarded as envisaged by the legislature in forbidding the offense."[341] Here the court is clearly second-guessing the legislature on the ground that it could not have wanted to punish that which could not be avoided, an application of Blackstone's "Tenth Rule," that "acts of parliament that are impossible to be performed are of no validity."[342]

Only one of the grounds for a de minimis dismissal really is about de minimis infractions, strictly speaking. It authorizes dismissal in cases where the proscribed conduct (1) "did not actually cause or threaten the harm or evil sought to be prevented by the law defining the offense," or (2) "did so only to an extent too trivial to warrant the condemnation of conviction." The Commentaries cast the first clause as a generalization of the utter impossibility (voodoo doll) cases in the law of inchoate crimes.[343] With the second clause, the drafters had in mind everyday occurrences such as "unconsented-to contacts" on subways, in ticket lines, or at rock concerts, which might technically count as assaults. A more direct way of dealing with this issue, of course, would

equivalents. See, e.g., Markus D. Dubber, American Plea Bargains, German Lay Judges, and the Crisis of Criminal Procedure, 49 Stan. L. Rev. 547 (1997). For comparative analysis, see Markus D. Dubber & Tatjana Hörnle, Criminal Law: A Comparative Approach ch. 5.C (2014).

339. For our discussion of consent, see § 11 below.
340. Perhaps not surprisingly, dismissal on this ground requires a written justification. § 2.12(3).
341. Excuses are discussed in § 12 below.
342. Commentaries § 2.12, at 404 n.18.
343. Id. at 403.

be to define the offense more narrowly, thus precluding even "technical" liability for de minimis harm—as the Code drafters did with the crime of assault, for instance.[344]

§ 6.2 Individual or Public Interests

The realm of criminal law is not defined only by a particular degree of interference—"substantial harm"—but also by a set of objects of that interference—"individual or public interests." These interests structure the special part of the Model Code, a vast improvement over the alphabetical ordering in previous efforts at statutory compilation. The federal criminal code, in Title 18, for instance, to this day begins with chapters on "aircraft and motor vehicles," "animals, birds, fish, and plants," "arson," "assault," "bankruptcy," and "biological weapons," and ends with "terrorism," "trafficking in contraband cigarettes," "treason, sedition, and subversive activities," "transportation for illegal sexual activity," "war crimes," "wire and electronic communications interception and interception of oral communications," and—reflecting a sudden loss of the will to alphabetize—"stored wire and electronic communication and transactional records access," followed by "prohibition on release and use of certain personal information from state motor vehicle records."[345]

The Code instead recognizes the following "private or public interests" as worthy of criminal protection:

existence or stability of the state (art. 200)[346]
person (arts. 210–13)[347]
property (arts. 220–24)

---

344. Id. at 404; see § 211.1 (by requiring at least recklessness in most cases and by limiting relevant harm to bodily injury, defined as "physical pain, illness or any impairment of physical condition" or serious bodily injury, defined as "bodily injury which creates a substantial risk of death or which causes serious, permanent disfigurement, or protracted loss or impairment of the function of any bodily member or organ").

345. For a systematic, interest-based ordering of federal crimes, one must instead refer to the federal sentencing guidelines. See Markus D. Dubber, Reforming American Penal Law, 90 J. Crim. L. & Criminology 49, 78 (1999).

346. Model Penal Code 123 (Proposed Official Draft 1962).

347. Actually, "offenses involving danger to the person."

family (art. 230)
public administration (arts. 240–43)
public order and decency (arts. 250–51)
miscellaneous[348]

Although the Code drafters organized their special part around these interests—or at any rate categories that could be translated into interests—it would be a mistake to think that they spent a great deal of time thinking about the nature and types of criminal harm. In fact, as we have seen again and again, they were not particularly interested in the phenomenon of harm. Their focus instead was on the diagnosis of abnormal criminal dangerousness and the prescription of appropriate peno-correctional treatment.

In fact, the formulation "private or public interests" was adopted only as an afterthought. Originally, § 1.02(1)(a) referred to "individual *and* public interests."[349] "And" became "or" only after a chapter on "Logic and Law" in a book optimistically entitled "Law and Electronics: The Challenge of a New Era—A Pioneer Analysis of the Implications of the New Computer Technology for the Improvement of the Administration of Justice," had pointed out some possible ambiguities in the original formulation.[350]

---

348. Model Penal Code 241 (Proposed Official Draft 1962) (narcotics, alcoholic beverages, gambling, tax, and trade).
349. Tentative Draft No. 4, § 1.02(1)(a), at 2 (Apr. 25, 1955) (emphasis added).
350. See Commentaries § 1.02, at 16 n.3 (citing Layman E. Allen, Logic and Law, in Law and Electronics: The Challenge of a New Era—A Pioneer Analysis of the Implications of the New Computer Technology for the Improvement of the Administration of Justice 187–98 (Edgar A. Jones, Jr. ed., 1962)).

[2]

JUSTIFICATION

Having completed our discussion of what qualifies behavior as a criminal offense, it is now time to consider what else it would take to impose criminal liability on a particular person engaging in that behavior. Counting as a criminal offense according to some criminal statute or other is a necessary precondition for behavior to be punished. Sufficient it is not. The question we will address in the remainder of this book is what else we need for punishability, besides matching the definition of some criminal offense.

§ 7 DEFENSES IN GENERAL

Traditionally, Anglo-American law has approached this issue not as a substantive question about the elements of criminal liability, but as a question of procedure, and more specifically, of evidence.[1] Procedurally speaking, our question is one of "defenses." Matching some offense definition makes out a prima facie case of punishability. That presumption of criminality (or, in the Model Penal Code's treatmentist terms, criminal dangerousness) then can be rebutted by the "defendant"—as opposed to, say, the "accused"—raising certain "defenses."

This procedural way of looking at things may reflect the roots of the Anglo-American criminal process in trial by combat. Even today, the American criminal process, not only at trial, is regarded as "adversarial,"

---

1. See Note, Justification: The Impact of the Model Penal Code on Statutory Reform, 75 Colum. L. Rev. 914 (1975).

rather than "inquisitorial," as a struggle, or at least a contest, between adversaries who deliver blows and launch counterattacks in a constant back-and-forth.

This procedural conception may be a little misleading, however, because it creates the impression that it is up to one side, the "prosecution," to establish the offense and to the other, the "defendant," to establish, well, the defense to that offense. We have already seen that "defenses" such as intoxication and mistake (or termination in complicity) are not for the defendant to prove, but for the prosecution to disprove, insofar as they are inconsistent with the prosecution's claim that the defendant had the requisite mens rea.

Now there *are* claims that count as defenses in the sense that it is up to the defense to raise them, and back them up with some modicum ("scintilla") of evidence, before the burden shifts onto the prosecution to disprove them.[2] The Model Code calls these "affirmative" defenses.[3] Some codes, the New York Penal Law being one example, go so far as to place the burden of *proof* as to certain defenses on the defense,[4] even to the point of requiring proof beyond a reasonable doubt.[5]

Still, the substantive question of whether the prerequisites for criminal liability have been met is distinct from the procedural question of who should have to prove that they have (or have not)—or even who should raise the issue, backed up with at least a shred of evidence, whether they have or not. In American law the procedural tail tends to wag the substantive dog, with the former question receiving far more attention than the latter. In fact, much of the constitutional law regarding the prerequisites for criminal liability is a branch of the law of evidence, with

---

2. See, e.g., Hoagland v. State, 240 P.3d 1043, 1047 (Nev. 2010) ("regardless of whether the evidence is weak, inconsistent, believable, or incredible").

3. § 1.12. To be precise, the Model Code does not require the defense to bear the burden of production even with respect to these issues. Evidence of an affirmative defense may also pop up—presumably unintentionally—in the prosecution's case. It is just that "typically" it is the defense that comes up with it. Commentaries § 3.01, at 6. The important point thus is that even in the case of an affirmative defense, what matters under the Model Code is that "there *is* evidence supporting such defense," not who introduces it. § 1.12(2)(a) (emphasis added).

4. See N.Y. Penal Law § 25.00.

5. Leland v. Oregon, 343 U.S. 790 (1952) (insanity).

fairly elaborate judicial dissertations on the distinctions among var
types and levels of evidentiary burdens (of production, of persuasion, or
proof; beyond a reasonable doubt, clear and convincing evidence, or preponderance of the evidence),[6] their assignment to—and then shifting
among—the parties (state, defendant),[7] during different stages of the
process (trial, sentencing),[8] and evidentiary presumptions that might
be used to alleviate evidentiary burdens, once assigned, without shifting
them altogether (rebuttable, irrebuttable, mandatory, permissive).[9]

The Model Code recognizes two types of defenses—or rather their
absence—as substantive prerequisites for criminal liability: justifications and excuses.[10] That is why it includes in its definition of offense
element "(i) such conduct or (ii) such attendant circumstances or
(iii) such a result of conduct as ... (c) negatives an excuse or justification for such conduct."[11] As the prosecution must prove every offense
element (beyond a reasonable doubt),[12] this means—procedurally
speaking—that it must also *disprove*—"negative"—justifications
and excuses.[13] All in all, criminal liability thus requires conduct that
matches (1) "the description of the forbidden conduct in the definition
of the offense," including (2) "the required kind of culpability," and that
does *not* match (3) "an excuse or justification for such conduct."[14]

6. In re Winship, 397 U.S. 358 (1970).
7. Mullaney v. Wilbur, 421 U.S. 684 (1975) (provocation); Patterson v. New York, 432
   U.S. 197 (1977) (extreme emotional disturbance); Martin v. Ohio, 480 U.S. 228
   (1987) (self-defense).
8. McMillan v. Pennsylvania, 477 U.S. 79 (1986).
9. Sandstrom v. Montana, 442 U.S. 510 (1979).
10. While the Code drafters refused "to draw a fine line" between justifications and
    excuses, they did make "a rough analytical distinction" between them. Commentaries
    art. 3, introduction, at 2. We will explore that distinction in the context of particular
    justifications and excuses.
11. § 1.13(9)(c).
12. § 1.12(1).
13. It retains that burden even if the defense is classified as affirmative, once some evidence
    of the defense has been introduced—ordinarily by the defendant—at trial. § 1.12(2)
    (a). The only exceptions to this rule are the super-affirmative defenses that the Code
    "plainly requires the defendant to prove by a preponderance of the evidence." See, e.g.,
    §§ 2.04(4) (ignorance of law), 2.07(5) (due diligence), 2.13(2) (entrapment), 5.07 (tem-
    porary possession), 213.6(1) (mistake about age).
14. § 1.13(9)(a)–(c).

.n this light, the elements of a defense appear like the elements of an .fense, only upside down. Set out in the general part, justifications and excuses are invisible attachments to any offense definition. So the *offense* of murder, for instance, is defined as purposely or knowingly causing the death of another human being. *Criminal liability* for murder, however, requires that we add "without justification or excuse."

What is more, the Model Code classifies (the absence of) justifications and excuses not merely as offense elements, but as *material* elements.[15] This means that its general culpability provisions apply not only to "the description of the forbidden conduct in the definition of the offense," but also to the justifications and excuses for this conduct. Think of justifications and excuses as having modes of culpability attached to their elements. To negative a justification or an excuse then would mean to negative that mental state. For instance, using (otherwise criminal) force in self-defense, as we will see shortly, is "justifiable when the actor *believes* that such force is immediately necessary for the purpose of protecting himself against the use of unlawful force by such other person on the present occasion."[16] Negativing the justification of self-defense thus requires showing that the actor did not have the requisite "belief" with respect to the elements of the defense (immediate necessity, unlawful force, etc.).

Note that it says "believes" rather than "knows." Knowledge—that is, an *accurate* belief—is not required.[17] Mistakes are allowed. On its face, the justification is available even if I turned out to be wrong about any or all of the conditions that I thought gave rise to my right to defend myself (maybe it was not strictly "necessary," for example, to body-check the skateboarder who raced toward me on the sidewalk).

Mistakes are allowed, but whether they are enough to justify my action is another question. For it turns out that the Model Code also provides that certain types of mistake make out what is sometimes

---

15. § 1.13(10).
16. § 3.04(1); see also §§ 3.02(1) ("conduct which the actor *believes* to be necessary to avoid a harm or evil to himself"); 3.03(3) ("actor *believes* his conduct to be required or authorized"); 3.06(1) ("actor *believes* that such force is immediately necessary"); 3.07(1) (same).
17. Cf. § 2.02(2)(b)(i) (defining knowledge regarding an attendant circumstance as awareness of its existence).

called an *imperfect* defense, that is, a defense that limits criminal liability, rather than doing away with it altogether. In particular, if my mistake regarding the elements of a defense was reckless or negligent then I will have a defense against offenses that require more than recklessness or negligence for conviction, that is, offenses that require purpose or knowledge (such as murder). But I will remain criminally liable for offenses that require less. If I was reckless in making the mistake, I will be liable for offenses that require recklessness (such as manslaughter). And if I was negligent, I will still be liable for negligence offenses (such as negligent homicide).

Note that the Model Code does not speak, at least not directly, in terms of "reasonable" beliefs, or mistakes. Under the common law, and in many American jurisdictions to this day, beliefs—even mistaken ones—about the conditions of my justification are enough, but only if they are reasonable. If I was unreasonably mistaken about the presence of the elements of self-defense, for instance, then I had no defense at all. The common law rule was an either-or, an all-or-nothing, proposition: justified if reasonable, not justified if not.[18]

The Model Code instead differentiates, indirectly, among different types of unreasonable mistakes. A reasonable belief, according to the Code, is "a belief which the actor is not reckless or negligent in holding."[19] But as we just saw, the fact that I was recklessly or negligently mistaken does not mean that I have no defense, and thus would be liable for any offense, even one requiring purpose or knowledge (such as murder). It means that I will escape liability for such serious offenses, and—assuming they exist—will be liable only for (lesser included) offenses in keeping with the nature of my mistake: recklessness offenses if reckless, negligence offenses if negligent.[20]

18. See People v. Goetz, 68 N.Y.2d 96 (1986).
19. § 1.13(16).
20. For an intermediate position, which reduces murder liability to manslaughter in the case of an unreasonable mistake regarding the conditions of self-defense, see Weston v. State, 682 P.2d 1119 (Alaska 1984). This doctrine, often referred to as "imperfect self-defense," resembles the Model Code position in that it does not bar the defense altogether in cases of unreasonable mistakes. Unlike the Code, however, it does not tailor liability to the nature of the actor's mistake. Reckless or negligent, unreasonable mistakes result in liability for manslaughter. Cf. State v. Bowens, 108 N.J. 622 (1987)

Now that we have a general understanding of the Model Code's approach to defenses, let us take a closer look at specific defenses, justifications first (then excuses, in Chapter 3). It is always a good idea to keep this general approach in mind as we make our way through the Code justification provisions, many of which are quite detailed, if not convoluted.

§ 8 NECESSITY

Necessity is the mother of all justifications, as the title of § 3.02 makes plain: "Justifications Generally: Choice of Evils." It is only right and proper that it appear ahead of all the other justification defenses addressed in article 3 of the Code. It is also the fallback justification that might apply if others fail.

The basic idea of necessity as a justification is that there are some circumstances in which conduct that is facially criminal is not unlawful in fact, in the context of the law generally speaking.[21] Assuming that the—or at least one—purpose of the law is to avert "harm or evil,"[22] and that criminal law, as a species of law, has that same purpose, then it is not contrary to law to engage in conduct that violates some criminal statute but advances the overall goals of law. If, in other words, I can avert "harm or evil" by violating a criminal statute designed to avert "harm or evil" then I am justified, assuming that the harm or evil I avert is greater than the harm or evil I commit. If I can save the town by burning down my neighbor's farm, then I am not acting unlawfully.

(rejecting imperfect self-defense in MPC jurisdiction). Note also that this defense, like that of provocation, is limited to homicide cases. On provocation, see § 16 below.

21. This reference to "the law generally speaking" must be taken with a grain of salt. The Code drafters did not set out, or endorse, a unitary theory of law, into which its various subjects fit like drawers into a cabinet, or slices into a pie chart. For one, they insisted that a justification in criminal law does not have any implications for "any civil action." § 3.01(2). There was no suggestion that the "privileges" in tort law cover the same ground as "justifications" in criminal law, which complicated their attempt to define unlawfulness in the context of the "unlawful force" requirement in the doctrine of self-defense. See § 9.1(D) below.

22. On the frequent appearance of this phrase in the Code, see § 4.2(B), note 40 above.

The necessity defense takes its name from its limitation to situations of necessity, or even "emergency."[23] Ordinarily, the balancing of potential costs and benefits of a given course of conduct occurs prospectively at the legislative level, among representatives of the political community. These—my—representatives have passed a criminal code that contains the criminal statute I have violated—arson, say. For me to second-guess their, and therefore my, judgment and act contrary to the norms they have defined in furtherance of the goal of averting "harm or evil," I must face extraordinary circumstances. In short, I must face necessity. Without necessity, I am not entitled to take the law into my own hands, breaking a statute to save the law, so to speak or, to put it more dramatically, violating the law for its own sake.

This sort of balancing in light of the underlying purpose of the law, and, in fact, of government generally, underlies all justification defenses. In necessity, or choice of evils, the rationale of justifications is most explicit, and least constrained. It is no accident that the Code's provision on necessity is so much shorter than those on, say, self-defense or law enforcement. The other justification defenses work out the details of the "choice of evils" in particular, and particularly common, scenarios. In these defenses, the legislature attempts to predict the extraordinary circumstances under which its criminal norms, poured into statutes, generate counterproductive results. Self-defense, for example, describes—in considerable detail—those cases in which the prohibition against harming other persons would cause greater harm than its violation.

The Code provision on necessity is refreshingly straightforward:

> Conduct which the actor believes to be necessary to avoid a harm or evil to himself or to another is justifiable, provided that...the harm or evil sought to be avoided by such conduct is greater than that sought to be prevented by the law defining the offense charged.[24]

23. N.Y. Penal Law § 35.05(2).
24. § 3.02(1).

What is more, the Commentaries illustrate the point of the defense in an oft-quoted passage that is worth reciting:

> [A] principle of necessity, properly conceived, affords a general justification for conduct that would otherwise constitute an offense. It reflects the judgment that such a qualification on criminal liability, like the general requirements of culpability, is essential to the rationality and justice of the criminal law, and is appropriately addressed in a penal code. Under this section, property may be destroyed to prevent the spread of a fire. A speed limit may be violated in pursuing a suspected criminal. An ambulance may pass a traffic light. Mountain climbers, lost in a storm may take refuge in a house or may appropriate provisions. Cargo may be jettisoned or an embargo violated to preserve the vessel. An alien may violate a curfew in order to reach an air raid shelter. A druggist may dispense a drug without the requisite prescription to alleviate grave distress in an emergency.[25]

This passage points out, first, that the very idea of codifying a general necessity defense was something new at the time of the Model Code. Even in legal systems with a long tradition of codification, the necessity defense remained uncodified. German courts, for instance, referred to the balance-of-evils defense as "suprastatutory necessity," precisely because its recognition flew in the face of the relevant criminal statute defining the offense. In this sense, necessity was not only uncodified, but uncodifiable as well.[26]

Note also that the Commentaries here invoke the requirements of "rationality and justice," which is a far cry from the talk of dangerousness that dominates the article on inchoate offenses, for instance. In

---

25. Commentaries § 3.02, at 9–10.
26. In Germany, the necessity defense was first recognized in an abortion case, where the doctor performed the abortion to save the life of the mother. RGSt 61, 242 (1927) (German Imperial Court). It was not codified until 1969. See StGB [German Criminal Code] § 34 (necessity as justification). For a more detailed comparative analysis, see Markus D. Dubber & Tatjana Hörnle, Criminal Law: A Comparative Approach ch. 13.B (2014).

fact, in the Commentaries on the Code's justification provisions, one is far more likely to come across references to what would be "unjust,"[27] or what does or does not have a "place in the penal law."[28] The drafters still do not set out an account of either "justice" or "the penal law" (or "law," for that matter), which would help us understand why one, or both, might require the adoption of a particular doctrinal rule. And yet, even in a code so thoroughly committed to treatmentism as the Model Code, talk of "justification" slips into talk of justice, talk of "unlawfulness"[29] into talk of law, of "wrongfulness"[30] into talk of wrong, of "claim of right" into talk of right,[31] and of "harm or evil"[32] into talk of, well, harm and evil.[33]

The Code section on necessity is not just unusually clear; it is also relatively generous. Unlike other statutes, most important the New York Penal Law, the Code does not include an "imminence" requirement.[34] It is not that imminence, or "urgency," does not matter under the Code. It is just that it does not matter any more, or less, than any other factor in evaluating the necessity for making a choice,

---

27. See, e.g., Commentaries § 3.04, at 36; see also Commentaries § 2.09, at 373, 375 (duress).

28. See, e.g., Commentaries § 3.04, at 39. Similarly, the justification Commentaries are littered with discussions—and frequently adoptions—of the treatment of analogous issues in the law of torts, a body of law concerned with remedying harms, and distinctly unconcerned with eliminating dangerousness. In fact, one entire justification provision in the Code does no more than refer to the law of torts. See § 3.10 (justification in property crimes).

29. See, e.g., Commentaries § 3.04(1) ("unlawful force"); see also §§ 2.09, 2.10 (unlawful order), 3.04(2)(a)(i) & 3.07(4) (unlawful arrest), 3.04(2)(a)(ii)(2) (unlawful dispossession), 3.06(1)(a) (unlawful entry and carrying away), 3.06(3)(c) (unlawful re-entry and recaption), 5.01(2)(d) (unlawful entry), 5.01(2)(e) (unlawful use).

30. See, e.g., § 3.06(6) ("wrongful obstructor"); see also §§ 2.08(4) & 4.01(1) (wrongfulness of conduct).

31. See, e.g., §§ 3.04(2)(a)(ii) & (b)(ii), 3.06(1)(b)(ii), (2)(c), (3)(d)(i), & (6)(a).

32. See, e.g., § 3.02(1); see also §§ 1.09(1)(c), 1.10(1), 1.13(10), 2.02(6), 2.11(1), 2.12(2).

33. That is not to say that one could not couch issues of justification in treatmentist terms, just that the drafters did not do so as often as one might expect. After all, the woman who burns down a house to save the village from an oncoming firestorm does not display the same criminal dangerousness as the woman who sets her neighbor's house on fire without a justification of any kind.

34. In fact, it does not even require, unlike other justification defenses in the Code, that the facially criminal conduct be "immediately" necessary. See, e.g., §§ 3.04(1) (self-defense), 3.06(1) (defense of property), 3.07(1) (law enforcement).

or the rightness of choosing one harm over the other. As an example of a case in which imminence might matter, the Commentaries mention the famous maritime cannibalism case of *Regina v. Dudley & Stephens*, in which three shipwrecked sailors killed and ate a fourth, only to be rescued within a few days.[35] The problem was that they might have been able to survive, even if not until their rescue, then at least for some time, without cannibalizing one of their number, and that the eventual victim was so sick that he might have died shortly on his own account, without the need to resort to murder. Under the Code, the absence of imminence would not automatically bar a necessity defense. Necessity thus can justify the prevention of a future harm, provided it is sufficiently likely and serious.

Moreover, a belief in necessity—including imminence, if relevant—will be enough. The general mistake provisions governing defenses apply here as well, so that a correct assessment of the need for action is not required.[36] A belief in the necessity will do, with the familiar allowances for imperfect defenses in the case of recklessly or negligently mistaken beliefs. (In New York, by contrast, the necessity defense on its face applies only to conduct that "*is* necessary as an emergency measure."[37]) So even if Dudley and Stephens were wrong in assessing the necessity of killing the cabin boy, and the imminence of their deaths, they would not be liable for murder, which under the Code requires purpose or knowledge. Depending on the nature of their mistake, however, they may be liable for manslaughter or negligent homicide.

---

35. Commentaries § 3.02, at 16 n.20 (citing Regina v. Dudley & Stephens, 14 Q.B.D. 273 (1884)). Note that the Code generally allows a necessity justification for homicidal arithmetic à la *Dudley*. Commentaries § 3.02, at 15. Without such a "numerical preponderance in the lives saved compared to those sacrificed," however, no justification is available. This is bad news for those who find themselves in the other classic shipwreck scenario—sharing a floating plank that can hold one, but not two. Here I would not be justified in pushing off my fellow sailor to save my own skin. Id. at 17. As it turns out, I do not even have an excuse defense here because, as we will see shortly, the Code does not recognize necessity as an excuse (or circumstantial, as opposed to personal, duress) in cases where I face a necessary choice, but not one in which the balance of evils favors me. See § 13 below.
36. N.Y. Penal Law § 35.05(2); Commentaries § 3.02, at 19–22.
37. See People v. Craig, 78 N.Y.2d 616 (1991) (necessity defense "objective only").

Note, however, that the Code's necessity provision does contain one objective element. A mistaken belief in the necessity of taking facially criminal action does not preclude the defense, but a mistaken "choice of evils" does.[38] This crucial limitation was meant to keep the necessity defense from justifying defendants such as the one who "genuinely believes that the life of another is less valuable than his own financial security."[39] The Commentaries distinguish mistakes about balancing from mistakes about necessity in that the former are about questions of law, and the latter about questions of fact:

> What is involved may be described as an interpretation of the law of the offense, in light of the submission that the special situation calls for an exception to the criminal prohibition that the legislature could not reasonably have intended to exclude, given the competing values to be weighed.[40]

Finally, the Code does not necessarily bar the defense in cases where the actor had some fault in bringing about the situation giving rise to the necessity.[41] In keeping with its general treatment of mistakes as to defense elements, the Code instead differentiates between types of causation: recklessly bringing about and negligently doing so.[42] Although purposefully or knowingly setting up the necessity to violate the law will not do, recklessly or negligently creating the situation of necessity gives rise only to liability for recklessness or negligence offenses.

---

38. See Commentaries § 3.02, at 12; § 3.02(1)(a) ("harm or evil sought to be avoided by such conduct *is* greater than that sought to be prevented by the law defining the offense") (emphasis added).

39. Commentaries § 3.02, at 12.

40. Id.; cf. § 2.12(3) (de minimis).

41. Contrast N.Y. Penal Law § 35.05(2) (specifically limiting defense to "situation occasioned or developed through no fault of the actor"). On forfeiture in the law of self-defense, see § 9.3 below.

42. Cf. § 3.09(2).

§ 9 DEFENSE OF PERSONS (SELF AND OTHERS) AND OF PROPERTY

The Code's treatment of self-defense distinguishes two types of cases, those that do not involve the use of "deadly force" and those that do.[43] Initially, both are governed by the same general standard, which is simple enough:

> [T]he use of force upon or toward another person is justifiable when the actor believes that such force is immediately necessary for the purpose of protecting himself against the use of unlawful force by such other person on the present occasion.[44]

So far, the self-defense provision looks a lot like that on necessity, simple and to the point. That is how it should be, in form and in substance, since self-defense is but one instance of necessity. As the provision makes clear, using force in self-defense is justified only if (1) it is *necessary* and (2) it fits a general situation where the "harm or evil" of a certain type of criminal conduct (assault, imprisonment, homicide) is *outweighed* by the "harm or evil" of another type of criminal conduct (assault, imprisonment, kidnapping, rape, or homicide), namely when I have to use the former to protect myself against an unlawful instance of the latter.

The drafters, however, could not leave well enough alone. They decided that if I want to claim a self-defense justification for using "deadly force," rather than just any "force," I will have to jump through some additional hoops, which they then proceeded to specify in considerable detail.

---

43. This cluster of defenses (of persons and property) are the only "defenses" in the true sense of the word. While any justification or excuse may count as a defense in some *procedural* sense, self-defense, defense of another, and defense of property (mine and another's) are defenses in the *substantive* sense. More specifically, these defenses are defenses in the procedural sense because they are defenses in the substantive sense—at their common core lies my right to defend my rights and those of another against rightless attack.

44. § 3.04(1).

§ 9.1 Self-Defense

But let us look at the basic requirements for self-defense first, especially since the provisions on deadly force tend to get all the attention.[45]

(A) Use of Force Upon or Toward Another Person

The first thing to notice is that this provision—as every other justification provision, with two exceptions—deals only with offenses involving the use of *force*, and more particularly of force against another person (codified in articles 210–213 of the Code's special part). The two exceptions are § 3.02, on necessity, which we just discussed, and § 3.10, on justification in property crimes, which we will not discuss in detail. As its title suggests, § 3.10 deals with defenses to crimes involving harm not to persons, but to property (codified in articles 220–224). The Code drafters were not particularly interested in this issue, dealing with it by a simple nod in the direction of the law of torts, equating "a defense of privilege in a civil action" with a justification in a criminal case. Here is how the Second Restatement of Torts illustrates the privilege "intentionally to invade interests in present and future possession of chattels": "A, while visiting in B's house, is assaulted by B, who seizes a valuable vase to hurl at him. To protect himself, A picks up B's umbrella, and with it knocks the vase out of B's hands and breaks it and the umbrella. A is not liable to B for the value of either the umbrella or the vase."[46] Under § 3.10, then, A would not be *criminally* liable either, say for criminal mischief.[47] The justification of all other crimes, not involving harm either to persons or to property, presumably is covered only by the general necessity provision, which is not limited to any particular type of crime.

(B) Belief

Next we find the familiar reference to belief, with the similarly familiar consequences for the treatment of mistakes. If they are reckless or

45. For a historical essay on self-defense, which itself is of more than historical interest, see Joseph H. Beale, Retreat from a Murderous Assault, 16 Harv. L. Rev. 567 (1903).
46. Restatement (Second) of Torts § 261.
47. § 220.3; see also N.Y. Penal Law § 145.00.

negligent—and therefore unreasonable—then there can only be liability for recklessness or negligence offenses, respectively. If they are neither reckless nor negligent—and therefore reasonable—then they do not stand in the way of a justification for the use of force.[48]

When it comes to the unlawfulness of the force against which I am defending myself, however, the Code clarifies that a mistake about un*law*fulness does not count if it is "due to ignorance or mistake as to the provisions of the Code [or] any other provision of the criminal *law*."[49] So if I use force to protect myself against your attempt to wrest your wallet out of my hand, firmly[50] believing that it is never lawful to use even moderate force to recover stolen property, that belief would not do me any good.

(C) Necessity

Like necessity, self-defense covers the use of force only if it is "necessary." Plus it requires a mental state of "purpose" with respect to its conduct element ("protecting himself"), much as necessity requires that the actor "sought to" avoid greater harm by engaging in facially criminal conduct. As we just saw, "belief" is enough with respect to its attendant circumstances ("immediately necessary," "unlawful")—once again echoing necessity ("necessary"[51]). So conduct that only turns out later to have met the prerequisites (or elements) for self-defense (say, because the assailant had, unbeknownst to the person claiming self-defense, concealed a bowie knife in her coat pocket) will not qualify as self-defense. On the flipside, however, conduct that turns out later *not* to have met the conditions for self-defense, but appeared to meet them to the actor at the

---

48. It is here, in assessing the nature of the defendant's belief regarding the conditions for the justified use of self-defensive force, that the Code would accommodate evidence of battered woman syndrome. See State v. Leidholm, 334 N.W.2d 811 (N.D. 1983); see also State v. Kelly, 97 N.J. 178 (1984).

49. § 3.09(1) (emphasis added).

50. But wrongly. § 3.06(1); Commonwealth v. Donahue, 148 Mass. 529 (1889) (assault to reclaim property).

51. Except, once again, regarding the balancing element, that the "harm or evil sought to be avoided by such conduct is greater than that sought to be prevented by the law defining the offense charged." Commentaries § 3.02, at 12.

time, will qualify, subject to the familiar provisions regarding reckless and negligent mistakes.

Unlike necessity, however, self-defense does not require a balance of evils, at least not explicitly. That balance has been struck in the abstract by the legislature in framing the conditions for self-defense. In a homicide case, for example, necessity would balance lives saved against lives sacrificed. So killing three to save one could never be justified on grounds of necessity. By contrast, killing three (or more) to save one in self-defense may well be justified. In effect, the lives of those who engage in "unlawful" conduct are not weighted as heavily as those who do not.

I have the right to use force in defending myself against one or more persons only if they use "unlawful" force. There is no similar limitation on the right to use force—or to engage in any other criminal conduct—in the name of necessity. To stick with homicide, I may throw Jill overboard to save myself and my friend Jack, even if she engaged in no unlawful conduct of any kind—on grounds of necessity. But I could not throw her overboard just to save myself—on grounds of self-defense—as her life counts as much as mine.[52]

(D) Unlawfulness

As so much in self-defense—and, as we will see later on, in duress as well[53]—turns on the "unlawfulness" of the aggressor's force, it is no surprise that the Code drafters took care to define just what they considered "unlawful force" to be. Unfortunately, their definition is not a model of clarity:

> "[U]nlawful force" means force, including confinement, which is employed without the consent of the person against whom it is directed and the employment of which constitutes an offense or actionable tort or would constitute such offense or tort except

---

52. Blackstone, without the concept of unlawfulness, would find self-defense here because "their both remaining on the same weak plank is a mutual, though innocent, attempt upon, and an endangering of, each other's life." 4 William Blackstone, Commentaries on the Laws of England 186 (1769). Dudley and Stephens tried a similar argument a century later, but failed. Regina v. Dudley & Stephens, 14 Q.B.D. 273 (1884).

53. See § 13 below.

for a defense (such as the absence of intent, negligence, or mental capacity; duress; youth; or diplomatic status) not amounting to a privilege to use the force.[54]

One might have expected the drafters simply to say that unlawful force meant unjustified force, as after all conduct is justified if it does not violate the law, generally speaking, even if it is facially criminal in the sense of matching the definition of a criminal offense. Under this formulation, self-defense would be justified only against unjustified force or, alternatively, self-defense would be lawful only against unlawful force. (So, for instance, using self-defensive force against force used in self-defense could not be justified.) Instead of referring to justification in general, the drafters make reference to one specific justification ("consent")[55] and to the rough tort analog of a justification ("privilege"), so that unlawful force is defined so as not to include force that is consented to or privileged.[56]

The Code formulation also makes clear that, although *justified* conduct may not be resisted by self-defensive force, conduct that is merely *excused* may. Once more, the drafters listed particular excuse defenses, however, rather than speaking of excuses in general; unlawful force includes force committed under circumstances giving rise to a defense of "mental capacity; duress; youth."[57]

The differential treatment of justified and excused attacks makes sense. Justified conduct means not unlawful conduct. Excused conduct, by contrast, bars criminal liability but does not challenge the unlawfulness of the conduct. My killing Roger under duress may be excused, but it cannot be justified. For that reason, Roger may use self-defensive force

---

54. § 3.11(1).

55. Originally, the section on consent was slated to appear in article 3 of the Code, on "general principles of justification." See Tentative Draft No. 8, § 3.11, at 81 (May 9, 1958). In the final version, it was placed in article 2, as § 2.11. For more on consent, see § 11 below.

56. According to the drafters, however, justifications do not match up perfectly with the analogous privileges. Sometimes they are broader, and sometimes narrower. Commentaries art. 3, introduction, at 2. A further complication is that consent for purposes of determining the unlawfulness of force differs from consent as a defense to nominal liability. Commentaries, § 3.11, at 157–59.

57. On the excuses of duress, insanity, and infancy, see §§ 13 & 17 below.

against my attempt to kill him. More dramatically, I would be justified in using self-defensive force, even deadly force, against attacks by an insane person (i.e., someone who qualifies for the excuse of mental disease or defect[58]) or a child (i.e., someone excused by reason of immaturity[59]).

Note that the Code here allows, in fact justifies, the use of self-defensive force against conduct that would not be punishable. In other words, I may kill someone in self-defense with impunity whom the state could not subject to any punishment whatsoever, however slight. In fact, the Code justifies the use of self-defensive force even against conduct that is not punishable because it is not even facially criminal (as opposed to facially criminal, but excused). For unlawful force—and therefore force against which I am justified in defending myself—includes not only force that "constitutes an offense," but also force that "would constitute such offense... except for a defense... such as the absence of intent [or] negligence." In other words, I am justified in using self-defensive force even if the person threatening me lacks the requisite mental state to match the definition of a criminal offense. As long as the "attacker" engaged in the proscribed *conduct*, even if without mens rea of any kind, including negligence, I am justified in using self-defensive force, including deadly force where appropriate. So, for instance, I may shoot the driver of a car that is about to hit me at high speed, even if I know the driver was not negligent in any way, and obeyed the traffic laws to the letter: "Whatever may be thought in tort, it cannot be regarded as a crime to safeguard an innocent person, whether the actor or another, against threatened death or injury that is unprivileged, even though the source of the threat is *free from fault*."[60] In this case, perfectly lawful conduct is treated as unlawful. Commenting on this sleight of hand, the drafters remarked with characteristic pragmatism that "[i]f the resulting concept is an awkward one, the difficulty is outweighed by the drafting advantages that it entails."[61]

---

58. § 4.01.
59. § 4.10.
60. Commentaries § 3.11, at 159 (emphasis added).
61. Id. The alternative of treating this scenario as a case of necessity is not available because the balance of evils would not come out in my favor—I would sacrifice the driver's life

By limiting self-defense to unlawful force, rather than unjustified force, the Code drafters avoided the need to draw a sharp line between justification and excuse. The problem of demarcating the boundaries of self-defense, however, is thereby merely shifted from the definition of justification to that of unlawfulness. And that definition in the Code is so broad, and so noncommittal, including cryptic references to the law of torts (and even the concept of "intent," shunned elsewhere in the Code), that it cannot bear the doctrinal weight the drafters assigned to it, or at least can bear it no better than an attempt to differentiate justification from excuse.

Before we move on to another condition for self-defense, it is important to note an exception to the general rule that protective force is justified against "unlawful force." When the justification of self-defense collides with that of law enforcement, the latter takes precedence. Contrary to the law of torts, the Code does not recognize a justification for the use of force against an unlawful arrest.[62] An arrestee's belief in the unlawfulness of an arrest is simply irrelevant. He will not be justified in defending himself against it either way.[63]

(E) Immediacy and Protection

By abandoning the explicit requirement of choosing the lesser of two evils, the self-defense justification exceeds the bounds of the necessity defense. At the same time, the Code restricts the scope of self-defense by limiting it to protection against *unlawful* attacks. Also, unlike the necessity provision, self-defense is limited to *immediate* necessity, presumably to exclude preventive strikes under the guise of self-*defense*. One of the

for my own. Necessity as an excuse also would not apply as the Code steadfastly denies a defense in cases of circumstantial, rather than personal, duress. See § 13 below.

62. § 3.04(2)(a)(i); Commentaries § 3.04, at 42 (citing Restatement (Second) of Torts § 67). On the flipside, the Code also exempts police attempting to make an arrest from the general retreat requirement imposed upon the use of *deadly* self-defensive force, even if the arrest is unlawful. The tort privilege, by contrast, is limited to lawful arrests. § 3.04(2)(b)(ii)(2); Commentaries § 3.04, at 57 (citing Restatement (Second) of Torts § 65(2)(c)).

63. The *arrester's* criminal liability for making an arrest *she* does not believe to be lawful is another matter. Cf. §§ 3.07(1) ("lawful arrest"); 3.09(1)(a) (mistake as to lawfulness of arrest). Plus, the separate offense of "resisting arrest" under the Code still requires a "lawful arrest" § 242.2; cf. People v. Peacock, 68 N.Y.2d 675 (1986).

distinctions between self-defense and necessity is, after all, that the former is *only* defensive, whereas the latter may be, and often is, offensive.[64]

Defensive, however, does not mean retrospective. Self-defensive force is by nature preventive, and therefore prospective. The point is to *protect* one's self, or someone else's self, or one's property, against future harm, not to retaliate for past harm, or even for past threats of harm. As Blackstone explained, "if the person assaulted does not fall upon the aggressor till the affray is over, or when he is running away, this is revenge and not defence."[65] Fear is justifiable, anger not.[66]

(F) Self- and Other-Defense

Self-defense is limited to force used by a person to protect "himself" (or herself), rather than someone, or something, else. The right to protect someone or something else is handled in separate provisions, which we will not spend much time discussing. Section 3.05, dealing with protection of someone else, does not require separate attention because the drafters decided, perhaps wisely, to treat the issue of other-defense in analogy to that of self-defense. In the succinct phrase of the Commentaries, "the rules are the same as those that govern self-defense."[67] That is, I will be justified in defending another against a third person if I, placing myself in the other's shoes, would have been justified in defending myself against that third person. Tricky cases involving Good—but mistaken—Samaritans who come to the aid of the wrong party in a dispute are handled just as any other mistake about the conditions of justification: if they are reasonable, they make a complete defense. If they are not, they make at least an incomplete defense against

64. Note, however, that the Code does not limit the use of force to immediate (or "imminent") threats of violence. Instead the attack must occur, or be feared to occur, on the "present occasion." This formulation is meant to be more generous than the traditional imminence requirement, by justifying the use of self-defensive force, for instance, "to prevent an assailant from going to summon reinforcements, given a belief that it is necessary to disable him to prevent an attack by overwhelming numbers." Commentaries § 3.04, at 39–40. Whether cases of this sort could also be reached under a flexible reading of an imminence requirement is another question.
65. 4 William Blackstone, Commentaries on the Laws of England 185 (1769).
66. See Weston v. State, 682 P.2d 1119 (Alaska 1984).
67. Commentaries § 3.05, at 62–63.

crimes that require more than recklessness or negligence, but do not work against crimes that do not.[68]

It is perhaps noteworthy, however, that the Code abandons any attempt to limit the class of third persons whom one would be justified in defending. Unlike the common law, which limited it to certain individuals who stand in a special relationship to the actor—relatives, superiors, subordinates[69]—the justification of vicarious self-defense under the Code applies to any person whatsoever ("person of another").

§ 9.2 Defense of Property

The connection between self-defense and defense of property is not quite as obvious as that between defense of self and defense of other persons. Still, a connection exists. The most important point about the Code's treatment of the right to use force in protection of property is that the right to property cannot trump the right to life.[70] As the Commentaries explain:

> [T]he general principle of the section is quite easy to state, though the drafting of it proved complex. The basic judgment that is reflected is that "the preservation of life has such moral and ethical standing in our culture and society, that the deliberate sacrifice of life merely for the protection of property ought not to be sanctioned by law."[71]

Pouring this "general principle" into statutory form turned out to be so "complex," and the resulting section so convoluted, because the

68. Id. at 65–66. The common law was not always so kind. See, e.g., Wood v. State, 128 Ala. 27 (1900) (third-party defender "enter[s] combat at his own peril").
69. 4 William Blackstone, Commentaries on the Laws of England 186 (1769) ("the principal civil and natural relations"); see also Restatement (Second) of Torts § 76, cmt. e.
70. Defense of property tracks defense of person in another way. Just as defense of another's person is handled analogously to defense of my person, so defense of another's property is handled analogously to defense of my property. There is, however, no separate section dealing with defense of another's property. § 3.06 (1)(a); Commentaries § 3.06, at 79.
71. Commentaries § 3.06, at 72 (quoting ALI Proceedings 285–86 (1958)) (statement of Herbert Wechsler).

principle proved less universal than the drafters, and Herbert Wechsler in particular, had thought.[72] Several ALI members stressed the need to draft a Code that did not drift too far afield of "basic sentiments of the community"[73] and "popular sentiment,"[74] reflected in a string of precedents clearly recognizing a basic right of every "householder"[75] to defend himself and "the members of his household"[76] against the paradigmatic nighttime burglar. Criminal law could not deny a man the right to "protection of his person and of his family,"[77] when confronted with blatant attacks on his home, or so the criticism went.

In response, Wechsler could do little more than reassert the contested principle. When pressed to provide arguments in its support, he replied, with uncharacteristic resignation: "I suppose that this is a kind of proposition that cannot be demonstrated, that involves in the end one's convictions. And one either holds convictions or one does not."[78] Apparently, many ALI members did not. Just what changes the critics advocated, however, was less than obvious. An exasperated Wechsler remarked at the end of the meeting: "I can only say on behalf of the Reporter that I hope the transcript will indicate to me what it is that I am supposed to do."[79]

What Wechsler ended up doing was to make some changes to the section while retaining the "general principle." The Commentaries neatly summarize the doctrinal core of the section on defense of property, in its proposed as well as in its final form:

> The general principle of the section is that moderate but not deadly force may be used to defend property against caption or

---

72. The controversy at the ALI annual meeting on this section is documented in a student note from the time, Note, The Use of Deadly Force in the Protection of Property under the Model Penal Code, 59 Colum. L. Rev. 1212 (1959).
73. Id. at 1223.
74. Id. at 1224 n.64.
75. Id. at 1223 n.56.
76. Id. at 1216.
77. Id. at 1216 n.19.
78. Id. at 1222 n.54 (quoting ALI Proceedings 285–86 (1958)).
79. Id. at 1223 n.59 (quoting ALI Proceedings 325 (1958)).

trespass, with specific exceptions allowing the use of deadly force in certain instances.[80]

Most significant for our purposes, the revised section included a provision specifically dedicated to the "use of deadly force" in defense of property, laying out the two "specific exceptions" to the general rule that life could not be sacrificed for property:

> Use of Deadly Force. The use of deadly force is not justifiable under this Section unless the actor believes that:
> (i) the person against whom the force is used is attempting to dispossess him of his dwelling otherwise than under a claim of right to its possession; or
> (ii) the person against whom the force is used is attempting to commit or consummate arson, burglary, robbery or other felonious theft or property destruction and either:
> (1) has employed or threatened deadly force against or in the presence of the actor; or
> (2) the use of force other than deadly force to prevent the commission or the consummation of the crime would expose the actor or another in his presence to substantial danger of serious bodily harm.[81]

Subsection (d)(i), dealing with the use of deadly force to prevent being kicked out of one's own home by anyone not acting under a claim of right, already appeared in the first draft of the section.[82]

Subsection (d)(ii) was new, but added nothing. Although on one hand it extends the right to use deadly force to prevent property crimes, on the other it limits it to cases of personal threat.[83] The right to use deadly force in the protection of persons, however, had never been in doubt, and is spelled out in the two preceding sections, 3.04

---

80. Commentaries § 3.06, at 72.
81. § 3.06(3)(d). On the broader conception of defense of property in the New York Penal Law, see, e.g., People v. Petronio, 192 Misc.2d 240, 746 N.Y.S.2d 781 (2002).
82. See Tentative Draft No. 8, § 3.06(2)(b), at 34 (May 9, 1958).
83. See generally Commentaries § 3.06, at 91–97.

(self-defense) and, by analogy, 3.05 (other-defense).[84] As the Mississippi Supreme Court had already explained in 1883:

> No man is required by law to yield possession of his property to the unlawful claim of another. He may defend his possession; and while he may not kill to prevent the trespass, he may kill to protect his own person against a deadly assault made by the trespasser on him. In other words, one who assaults a trespasser to prevent the injury threatened is the actor but not the aggressor in the difficulty, and he does not lose the right of self-defence because he makes the attack.[85]

The Code's approach to the use of force, and deadly force in particular, in defense of property is exemplified by its handling of spring guns and similar devices. Their use is justifiable under the Code only if they do not amount to the use of deadly force against intruders.[86] Given the general principle that life cannot be sacrificed for the sake of property, this comes as no surprise. As subsection (d)(ii) makes clear, using deadly force against an intruder is justifiable only to prevent death or serious bodily harm to one or more persons. A machine, however, is not a person, nor can it assess whether, under the circumstances, a person interfering with, or threatening to interfere with, my right to property also poses a threat to myself or others.[87]

§ 9.3 Deadly Force

The use of deadly force against attacks on myself or another is justified if certain additional requirements, beyond those imposed on self-defensive force generally speaking, are met. In other words, there is no general principle prohibiting the sacrifice of one life to save another,

---

84. Contrast N.Y. Penal Law § 35.20 (right to use deadly force to prevent arson or burglary without showing of personal threat); see N.Y. Penal Law § 35.25 (no right to use deadly force to prevent larceny or criminal mischief).
85. Ayers v. State, 60 Miss. 709 (1883).
86. Compare § 3.06(5)(a) with § 3.11(2).
87. Cf. People v. Ceballos, 12 Cal. 3d 470 (1974).

or to protect myself—or another—against certain nonlethal harm, including "serious bodily harm, kidnapping or sexual intercourse compelled by force or threat."

The deadly force issue is central to the law of self-defense. In fact, the recognition of self-defense as a general defense applicable to any offense is a fairly recent development. Historically, self-defense was an issue not for the general part, but for the special part of Anglo-American criminal law. More specifically, self-defense was an issue in the law of homicide.[88] Self-defense was a defense *only* in cases involving the use of deadly force. Even today, the vast bulk of self-defense cases—and law school hypotheticals—deal with self-defense as a defense against homicide, and yet more specifically, against murder.

Having said that, it is important to note that the Model Penal Code defines deadly force more broadly than homicidal force. Deadly force under the Code also includes the purposeful, knowing, or reckless (but not negligent) use of force that, if applied successfully, would result not in death but in "serious bodily harm," and therefore in liability for aggravated assault,[89] rather than for homicide.[90]

The basic rule governing the use of deadly force is that it may be used if, in addition to the general conditions for self-defense already discussed, "the actor believes that such force is necessary to protect himself against death, serious bodily harm, kidnapping or sexual intercourse compelled by force or threat." The nature of the threat thus determines the nature of the justified response. The response must be proportional to the threat, but it need not be equivalent. I may use deadly force to prevent not only death, but also lesser—though still serious—harm to myself, or another.

In addition to the general, if implicit, requirement of proportionality between serious threat and deadly response, the Code imposes several other constraints on the use of deadly force. The first provision denies the right to use deadly force to anyone who "with the purpose of causing

88. Self-defense's excuse analog, provocation, has remained there to this day. See § 16 below.
89. § 211.1(2).
90. § 3.11(2). Aggravated assault, not simple assault, because the potential of nonserious physical harm is not enough, nor is the threat of serious physical harm.

death or serious bodily harm, provoked the use of force against himself in the same encounter."[91] Note that the Code does more than restate the common law's traditional initial aggressor limitation on the right to use deadly force in self-defense. As in the case of necessity, the Code rejects the idea that anyone who is not without fault in creating the conditions giving rise to a justification thereby forfeits that justification.[92] So if I should pick a fight with a fellow driver over a traffic incident, I would not automatically be precluded from claiming the right to use deadly force in self-defense later in the encounter. If, for instance, my fellow motorist raises the stakes in the middle of our impromptu roadside shoving match by pulling a gun out of his pants pocket and firing it at me, I may even be justified in using deadly force—by retrieving my very own firearm from the glove compartment—to protect myself (unless, of course, I started the initial altercation "with the purpose of causing death or serious bodily harm," rather than, say, of punching the victim of my road rage in the nose).

If the victim of my initial aggression escalates the struggle to the level of deadly force, in other words, I will be justified, under the Code, in using deadly force in response. Because now it is he who is the one using unlawful force by responding, excessively, with deadly force to nondeadly force. He is now using not only unlawful force, but unlawful *deadly* force against me, which turns the justificatory tables entirely by putting me in the position of being authorized to use not just force, but *deadly* force, in response.[93]

The initial aggressor (or forfeiture) rule in this way supplements the other exception to the justifiability of deadly force in self-defense,

<hr />

91. § 3.04(2)(b)(i).

92. See § 8 above. Cf. 4 William Blackstone, Commentaries on the Laws of England 186 (1769).

93. See the classic case of Rowe v. United States, 164 U.S. 546 (1896). There the eventual homicide victim, a white man named Frank Bozeman, provoked a Cherokee by the name of David Cul Rowe by a racial slur into a minor assault (which was concededly unlawful and wrongful, however understandable), to which Bozeman responded with the use of deadly force, prompting the use of deadly force by Rowe in turn, resulting in Bozeman's death. The Court held that Rowe, though the initial aggressor, was not precluded from justifying his use of deadly force on the grounds of self-defense.

the retreat rule.[94] I cannot with justification use deadly force if I "know that [I] can avoid the necessity of using such force with complete safety by retreating."[95] If, in our example, I could avoid having to return fire by speeding away, I would not be justified in shooting even after having been shot at, provided I could get away "with complete safety," and I knew I could. The flipside of the retreat rule is that, once I *have* retreated as far as I could ("to the wall," in the language of the common law), I am justified under the Code in using deadly force.[96]

It being a general rule, however, also means that the retreat requirement applies to anyone wishing to justify the use of deadly force in self-defense, not just to initial aggressors. It is a familiar rule from the common law, which—once again concerned with the paradigmatic case of "combat"—required that anyone claiming self-defense "must show, that before a mortal stroke given, he had declined any farther combat, and retreated as far as he could with safety."[97]

Just what the retreat rule adds to the necessity requirement, which is all over the Code's section on self-defense, is not clear. If a person can "protect[] himself against the use of unlawful force by [an]other person on the present occasion" by retreating, then "the use of force upon or toward another person" is *not* "immediately necessary." And if no force of any kind would be necessary, then *deadly* force certainly would not be necessary either. The drafters, however, preferred to view the possibility of safe retreat as distinct from necessity, partly because "all agree" that the use of *nondeadly* force can be "necessary" even though safe retreat would be possible, allowing the actor to "stand his ground and estimate necessity upon that basis."[98] Not so in the case of deadly self-defensive force, however. Here necessity still does not require the absence of retreat options as a matter of "logic"; the retreat requirement instead flows from the Code's placing "a high value on the preservation

94. See generally Joseph H. Beale, Retreat from a Murderous Assault, 16 Harv. L. Rev. 567 (1903).
95. § 3.04(2)(b)(ii).
96. Cf. Stoffer v. State, 15 Ohio St. 47 (1864).
97. General Summary of Crimes, and Their Punishments, in 2 Laws of the Commonwealth of Pennsylvania 558, 571 (1810).
98. Commentaries § 3.04, at 53.

of life."[99] Joseph Beale, in 1903, expressed the basic sentiment underlying the duty to retreat with unusual force, and even a touch of pathos:

> A really honorable man, a man of truly refined and elevated feeling, would perhaps always regret the apparent cowardice of a retreat, but he would regret ten times more, after the excitement of the contest was past, the thought that he had the blood of a fellow-being on his hands. It is undoubtedly distasteful to retreat; but it is ten times more distasteful to kill.[100]

Even in deadly force cases, however, the retreat rule is not without its exceptions. The first exception to the retreat exception to the justifiability of deadly force in defense against "death, serious bodily harm, kidnapping or sexual intercourse compelled by force or threat" is the house-or-work exception. There is no need to retreat if I am attacked at home,[101] or at work. This exception, however, has its own set of exceptions: (1) I have to retreat at home *or* at work if I was the "initial aggressor,"[102] and (2) I have to retreat at work if I was attacked by someone I recognize as a coworker (but, unlike in some jurisdictions, not if I was attacked at home by a cohabitant).[103]

Besides the house-or-work exception—with its various subexceptions—to the retreat requirement, there is the police (or "public officer") exception. So, for instance, a police officer may kill someone who resists arrest, rather than abandoning her efforts and leaving the

---

99. Id. at 55.

100. Joseph H. Beale, Retreat from a Murderous Assault, 16 Harv. L. Rev. 567, 581 (1903). Beale went on to favorably compare these sentiments of a cultivated gentleman (like himself) with the "talk of dishonor and cowardice" by "the border-ruffian, who walks about the earth with one hand on his hip-pocket." Id. at 582.

101. More precisely, in my "dwelling," defined generously as "any building or structure, though movable or temporary, or a portion thereof, that is for the time being the actor's home or place of lodging." § 3.11(3). For a case interpreting the home exception in the New York Penal Law, see People v. Jones, 3 N.Y.3d 491, 821 N.E.2d 955 (2004) (affirming application of home exception even to attacks by co-occupant in light of its "importance in cases of domestic violence, most often against women").

102. To be distinguished from the initial aggressor who is not entitled to use deadly force in the first place because he started the fracas with "the purpose of causing death or serious bodily harm." § 3.04(2)(b)(i).

103. See, e.g., N.D. Crim. Code § 12.1–05–07(2)(b) (discussed in State v. Leidholm, 334 N.W.2d 811 (N.D. 1983)).

arrest for another, hopefully better, day, even if safe retreat is possible.[104] Note, however, that the other constraints on the use of deadly force remain; the police exception is only an exception to the retreat exception to the familiar rule justifying the use of deadly force under certain, limited circumstances. Even a police officer, or his private helper, therefore can use deadly force against an arrest resister only if he "believes that such force is necessary to protect himself against death, serious bodily harm, kidnapping or sexual intercourse."[105]

It is unclear whether the Code drafters struck the right balance between clarity and complexity in the section on self-defense, or more precisely in the cluster of provisions on self-defense and closely related topics. It is difficult to imagine that they hoped to provide potential offenders with notice about the possible consequences of their contemplated behavior. (In fact, the provisions on self-defense seem to reflect the kind of "acoustic separation," that is, a distinction among audiences and related modes of communication, that Meir Dan-Cohen has traced and that Paul Robinson has advocated.[106]) But even as "principles of adjudication" (rather than "rules of conduct"), these provisions appear to err on the side of micromanaging decision-making processes instead of guiding the exercise of discretion by presumably qualified state officials.

§ 10 LAW ENFORCEMENT

The general justification for the use of force in making an arrest appears in § 3.07. Arrests, after all, generally imply the use of force, even in the absence of affirmative resistance by the arrestee and beyond the right of the arrester to use force in self-defense, which is handled

---

104. And even if she is making an unlawful arrest. Commentaries § 3.04, at 57.
105. For a case that nicely illustrates the interplay of the rules governing the use of force, deadly and moderate, in defense of one's property and of one's person, including the initial aggressor rule and the duty to retreat, see United States v. Peterson, 483 F.2d 1222 (D.C. Cir. 1973).
106. Meir Dan-Cohen, Decision Rules and Conduct Rules: On Acoustic Separation in Criminal Law, 97 Harv. L. Rev. 625 (1984); Paul H. Robinson, Rules of Conduct and Principles of Adjudication, 57 U. Chi. L. Rev. 729 (1990).

in § 3.04.[107] Viewed in this light, the Code provision on law enforcement resembles other justification sections dealing with types of
conduct that are as commonplace as they are facially criminal,
"Execution of Public Duty"[108] and "Use of Force by Persons with
Special Responsibility for Care, Discipline or Safety of Others."[109]

The first thing the law enforcement section does then is explain
why—and ensure that—arrests are justified, and therefore not punishable, even though they may formally constitute an assault.[110] Note here,
once again, that an arrest is justified—and thus not unlawful—even if
it is in fact unlawful:[111] I am justified in using force incident to an arrest
even if the arrest turns out to have been unlawful (because I lack probable cause, in the case of a warrantless arrest, or because the warrant
turns out to be defective), as long as I believe in the lawfulness of the
arrest. Armed with this belief—subject to the familiar provisos regarding reckless and negligent mistakes, and the irrelevance of mistakes of
law[112]—I can use force (that I believe to be) "immediately necessary"
to make the arrest. The justification for using force is complete when
the (belief in the) immediate necessity of using it and the (belief in the)
lawfulness of the arrest are joined by the arrestee's actual, or constructive, notice of "the purpose of the arrest," that is, my reason for subjecting her to otherwise criminal conduct, particularly assault. This notice

107. The arrest itself, which constitutes facially criminal conduct even if made without
     force (e.g., kidnapping (§ 212.1), false imprisonment (§ 212.3)), is justifiable under
     § 3.03, execution of public duty.
108. Justifying "the policeman who exceeds posted speed limits in apprehending a fugi-
     tive, the marshal who trespasses to execute a warrant, the sheriff who seizes property
     to satisfy the judgment of a court," Commentaries § 3.03, at 23, and, to cite the typical
     case invoked in common law sources, the executioner, who "in the *execution* of pub-
     lic justice,... put[s] a malefactor to death, who hath forfeited his life by the laws and
     verdict of his country." 4 William Blackstone, Commentaries on the Laws of England
     178 (1769) (emphasis added). On the Code's ambiguous stance on capital punish-
     ment, see § 2.2, note 43 above.
109. Justifying, among others, parents who punish their children, and wardens their
     inmates, as well as surgeons who slice open their patients, all facial assaults, simple or
     aggravated. § 3.08.
110. Under a suitably broad definition of assault as any touching, every arrest is an assault.
     The Code's definition is narrower. See § 211.1.
111. Commentaries § 3.07, at 107–09.
112. § 3.09(1); but see § 2.04(3).

requirement too is phrased broadly, requiring me to inform the suspect of the purpose of her arrest, unless I believe that purpose "is otherwise known" or "cannot reasonably be made known" to her.[113]

Before we get to the details, two characteristics of the Code's law enforcement provision are worth noting. First, it deals with "law enforcement," not with law enforcement officials, or, put another way, with law enforcement as an activity rather than as an institution. It applies to anyone, any "actor," police officer or not. The justification for the use of force in an arrest springs not from the occupation, or special status, or the person using it, but from the purpose for which it is used—namely law enforcement. This point is as crucial as it is easily forgotten.

Second, the law enforcement section deals almost exclusively with arrests.[114] It thus focuses on defining the justificatory limits placed upon the use of force in a particular, and particularly central, aspect of law enforcement, one that involves the use of force by definition and raises the specter of additional force by experience, given the tendency of many suspects to resist becoming arrestees, triggering the need to subdue them in return.

Defining the justifiability of using force to arrest in terms of "immediate necessity" is familiar from the Code's self-defense provision, and so is the two-pronged layout of the provision on "the use of force in law enforcement," one prong dealing with force, the other with deadly force. Also, as in self-defense, things do not really get interesting until the second prong, the one dealing with the use of deadly force.

Like self-defense, law enforcement places additional constraints on the use of deadly force, supplementing the general limitation on the use of force, period—that the actor believe the force to be "immediately

113. § 3.09(2)(a)(i).
114. Other facially criminal conduct by state officials—including the use of force unrelated to an arrest, or criminal conduct not involving the use of force (such as searches and seizures of property)—is justified under use of force in crime prevention (§ 3.07(5)), the other topic addressed in the section on law enforcement, and execution of public duty (§ 3.03). State officials of course also are entitled to the same justifications available to all persons, most important self-defense (and defense of another). Plus, the Model Code section on self-defense includes certain special—and more generous—provisions applicable to state officials. See, e.g., § 3.04(2)(a)(ii)(1) & (2) (b)(ii)(2).

necessary to effect a lawful arrest," plus actual, or constructive, notice. These supplemental constraints are straightforward, and quotable:

(i) the arrest is for a felony; and

(ii) the person effecting the arrest is authorized to act as a peace officer or is assisting a person whom he believes to be authorized to act as a peace officer; and

(iii) the actor believes that the force employed creates no substantial risk of injury to innocent persons; and

(iv) the actor believes that:

(1) the crime for which the arrest is made involved conduct including the use or threatened use of deadly force; or

(2) there is a substantial risk that the person to be arrested will cause death or serious bodily harm if his apprehension is delayed.[115]

These constraints on the use of deadly force to make an arrest have since been constitutionalized, in *Tennessee v. Garner*.[116] The Model Code, and *Garner*, did away with the old common law rule that permitted the use of deadly force to arrest any felon, where a felony in turn was (often) defined in terms of its prescribed punishment, death.[117] Using death to arrest a felon, then, was justifiable because it merely accelerated the criminal process.[118] Whatever sense this rule made at a time when all (or most) felonies were capital, it made even less sense when all (or most) felonies were no longer capital.

115. § 3.07(2)(b). As the Commentaries stress, the use of deadly force by the arrester may be justified on other grounds, including self-defense or defense of others. This provision deals only with cases where no justification for using deadly force other than law enforcement, and more specifically, law enforcement through an arrest, is available. The question is when a police officer may use deadly force to effect an arrest, period.

116. 471 U.S. 1 (1985).

117. Blackstone disagreed, instead defining "felony" in terms of another punishment, forfeiture, and thereby making room for noncapital felonies. 4 William Blackstone, Commentaries on the Laws of England 94–97 (1769).

118. Provided, of course, the felon was indeed a felon. In the common law, greater authority to kill fleeing felons tended to go along with greater liability for killing a nonfelon.

Still, the Code retains the limitation of deadly force to felonies. The commission, or suspected commission, of a felony is no longer a sufficient condition for the use of deadly force to arrest, but it is still necessary. In the Code, the commission of a felony, without more, is an insufficient indicator of the offender's criminal disposition, or dangerousness, the central factor in the justifiability of deadly force:

[T]he character of the offender as it can be inferred from the available information, rather than from an abstract classification of the offense he is thought to have committed, should be determinative as to the use of deadly force. Specifically, the judgment is that the use of deadly force should be sanctioned only in cases where the offender is thought to pose such a danger to life or limb that his immediate apprehension overrides competing considerations.[119]

So the Code limits the justifiability of deadly force to certain felonies, namely those that "involved conduct including the use or threatened use of deadly force." In this way, the Code maintains a certain proportionality, but now—as in the case of self-defense—between the act to be justified and the offense, rather than between the act to be justified and the *punishment* for the offense. Alternatively, even if no fatal, or potentially fatal, felony was committed, the Code permits the use of deadly force as an incapacitative measure if—in the absence of evidence in the form of a suspected crime already committed—there "is a substantial risk that the person to be arrested will cause death or serious bodily harm if his apprehension is delayed."

Note that when it comes to deadly force, the distinction between police ("law enforcement") and others becomes decisive. Only a "peace officer,"[120] or someone (who believes she is) assisting a peace officer, may use deadly force to arrest.

And, finally, the Code denies even a peace officer the right to use deadly force to arrest unless she believes doing so will not create a

See, e.g., Petrie v. Cartwright, 70 S.W. 297 (Ky. App. 1902) (officer using deadly force to arrest suspected felon "does so at his peril" and "must proceed very cautiously").
119. Commentaries § 3.07, at 119–20.
120. The Code does not define "peace officer." Just who counts as a peace officer is not necessarily a simple matter. See People v. Marrero, 69 N.Y.2d 382 (1987).

substantial risk of "injury" to innocent bystanders. This means that she will have no defense if she believed that using deadly force would in fact create such a risk (i.e., she acted recklessly)[121] or held no particular belief on the matter, perhaps because she was unaware of the risk (i.e., she may have acted negligently). This provision is meant to "emphasiz[e] and articulat[e] the priority that law enforcement personnel ought to accord to safeguarding innocent persons against injury from deadly force directed against persons fleeing from arrest."[122]

§ 11 CONSENT

The last justification that deserves a closer look before we turn our attention to the next, and final, level of analysis—excuses—is consent. Unlike the other justifications we have discussed up to this point, consent is not codified in article 3 of the Code, expressly dedicated to "General Principles of Justification." It appears in article 2 instead, dedicated to "General Principles of Liability," which includes not only provisions dealing with the first level of analysis (offense definition)—such as actus reus, mens rea, causation, complicity, and the like—but, as we will see shortly, also codifies several level three defenses (excuses)—such as duress, military orders, and entrapment—as well as defenses that straddle two levels of analysis—such as mistake and intoxication, which, as we have seen already, appear both as level one (failure of proof) and level three defenses.

Consent finds a home in article 2 because, like mistake and intoxication, it stands with one foot in level one, the subject of the bulk of article 2. Unlike mistake and intoxication, however, its other foot rests in level two, rather than in level three. In other (Model Code) words, consent either "negatives an element of the offense" or it "precludes the infliction of the harm or evil sought to be prevented by the law defining the offense." Given consent's dual status as a failure-of-proof defense and a justification, it is no surprise that it started out in the article on

---

121. Cf. N.Y. Penal Law § 35.30(2); see People v. Pena, 169 Misc. 2d 75 (N.Y. Sup. Ct. 1996).
122. Commentaries § 3.07, at 118.

justification (as § 3.11), but ended up in the article on principles of liability (as § 2.11).[123]

The provision on consent as a level one defense is as straightforward, and as redundant, as are the analogous provisions on mistake and intoxication. It should go without saying that consent would bar even facial criminal liability if it negatived an element of the offense: if the offense definition included the absence of consent, then the presence of consent would mean that the offense had not been committed. So, for instance, the Code defines joyriding as "operat[ing] another's automobile, airplane, motorcycle, motorboat, or other motor-propelled vehicle *without consent* of the owner,"[124] cruelty to animals as "kill[ing] or injur[ing] any animal belonging to another *without... consent* of the owner,"[125] and violation of privacy as "install[ing] in any private place, *without the consent* of the person or persons entitled to privacy there, any device for observing, photographing, recording, amplifying or broadcasting sounds or events in such place, or us[ing] any such unauthorized installation."[126] Similarly, rape traditionally has been defined as sexual intercourse "by force or threat of force against the will and *without the consent* of the other person."[127]

More interesting are cases where consent operates as a justification, rather than as a failure-of-proof defense.[128] The justificatory aspect of consent shines through in the reference to "the harm or evil sought to be prevented by the law defining the offense," which echoes the Code's formulation of the necessity defense as a justification for facially criminal

123. See Tentative Draft No. 8, § 3.11, at 81 (May 9, 1958).
124. § 223.9 (emphasis added).
125. § 250.11(3) (emphasis added).
126. § 250.12(1)(b) (emphasis added).
127. Md. Crim. Code § 463(a)(1) (emphasis added). The Code defines "rape" as sexual intercourse by a male with "a female not his wife... if he compels her to submit by force or by threat of imminent death, serious bodily injury, extreme pain or kidnapping, to be inflicted on anyone." (Yes, the Code retained the "marriage exemption," long since abandoned. See, e.g., People v. Liberta, 64 N.Y.2d 152 (1984).) The ALI is currently considering revisions of the Code's outmoded sexual offense provisions. See Model Penal Code: Sexual Assault and Related Offenses, Tentative Draft No. 1 (Apr. 30, 2014).
128. Rape, as defined in the Code, appears to be an example. Although the absence of consent does not appear in the Code's definition of rape, the Commentaries explain that "it is essential to the commission of the crime that there be an unwilling victim of the actor's conduct." Commentaries § 2.11, at 394.

conduct if "the harm or evil sought to be avoided by such conduct is greater than that sought to be prevented by the law defining the offense charged."[129]

Other traces of consent's justificationness are strewn about the Code.[130] Perhaps most important, consent occupies a central role in the Code's provision on the justification of the use of force in medical treatment, which requires, among other things, that the treatment be administered

> with the consent of the patient or, if the patient is a minor or an incompetent person, with the consent of his parent or guardian or other person legally competent to consent in his behalf, or the treatment is administered in an emergency when the actor believes that no one competent to consent can be consulted and that a reasonable person, wishing to safeguard the welfare of the patient, would consent.[131]

Just when the victim's consent "precludes the infliction of the harm of evil sought to be prevented by the law defining the offense" of course depends on one's view of the point of criminal law. If criminal law is designed to prevent harm inflicted on individuals, then consent would justify any facially criminal conduct. For if individuals are to be protected, then individuals should be entitled to waive that protection as well.

American criminal law, however, is not only, or even primarily, about protecting persons against suffering harm (or evil, for that matter) or, if that fails, about punishing those who inflicted it. Recall that the Model Code defines crime as "conduct that unjustifiably and inexcusably inflicts or threatens substantial harm to individual *or public interests*," with a distinct emphasis on "public."[132] Of the interests recognized

129. § 3.02(1)(a).
130. So consent precludes a finding of unlawfulness, not only because the Code's definition of "unlawful force" says so, but also because it is a key "privilege," the tort analog to a criminal justification. See § 9.1(D) above.
131. § 3.08(4)(b).
132. This emphasis is nothing new. The vast bulk of Blackstone's discussion of substantive criminal law, the law of "public wrongs," is dedicated to offenses against public

by the Code drafters, only one, "the person," qualifies unequivocally as an individual interest. Even "property" the Code treats as a public interest, or a "system."[133] The remaining interests protected by the criminal law against harm are clearly public (or institutional, as arguably in the case of the family): "the existence or stability of the state,"[134] "the family," "public administration," and "public order and decency," as well as the interests safeguarded by "miscellaneous offenses,"[135] such as those involving "narcotics," "alcoholic beverages," "gambling," and "offenses against tax and trade laws."

And so the consent defense in American criminal law, and in the Model Code, is not really a general defense. Having announced the general principle of consent as a justification, the Model Code proceeds to exclude cases involving the infliction of serious bodily injury.[136] The leading American criminal law treatise goes even farther, declaring that "[c]onsent by the victim is not a defense in a criminal prosecution."[137] The reason generally cited for limiting, or even rejecting, consent as a justification is that the criminal law, unlike torts, is about "public wrongs," not "private wrongs," a distinction familiar since at least Blackstone.[138]

interests. Here is Blackstone's list of public wrongs, in order: Offences against God and Religion; Offences against the Law of Nations; High Treason; Felonies, injurious to the King's Prerogative; Praemunire ("maintaining the papal power"); Misprisions and Contempts, affecting the King and Government; Offences against Public Justice; Offences against the Public Peace; Offences against Public Trade; Offences against the Public Health, and the Public Police or Oeconomy; Homicide; Offences against the Persons of Individuals; Offences against Private Property. 4 William Blackstone, Commentaries on the Laws of England (1769).
133. Commentaries § 223.1, at 157 ("[p]ersons who take only property to which they believe themselves entitled *constitute no significant threat to the property system*") (emphasis added).
134. Model Penal Code 123 (Proposed Official Draft 1962).
135. Id. at 241.
136. The main exception to this exception is the boxing/hockey rule—"joint participation in a lawful athletic contest or competitive sport." § 2.11(2)(b). Some states have added a potentially far-reaching exception covering "reasonably foreseeable hazards of…[t]he victim's occupation or profession." Rev. Stat. Mo. § 565.080 (1986); see State v. George, 937 S.W.2d 251 (Mo. App. 1996) (hospital security guard).
137. Wayne R. LaFave & Austin W. Scott, Jr., Criminal Law 477 (2d ed. 1986).
138. See 4 William Blackstone, Commentaries on the Laws of England 5 (1769) ("public wrongs, or crimes and misdemeanors, are a breach and violation of the public rights

A "criminal offense is," we are told, "a wrong affecting the general public, at least indirectly, and consequently cannot be licensed by the individual directly harmed."[139] Similarly, we learn that "[t]he interest of the state is paramount and controls prosecutions . . . [f]or it is the public, not a complainant, that is injured by the commission of a crime."[140]

Assuming that consent matters, either as a level one or as a level three defense, in a particular case, considerable doctrinal attention has been devoted to the secondary question of whether consent actually was present. The *law* on this central issue of *fact*—was it *really* consent, or was it just "assent," or, alternatively, if it was consent, was that consent "effective"?—is fairly complex (if not convoluted), and the Code does a nice job of summarizing it. Not surprisingly, consent by those who are not authorized to give it does not count; third-party consent is ineffective except in a very few circumstances—such as in the cases of medical emergency mentioned above. Consent by those incapable of consenting, for one reason or another, is likewise irrelevant. Interestingly, the Code includes not only "youth, mental disease or defect"—that is, conditions that would make out the incapacity excuses of infancy or insanity[141]— among the reasons for an incapacity to consent, but intoxication as well.[142] Recall that intoxication does not make out an incapacity excuse unless it is not self-induced.[143] In other words, voluntary intoxication can make me incapable of consenting to someone else's crime, but not of committing a crime myself.

As one might expect, consent obtained by force or duress (another excuse) also will not do. Then there is consent induced by deception, more precisely by "deception of a kind sought to be prevented by the law defining the offense." This is the Code's attempt to make room for the common law distinction between, in good Law Latin, "fraud in

and duties, due to the whole community, considered as a community, in its social aggregate capacity").

139. Wayne R. LaFave & Austin W. Scott, Jr., Criminal Law 477 (2d ed. 1986).

140. Id. at 481 (quoting People v. Brim, 199 N.Y.S.2d 744 (1960)).

141. See § 17 below.

142. "Improvident" consent is also ineffective. Here the drafters had in mind statutory rape. Commentaries § 2.11, at 398.

143. See § 4.3(a) above.

the factum" and "fraud in the inducement." In short, at common law, fraud in the factum "vitiates" consent, fraud in the inducement does not. If I get you to agree to let me install in your apartment what you think is a smoke detector, but what actually is a surveillance camera, then I am still guilty of "violation of privacy," as defined by the Code as "install[ing] in any private place, without the consent of the person or persons entitled to privacy there, any device for observing, photographing, recording, amplifying or broadcasting sounds or events in such place."[144] That is because I perpetrated a fraud in the factum—I deceived you about a fact relevant to an element of the offense to which I claim you consented. You consented not to the installation of a "device for observing, photographing, recording, amplifying or broadcasting sounds or events," but of a smoke detector. Now imagine that I am upfront about installing a surveillance camera, but tell you—falsely—that I am doing this as part of a science experiment at school. This time, I fooled you into consenting to what I was doing, as opposed to fooling you about what I was doing. I lied not about an element of the offense, but about a "collateral matter," a reason for committing the offense. In this scenario, your consent counts; in the previous one, it does not.

Instead of excluding consent obtained by a fraud in the factum—but not in the inducement—the Code disregards any "deception of a kind sought to be prevented by the law defining the offense." This provision is not particularly helpful, however. There are of course many offenses that aim to prevent all manner of deception, but presumably the drafters did not have just those in mind when they drafted the provision on consent.[145] It would seem that consent based on a fraud in the factum still would not count as consent, but not because it is a "deception of a kind sought to be prevented by the law defining the offense," but because the victim did not really consent to the offense at all, as she was not aware of the fact that she was consenting to it, and in fact thought she was consenting to something different altogether.

<hr/>

144. § 250.12(1)(b).
145. See, e.g., §§ 210.5(1) (causing suicide), 212.1 (kidnapping), 220.3(1)(c) (criminal mischief), 223.3 (theft by deception), & 223.7(1) (theft of services), art. 224 (forgery and fraudulent practices), § 241.6(1) (witness tampering).

[3]

EXCUSE

We have now arrived at the third, and last, step in our stroll through the analysis of criminal liability. To make it to this point in the inquiry, a case (hypothetical or real) already would have to clear two previous hurdles—facial criminality and unlawfulness. In Model Penal Code terms, the behavior in question would have to qualify as "conduct that inflicts or threatens substantial harm to individual or public interests" (level one). Put yet another way, the conduct would have to match the face of some criminal statute, satisfying each element in the offense definition it contains. Moreover, stepping outside the confines of the universe of offense definitions, we must have decided that this instance of prima facie criminality also qualified as unlawful, broadly speaking (level two).

§ 12 EXCUSES IN THE MODEL PENAL CODE

Before we can impose criminal liability on the person who engaged in this concededly criminal and unlawful conduct, however, we need to check one more thing. We need to see if she can be held responsible for her conduct, taking into account her relevant personal characteristics as well as the relevant circumstances of her behavior in this particular case.

Here, as in its treatment of justifications, the Model Code speaks far more in terms of justice, and morality, than one might expect, given its comprehensive effort to transform the criminal law into a system for the identification, diagnosis, and treatment of those displaying criminal dispositions of various types and degrees. Consider, for instance, the following passage from the Commentaries on the duress excuse, which in no uncertain terms gives precedence to considerations of justice over those of deterrence, or of incapacitation for that matter:

> [L]aw is ineffective in the deepest sense, indeed…it is hypocritical, if it imposes on the actor who has the misfortune to confront a dilemmatic choice, a standard that his judges are not prepared to affirm that they should and could comply with if their turn to face the problem should arise. Condemnation in such a case is bound to be an ineffective threat; *what is, however, more significant is that it is divorced from any moral base and is unjust.*[1]

This much is true, but a reference to moral foundations and justice, without more, does not a theory of excuses make. There is no such theory in the Code, or the Commentaries, just as there is no theory of justifications. Perhaps the most that could be said about the Code's view of excuses in general is that they are not justifications. So the Commentaries dismiss a provision in the Criminal Code of Western Australia recognizing a necessity defense under "such circumstances of sudden or extraordinary emergency that an ordinary person possessing ordinary power of self-control could not reasonably be expected to act otherwise" with the remark that it "deals with the matter as one rather of excuse than of justification."[2]

As the Commentaries explain, "[t]o say that someone's conduct is 'justified' ordinarily connotes that the conduct is thought to be right, or at least not undesirable." By contrast, "to say that someone's conduct is 'excused' ordinarily connotes that the conduct is thought to be undesirable but that *for some reason the actor is not to be blamed for it.*"[3] The Code's excuse provisions set out those reasons, one by one, without trying to reduce them to some common principle, except perhaps for the general, and undeveloped, notion of "blame." Occasionally reference is

---

1. Commentaries § 2.09, at 374–75 (emphasis added).
2. Commentaries § 3.02, at 11 n.2.
3. Commentaries art. 3, introduction, at 3 (emphasis added).

made to fairness and responsibility; a promising candidate, the notion of avoidability, remains unexplored.

There is a startling drop in sophistication, and ambition, in the Code drafters' handling of questions of justification and excuse. Occasional remarks aside,[4] no serious attempt is made to fit these concepts into the Code's overall treatmentist approach, laid out with great enthusiasm and care by Wechsler in "A Rationale of the Law of Homicide" and again in "The Challenge of a Model Penal Code." Nor is there an attempt to motivate the vague references to justice, blame, and fairness, never mind to locate the various justifications and excuses in an alternative, or supplementary, theoretical account that could match Wechsler's detailed treatmentist program, which revolved around general principles of criminality (and in particular the question of mens rea) and, in keeping with its driving ideology of treatmentist science, placed great emphasis on the Correctional aspect of the Model Penal and Correctional Code.

Like justifications, excuses have an article of their own, article 4, entitled "responsibility." That article, however, is more underinclusive than its justification analog, article 3, which includes every justification other than consent. Article 4 instead deals with only two excuses: insanity and infancy. Other excuses appear in article 2, including ignorance of law and intoxication (which we already discussed), as well as duress, military orders, and entrapment.[5] Another excuse, provocation or extreme emotional disturbance (EED), in Model Code language, does

4. See, for instance, the provision on the use of deadly force in arrest, which replaces the categorical common law rule with a flexible standard that turns on an assessment of the suspect's dangerousness. See § 10 above.

5. Of these three, only duress clearly qualifies as an excuse. Military orders can be a justification or an excuse, depending on whether one views the defense as a way to advance some general interest in the smooth functioning of the military (in which case it would appear as a justification) or on the uniquely coercive power a military order exerts upon its recipient (in which case it would look more like an excuse). Compare § 2.10 with Rules for Courts-Martial 916(d) (justification); United States v. Calley, 22 U.S.C.M.A. 534 (1973). Entrapment, as we will see, will not be mistaken for a justification. Some jurisdictions instead appear to treat it as a level one defense relating to mens rea, akin to mistake, see, e.g., Jacobson v. United States, 503 U.S. 540 (1992) (state bears burden of disproving entrapment beyond a reasonable doubt), while the Model Code frames it in objective terms, entirely unrelated to the actor's culpability, or blameworthiness.

not appear in the general part at all. Limited to homicide, it is codified in the section of the special part dealing with that crime. Finally, the Commentaries acknowledge that, despite their treatment in the article on justifications, cases of putative self-defense—or of mistaken beliefs regarding the conditions of a justification generally—"might more precisely be labeled excuses" insofar as "in some of the cases, at least, it might be said that the actor is really offering an excuse for his conduct rather than a full-fledged justification."[6]

Excuses in the Code thus are a disparate lot, as they are in criminal law generally, and are best treated one at a time.

§ 13 DURESS

One way of thinking about duress in the Model Penal Code is to view it as the excuse analog to the justification of necessity.[7] If with necessity you do not succeed, try duress. In a sense, duress is more about necessity than is the necessity defense. It is choice of evils without the choice of evils. Necessity is all there is in duress, without any claim of right, or lawfulness. The person acting under the justification of necessity has done the right thing, or at least not the wrong thing. The person acting under duress has done the wrong thing, and yet cannot be held responsible (or blamed) for doing what she did. The person justified under necessity made the right choice. The person excused under duress was forced to make the wrong choice, and in this sense made no choice at all. One is justified by her choice, the other excused by the absence of choice. One made the right choice; the other had no choice.

Duress, however, also shares much with self-defense, and defense of others (though not with defense of property[8]). Force used under duress, for instance, is self-defensive force directed not against the source of the

---

6. Commentaries art. 3, introduction, at 2–3.
7. The classification of duress as an excuse is somewhat controversial. See, e.g., Peter Westen & James Mangiafico, The Criminal Defense of Duress: A Justification, Not an Excuse—And Why It Matters, 6 Buff. Crim. L. Rev 833, 937–39 (2003); R. v. Perka, [1984] 2 S.C.R. 232 (Can.).
8. Commentaries § 2.09, at 375 ("perils to property" insufficient).

threat—as in self-defense—but against a third, innocent person. To protect myself, I harm not the person who threatens me with harm, but someone else altogether.[9] Duress also resembles self-defense in that it comes in a direct and in a vicarious version. I am excused under duress to prevent harm to myself and to "the person of another," just as I am justified in using force to protect myself or "the person of another" against an attacker. Here, as in self-defense, the traditional limitation to members of my household has been replaced by a universal reference to all persons.[10]

Note also that, like self-defense but unlike necessity, duress requires "the use of, or a threat to use, *unlawful* force." This reference to unlawfulness is confusing, as duress, unlike the justification of self-defense (or necessity, for that matter), does not render facially criminal conduct lawful. The threatened force in self-defense must be unlawful, so that my use of self-protective force against it can be lawful. I cannot lawfully use force against force lawfully used against me. As an excuse, duress lays no such claim. The rationale of duress is not the right to respond to unlawful force, it is the inevitability of responding to any force, lawful or not, provided it is great enough to force my hand (or rather my mind).

The point of the reference to "unlawful force" appears to have been to clarify that duress is limited to coercion caused by persons (personal duress), and not to compulsion by natural causes or circumstances

---

9. There is no requirement that I harm anyone, of course. The Code specifically recognizes the applicability of duress to escape, for instance. The prison escape cases, which tend to be regarded as the paradigm of duress in American criminal law, are problematic, in that no one ever coerces the defendant to commit the offense he is charged with: escape. Instead, the defendant claims to have escaped to avoid some other harm, usually physical or sexual abuse by fellow inmates or prison guards. The Code makes clear that even if the balance of harms does not come out in his favor, so that a necessity justification is unavailable, the escapee would not be precluded from claiming duress simply because "the crime committed by the victim of coercion is [not] one the author of coercion demands." Commentaries § 2.09, at 377 (citing People v. Lovercamp, 43 Cal. App. 3d 823 (1974)).
10. German criminal law, by contrast, retains this limitation in the case of duress, but not self-defense (or necessity). Contrast § 35 StGB (duress; "relative or other person close to him") with §§ 32 (self-defense; "another") & 34 (necessity; "another"). For a more detailed comparative analysis, see Markus D. Dubber & Tatjana Hörnle, Criminal Law: A Comparative Approach ch. 14.B (2014).

(circumstantial duress). That point, however, could have been made without reference to unlawfulness, for instance, by specifically requiring a personal threat.[11] The reason, in turn, for excluding natural compulsion, or coercion by circumstance, appears to have been that, in the case of a personal threat, "the basic interests of the law may be satisfied by prosecution of the agent of unlawful force." Natural causes, however, cannot be punished—or penally treated—so that, "if the actor is excused, no one is subject to the law's application."[12] Just what "the basic interests of the law" might be in this context, other than an apparent need to "apply" itself as widely as possible, remains unclear.

As the Code rejects duress from circumstances, it must resolve cases such as *Dudley & Stephens* (the cannibalism on the high seas case) under the rubric of choice of evils.[13] Even in extreme natural emergencies, facing almost certain death, the Code thus allows a defense only if the actor balances the potential harms of action and inaction, to herself and others, and then chooses the less harmful course of action (or inaction). This means also that in the yet more dramatic case of the floating plank meant for one but grabbed by two—in a situation, in other words, where I must take your life to save my own—the Code would not allow a defense, because your life is worth as much as mine, no matter how dire my (and your) straits might be. It is never the direness of the straits that matters; only a lesser harm will do, except if the direness has a personal, rather than a natural, cause. Then duress comes to the rescue.

When the Code drafters speak of prosecuting the source of the threat, they have two things in mind. To begin with, the coercer would be held accountable for the coerced's conduct. Recall that the Code specifically provides, in its "complicity" section, that a "person is legally accountable for the conduct of another person when…acting with the kind of culpability that is sufficient for the commission of the offense, he causes an innocent or irresponsible person to engage in such conduct."[14]

11. See, e.g., the alternative statutory formulations listed in Commentaries § 2.09, at 383 n.59 ("another's threat," "threats by another," "compulsion by another").

12. Commentaries § 2.09, at 379.

13. See § 8 above.

14. § 2.06(2)(a).

Here, the duress defense is usefully contrasted not to a level two defense—such as self-defense or necessity—but to a level one "defense" negativing actus reus. In the eyes of the Code drafters, duress stands to involuntariness as "psychological incapacity" stands to "physical incapacity."[15] Just as mistake and intoxication (and consent, where appropriate) make out a defense by negativing a crime's mens rea element, so certain types of coercion negative a crime's actus reus requirement. For instance, if I toss you over my neighbor's fence into her backyard, it may appear that you have committed a criminal trespass (defined as " enter[ing] . . . any place as to which notice against trespass is given by . . . fencing"[16]), except of course that you would not have committed the requisite voluntary act. In fact, your entering would have been distinctly involuntary, as "a bodily movement that . . . is not a product of the effort or determination of the actor."[17]

In the absence of a voluntary act, there would not even be facial criminality—that is, you would not even make it past the first level of analysis. Instead, I would be the one who would have done a voluntary act, merely using you as a tool. It is as though I had tossed myself over the fence.

By contrast, if I merely chased you over the fence with a pitchfork, you would have committed a voluntary act, and to escape criminal liability, would have to raise the excuse of duress. As you were the person who committed the relevant act, I could not be straightforwardly liable as the one who "really" did it. Instead, I would have to have *your* act imputed to me; in other words, I would have to be held accountable for your act, under the Code's provision on derivative liability.[18]

More interestingly, if the attempt at duress falls flat, the coercer *manqué* would qualify for the aptly named, and broadly framed, offense of "criminal coercion."[19] In fact, criminal coercion can be thought of as the offensive side of the coercion coin, with duress on the

---

15. Commentaries § 2.09, at 373–74.
16. § 221.2.
17. § 2.01(2)(d).
18. § 2.06(2)(a) ("causes an innocent or irresponsible person to engage in" criminal conduct).
19. § 212.5.

other, defensive, side. Duress consists of being "coerced" by another to commit a crime; criminal coercion is doing the coercing. The fit is not perfect, because criminal coercion covers threats "to commit any criminal offense" and duress only "the use of, or a threat to use, unlawful *force*." It is closer, however, than it would have been under the common law; the Code drafters rejected a further limitation on the nature of the threat in duress to death, seriously bodily injury, or other violent crimes.[20]

The duress provision places no limitations on the severity, or immediacy, of the threat, even if the defense is raised to excuse the use of deadly force.[21] The drafters also rejected the categorical exclusion of homicide from the class of offenses against which a duress defense could be raised.[22]

The Code's duress provision, in other words, contains no specific, and additional, constraints on the use of deadly force under duress. Unlike in the case of the self-defense justification, there is no requirement, for instance, that threatened force match defensive force, so that only a threat of deadly force could excuse the use of deadly force against another. Nor is there an explicit retreat requirement, with its very own set of exceptions and sub-exceptions.

In the absence of specific rules, the duress provision instead appeals to a single standard, or rather a single thought experiment: what "a person of reasonable firmness" would have done, or not done, in the defendant's "situation." The basic idea here is to inject some objectivity into the duress defense, without requiring any type of proportionality—or other—principle. It is not enough that a particular person has been overwhelmed by threats, as a matter of fact. Instead, we are to be held to a higher standard of fortitude, not actual but "reasonable" firmness. Just what reasonable firmness is, and whether I displayed whatever it

20. Commentaries § 2.09, at 369.
21. When the drafters stressed that "long and wasting pressure may break down resistance more effectively than a threat of immediate destruction," they were thinking specifically of the "brainwashing" of American prisoners of war during the Korean War. Commentaries § 2.09, at 376.
22. Commentaries § 2.09, at 371; but see State v. Toscano, 74 N.J. 421 (1977) (N.J. Code Crim. Just. § 2C:2–9).

is, would be left up to the jury, the paradigmatic, if exceedingly rare, receptacle—and arbiter—of reasonableness in American criminal law.

Having imagined the "person of reasonable firmness," the jury is then to place that construct—but not themselves—into the defendant's "situation," to see how she (or he[23]) might have fared. As the Commentaries, but not the Code itself, tell us, the "situation" includes certain circumstances, but not others:

> Stark, tangible factors that differentiate the actor from another, like his size, strength, age, or health, would be considered in making the exculpatory judgment. Matters of temperament would not.[24]

In the Commentaries we also learn that there are certain threats that are categorically declared irrelevant to the inquiry into "reasonable firmness": "when the claimed excuse is that duress was irresistible, threats to property or even reputation cannot exercise sufficient power over persons of 'reasonable firmness' to warrant consideration in these terms."[25] The excuse of duress thus deviates from the justification of defensive force against unlawful attack, codified in §§ 3.04–.06, by requiring a threat against the person (mine or another's), while disregarding threats to property.[26]

The Code drafters further restricted the scope of the duress defense by declaring that recklessly placing myself "in a situation in which it was probable that [I] would be subjected to duress" bars the defense entirely, rather than mitigating liability to recklessness offenses. Recall that, in the case of the justification defense of necessity, recklessness in this regard did not render the defense inapplicable, but instead reduced liability to a recklessness offense, as negligence reduced liability to a negligence offense. In the case of duress, this general rule of mitigation

---

23. Note that gender is not among the relevant characteristics listed.
24. Commentaries § 2.09, at 375.
25. Id. The Commentaries suggest that the categorical irrelevance of threats to property or reputation is implied by the reference to threats "against [the defendant's] person or the person of another."
26. Attacks on one's reputation are never grounds for self-defense.

to match the actual mode of culpability applies only to negligence; if I am reckless in creating the probability of coercion, such as by "connect[ing myself] with criminal activities," I cannot use that coercion to defend against any crime, including one that requires purpose or knowledge.[27] The Commentaries justify, or rather explain, this "deliberate departure" from the principle that liability match culpability by pointing to "the exceptional nature of the defense."[28] The Model Code, it helps to remember at these moments of undermotivated and underexplained inconsistency, is just that, a *model* code, whose drafters are in the business, ultimately, of producing a piece of model legislation that can not only win the approval of the American Law Institute, a national group of lawyers, judges, and law professors, but also exert influence on local legislatures and stakeholders throughout the country.

§ 14 ENTRAPMENT

You might think of entrapment as official duress, or as the carrot to duress's stick.[29] In duress, a private person "coerce[s]" me through "the use of, or a threat to use, unlawful force" to commit a crime. In entrapment, a "public law enforcement official…induces or encourages" me to do the same through other improper, though not necessarily "unlawful," means:

(a) making knowingly false representations designed to induce the belief that such conduct is not prohibited; or

(b) employing methods of persuasion or inducement which create a substantial risk that such an offense will be committed by persons other than those who are ready to commit it.[30]

---

27. Commentaries § 2.09, at 379 & n.48.
28. Id.
29. Cf. People v. Calvano, 30 N.Y.2d 199, 205 (1972) (entrapment and duress "differ only in respect of the pressures exerted").
30. § 2.13(1).

Note that this definition of entrapment says a great deal about the entrapper, but virtually nothing about the entrappee. This is so because the Model Penal Code opted for entrapment of the objective, rather than subjective, variety.[31] Objective entrapment focuses on the police, rather than on the defendant. It is designed "to deter wrongful conduct on the part of the government."[32] The innocence of the defendant is entirely irrelevant: "the defendant is just as guilty, with or without the entrapment."[33]

By contrast, the defendant's innocence is all that matters for purposes of subjective entrapment. In its subjective version, entrapment is only available to the innocent, or more precisely to one not "predisposed" to commit the offense without government inducement.[34] In fact, it is this very limitation to the innocent that induced the Code drafters to opt for objective, and only objective, entrapment. Here the drafters quote Justice Felix Frankfurter, also not a fan of subjective entrapment:

> Permissible police activity does not vary according to the particular defendant concerned; surely if two suspects have been solicited at the same time in the same manner, one should not go to jail simply because he has been convicted before and is said to have a criminal predisposition.[35]

The drafters' choice of objective entrapment also explains why entrapment (b) requires only the use of tactics that "create a substantial risk" that a crime will be committed by someone who is not "ready to

---

31. Contrast People v. Missrie, 300 A.D.2d 35, 751 N.Y.S.2d 16 (2002) (discussing "subjective" entrapment provision in New York Penal Law).
32. Commentaries § 2.13, at 406.
33. Id. at 412.
34. See, e.g., Jacobson v. United States, 503 U.S. 540 (1992) (detailed inquiry into defendant's predisposition).
35. Commentaries § 2.13, at 412 (quoting Sherman v. United States, 356 U.S. 369, 383 (1958) (Frankfurter, J., concurring)). Justice Frankfurter notwithstanding, objective entrapment hangs on in federal criminal law only by the thinnest of constitutional threads, as a due process defense of "outrageous governmental misconduct." Compare United States v. Mosley, 965 F.2d 906 (10th Cir. 1992) (defense exists) with United States v. Boyd, 55 F.3d 239, 241 (7th Cir. 1995) (defense does not exist).

commit it." Entrapment seeks to deter "unsavory police tactics,"[36] and these tactics are just as unsavory when they succeed as when they do not. Of course, for the defense of entrapment to come into play in a particular case, they must have succeeded in the sense that an offense has been committed; but the point of the defense is to combat police misconduct, and its effect on the criminal liability of the defendant is incidental.

The Code's entrapment standard thus does away with the traditional inquiry into the defendant's "predisposition" to commit an offense. The entrapment defense is available to all defendants, predisposed or nonpredisposed.[37] Note that, from a treatmentist perspective, a subjective approach to entrapment could be seen as a nuanced inquiry into the entrappee's criminal dangerousness; the "predisposed" defendant is not entitled to the defense insofar as her criminal dangerousness is independent of, and prior to, the efforts at police inducement.[38]

It is unclear in what sense objective entrapment under the Code amounts to an excuse (or any other kind of defense). Subjective entrapment might be a different story; for instance, evidence of entrapment could be regarded as rebutting the ordinary presumption of dangerousness attaching to the commission of an offense.[39] To explain what makes entrapment an excuse, however, would have required some general account of what might make anything an excuse, which the Code drafters did not provide.[40]

---

36. Commentaries § 2.13, at 412.

37. As long as they are not charged with an offense that includes "causing or threatening bodily injury" as an element. Punishing someone entrapped into an assault, say, would "not seem generally unfair," according to the Commentaries. Commentaries § 2.12, at 420.

38. Thanks to Dragana Rakic for bringing this point to my attention.

39. As the Commentaries note in passing, after all, "it is unfair to prosecute a person persuaded or deceived into criminality *by the state*." Id. (emphasis added). This suggests an analogy to the Code's treatment of mistake of law as a form of executive estoppel. See § 15 below.

40. For a discussion of different approaches to the issue of entrapment, including potential criminal liability of the entrapper, sentence mitigation, and procedural mechanisms, see Markus D. Dubber & Tatjana Hörnle, Criminal Law: A Comparative Approach ch. 14.B (2014).

§ 15 IGNORANCE OF LAW

Under the Code, successful "entrapment by estoppel" (also known as "executive estoppel") is an ignorance of law problem, rather than a matter of entrapment. As we noted in our discussion of mistake as a level one defense, the Code makes room for a limited excuse of ignorance of law, the venerated common law maxim *ignorantia legis non excusat* notwithstanding.[41] That excuse comes in two varieties, "reasonable reliance upon an official statement of the law, afterward determined to be invalid or erroneous"[42] being one, and nonpublication of the law the other, and far less important, one.[43]

Note, however, that the Model Code version of the ignorance of law excuse does not require a *knowing* misstatement, never mind an intentional one specifically "designed to induce the belief that such conduct is not prohibited," as entrapment would require. The Code does limit the defense to "official" misstatements of the law, thus excluding reliance, no matter how reasonable, on my—or any other—lawyer's nonofficial advice that, by a subsequent official statement, turns out to have been bad, or at least wrong.[44] Perhaps not surprisingly, reliance on the actor's own interpretation of the law, "afterward determined to be ... erroneous," will not do either.[45] "Official" statements of the law encompass statements issued by members of any branch of government, legislature ("a statute or other enactment"), judiciary ("a judicial decision, opinion or judgment"), and executive ("an administrative order or grant of permission"; "an official interpretation of the public officer or body charged by law with responsibility

---

41. See § 4.3(B) above.
42. An "invalid" statement would include a statute later determined to be unconstitutional. See State v. Godwin, 123 N.C. 697 (1898) (cited in Commentaries § 2.04, at 278 n.28). For a case interpreting an MPC-based ignorance provision, see People v. Studifin, 132 Misc. 2d 326 (N.Y. Sup. Ct. 1986).
43. The question of publicity was not always of little practical relevance. See, e.g., The Cotton Planter, 6 F. Cas. 620 (Cir. Ct. D.N.Y. 1810). Lambert v. California, 355 U.S. 225 (1957), has done little to revive the issue.
44. Commentaries § 2.04, at 279–80.
45. See People v. Marrero, 69 N.Y.2d 382 (1987) (good-faith (mis)reading of ambiguous statute not enough).

for the interpretation, administration or enforcement of the law defining the offense").

That ignorance of law under the Code is an excuse, rather than a level one "defense," is clear enough.[46] Why this should be so is not quite so obvious. Unlike duress, provocation, diminished capacity, infancy, and insanity—and perhaps even entrapment, at least in its subjective form—ignorance of law does not involve a loss of self-control, however partial. In the case of ignorance, the "reason the actor is not to be blamed for"[47] her concededly "undesirable" conduct may be thought instead to lie in its *unavoidability*. If the actor did not know, or could not reasonably have known, of the criminal statute she is charged with violating, she could not have avoided violating it. Similarly, if she did everything she could do (or could be expected to do) to determine the meaning of a statute familiar to her, and thus to avoid violating it, it might seem unfair to blame her for finding out, after the fact, that she failed, no matter how "undesirable" her conduct might have turned out to be. Under the Code's treatmentist approach, too, it would appear that someone who commits a mistake of law that is unavoidable in this sense could rebut whatever presumption of criminal dangerousness might attach to her for having engaged in the proscribed conduct.[48]

Perhaps the idea of unavoidability could be seen as undergirding the inability and incapacity excuses such as duress, insanity, and so on. In the case of duress, giving in to the coercion was as unavoidable under the circumstances as was succumbing to the inducement of entrapment. Provocation and diminished capacity, too, would appear as unavoidability defenses, though what was unavoidable—or at least too difficult to avoid—there was the violent response triggered by the provocation.

---

46. Cf. § 2.02(9) (knowledge of illegality not offense element).
47. Commentaries art. 3, introduction, at 3 (emphasis added).
48. Despite its limited scope, the Model Penal Code's mistake of law provision proved too broad for many American jurisdictions, including New York. See People v. Marrero, 69 N.Y.2d 382, 382 (1987). Other (civil law) jurisdictions provide for a more generous defense; see generally Markus D. Dubber & Tatjana Hörnle, Criminal Law: A Comparative Approach ch. 8.C (2014).

§ 16 PROVOCATION AND DIMINISHED CAPACITY

"Provocation," or "extreme mental or emotional disturbance" in Model Code language, differs from duress and other excuses because it is not a general defense. It is a defense to murder, and to murder only. That is why it does not appear in the Code's general part (part I), but in its special part, more specifically, in the article dealing with homicide, and still more specifically, in the section defining manslaughter.

Yet an excuse it clearly is, at least in the Model Code's scheme of things. Provocation carries its excuseness on its sleeve; it covers acts committed "under the influence of extreme mental or emotional disturbance for which there is reasonable explanation or *excuse*." But before we get to provocation as a mini excuse, we need to take a quick detour into the special part's homicide provisions.

What the common law called "voluntary manslaughter" is murder plus provocation, or rather murder minus malice aforethought, on account of provocation. Voluntary manslaughter is still murder in that it is still intentional, however, and is—in that misleading sense—"voluntary." The provocation, no matter how outrageous, did not change the fact that the defendant hit the victim over the head with a club with the conscious object of killing him (to speak in Model Code terms). It instead explained why he might have had that conscious object. *Involuntary* manslaughter, by contrast, was manslaughter, period, or nonintentional homicide, that is, homicide that was committed with neither desire nor awareness that death would result.

The Code, probably wisely, jettisons talk of voluntary and involuntary manslaughter (just as it does not like speaking of voluntary and involuntary intoxication, voluntariness being reserved for questions of actus reus, not mens rea[49]). It instead sets out two types of manslaughter, without naming them: reckless homicide (recklessly causing the death of another human being)—the Code's version of involuntary

---

49. On intoxication, see § 4.3(A) above.

manslaughter, which does not interest us here—and its version of voluntary manslaughter, which does interest us:

> Criminal homicide constitutes manslaughter when:…a homicide which would otherwise be murder is committed under the influence of extreme mental or emotional disturbance for which there is reasonable explanation or excuse. The reasonableness of such explanation or excuse shall be determined from the viewpoint of a person in the actor's situation under the circumstances as he believes them to be.[50]

As it appears in the definition of a criminal *offense*, and a serious one at that (manslaughter is a second degree felony in the Code), provocation differs from duress, and other excuses, in another way: not only does it apply only to a single offense, it is not even a complete defense to that offense.[51] Provocation turns murder into manslaughter, and that is it.

Still it is important to see why disturbance works as an excuse. It is clearly not a justification. The person who kills under the influence of extreme mental or emotional disturbance cannot claim a right to kill. If she could, she might qualify for self-defense. "Disturbance" is not a level one (or failure of proof) defense, either. The point of the disturbance is to provide an "explanation or excuse" for purposeful or knowing conduct—murder—rather than to deny that it was purposeful or knowing. That, again, is why provocation manslaughter is voluntary; it is intentional, but excusable.

Provocation is a partial, rather than a complete, excuse because it mitigates the actor's responsibility, rather than precluding it. It amounts to a "disturbance," however "extreme," rather than to an "inability" (as in the case of duress) or an "incapacity" (as in insanity). Disturbance does not negate the inference of "moral depravity"[52] (or exceptional

---

50. § 210.3(1)(b).

51. In fact, it is not even clear that it is a defense of any kind, rather than being an element of the offense of manslaughter. This was the issue in Patterson v. New York, 432 U.S. 197 (1977). There, the Supreme Court held that the federal constitution does not preclude a legislature from classifying provocation not only as a defense, but as an affirmative defense upon which the defendant bears the burden of proof.

52. Commentaries § 210.3, at 61.

dangerousness) from facially criminal conduct; it reduces the grade of the "depravity" (or dangerousness) inferred, from that ordinarily associated with purposeful or knowing homicide (murder) to that ordinarily associated with reckless homicide (manslaughter). In short, disturbance requires a downward adjustment in the diagnosis of the actor's criminal disposition, and therefore of her need for peno-correctional treatment.

Doctrinally, provocation falls somewhere in between self-defense, duress, and insanity. As you might think of duress as the excuse alternative to the justification of necessity, so provocation can be seen as the excuse alternative to the justification of self-defense. Unlike self-defense, it is not limited to the use of force against unlawful attacks, nor does it require a showing that my use of force was (nor even that it was believed to be) immediately necessary, never mind the initial aggressor or retreat constraints on the use of deadly force in self-defense. Like self-defense, provocation too has a vicarious analog; as self-defense has defense of others, so provocation is not limited to cases where I am the target of the provocation: "the Code does not require that the actor's emotional distress arise from some injury, affront, or other provocative act perpetrated upon him by the deceased."[53] This also means that, unlike self-defense (or other-defense)—but like duress—I can use provocation as a defense against inflicting harm (deadly harm, in fact) on someone other than the person who is doing the provoking, as "where [I] strike[] out in a blinding rage and kill[] an innocent bystander."[54]

Like duress, provocation is defined in terms of reasonableness. It is not enough for duress that I was unable to withstand the threats, nor is it enough for provocation that I was so disturbed that I could not control myself after being provoked. To inject some objectivity into the inquiry, the Code limits both excuses to cases where it was "reasonable" for me to behave as I did. Once again, this apparently objective inquiry into what "the hypothetical reasonable man"[55] might have done is then tailored to

---

53. Id. at 60–61.
54. Id. The victim thus need have engaged in neither unlawful, nor even provocative conduct. This is one reason the Code refers to emotional disturbance rather than provocation. See id. at 61.
55. Id. at 62.

my "situation." As in duress, this means that the factfinder gets to take into account certain, but not all, of my characteristics or "personal handicaps," including "blindness, shock from traumatic injury, and extreme grief," but not "idiosyncratic moral values" like something "as integral a part of moral depravity as a belief in the rightness of killing."[56]

The Code's flexible reasonableness standard sweeps away a host of more or less hard and fast common law rules defining the scope of the provocation defense. The common law barred the provocation defense in the face of sufficient opportunity to "cool off" and regain self-control after a provocation, and declared that words alone could never provoke. The Code instead throws these considerations, along with anything else that might be relevant to the actor's "situation," into the pot of reasonableness. So no particular temporal connection between provocative cause and effect is required, nor is any type (or source or target) of provocation excluded, not even attacks on "property or...reputation,"[57] which were declared categorically irrelevant to the reasonableness inquiry in cases of duress.

As we have seen, provocation under the Code is not really—or just—provocation, but "extreme emotional or mental disturbance." While the reference to *emotional* disturbance covers all cases of provocation, and then some, the reference to *mental* disturbance highlights the connection between provocation and insanity. That connection consists of a multifaceted defense called "diminished capacity," or "diminished responsibility" as the Model Code prefers to call it.

Diminished responsibility, like so many other defenses, comes in two varieties. On one hand, it is a level one defense. Evidence of mental incapacity or abnormality short of full-fledged insanity is relevant to mens rea. This straightforward, evidentiary aspect of diminished responsibility—familiar from other failure of proof defenses such as mistake or intoxication—is codified, however redundantly, in § 4.02 of the Code, immediately following the definition of insanity.[58]

<hr/>

56. Id.
57. Commentaries § 2.09, at 375. The Commentaries suggest that the categorical irrelevance of threats to property or reputation in duress is implied by the reference to threats "against [the defendant's] person or the person of another."
58. See State v. Breakiron, 108 N.J. 591 (1987).

On the other hand, diminished responsibility can be construed as a level three defense, an excuse. No Code section is specifically dedicated to diminished responsibility as an excuse. Instead, this aspect of the defense is covered by the "mental disturbance" language in the Code's provocation provision. Diminished responsibility as an excuse thus functions like provocation as an excuse—in fact, it *is* provocation as an excuse. It would reduce the actor's liability from murder to manslaughter, rather than leading to an outright acquittal (as a successful level one defense might), and apply to no offense other than murder.[59]

§ 17 INSANITY AND INFANCY

The Code drafters devoted a great deal of time and effort to the insanity defense. In their view, "[n]o problem in the drafting of a penal code presents greater intrinsic difficulty than that of determining when individuals whose conduct would otherwise be criminal ought to be exculpated on the ground that they were suffering from mental disease or defect when they acted as they did."[60] The importance of the insanity defense to the Code project did not reflect its practical significance; as is well-known, the insanity defense is very rarely invoked, and almost never successful. The problem instead was a systematic, or "intrinsic" one. Having reformed criminal law from an atavistic ritual of punishment to a scientific system of treatment, the Code drafters struggled to make room for the insanity defense. If all of criminal law is about identifying, diagnosing, and treating persons suffering from some penological abnormality, what is the point of excusing certain persons from punishment on account of some mental abnormality, and subjecting them to treatment instead? If all criminals are mentally abnormal, what is so special about the criminally insane?

---

59. Note, however, that diminished responsibility is not an independent defense. It is relevant only insofar as the "mental abnormalities" giving rise to it are relevant to the jury's (or factfinder's) general reasonableness inquiry and, more specifically, to the "actor's situation" defining that inquiry. Commentaries § 210.3, at 72.
60. Commentaries § 4.01, at 164.

In a system of criminal law as punishment—rather than as "peno-correctional treatment"—the question of insanity has a straightforward answer. The criminally insane are those persons to whom the general presumption of sanity—of normality—does not apply. Deprived of the mental or affective capacities necessary for choice and therefore for wrongful conduct, they cannot be proper objects of blame. Without blame, they must be without punishment. Instead of deserving punishment, they require treatment.

Given their treatmentist view of criminal law, which excised punishment from its vocabulary, the Model Code drafters instead were forced to frame the problem of insanity in a different, and more roundabout, way. The difference between the sane and the insane, the normal and the abnormal, was not that between punishment and treatment, but between different "modes of disposition" through treatment, and, more specifically, between different administrators of treatment. As the drafters saw it, "the problem is to etch a decent working line between the areas assigned to the authorities responsible for public health and those responsible for the correction of offenders."[61]

The result of the drafters' extended struggle to craft a treatment exception to their treatmentist vision of punishment was a long and highly detailed article entitled "responsibility" (art. 4). Despite its broad title, this article is devoted entirely to the defense of insanity, except for one brief section at the very end, on the traditional excuse of infancy (or "immaturity," in Model Code terms).

At common law, infancy worked very much like insanity; it was a substantive defense in a criminal proceeding. The infant, along with the "idiot" or "lunatic," was exempt from criminal liability because he was not among the "persons capable of committing crimes."[62] By the time of the Code, infancy had, for at least half a century, been a procedural, and more precisely a jurisdictional, issue, rather than a substantive one. And so, rather than addressing the conditions under which—and the general reasons that—immaturity might work as an excuse for otherwise

61. Commentaries § 4.01, at 165.
62. 4 William Blackstone, Commentaries on the Laws of England ch. 2 (1769).

criminal conduct, the Code sets up some general jurisdictional rules regarding the "transfer of proceedings to juvenile court."[63]

Immaturity, however, is an excuse for the same reason that insanity is. A child is not responsible for her conduct, or at least not sufficiently responsible for it, to warrant blame. Like the insane person, the child "lacks substantial capacity either to appreciate the criminality [wrongfulness] of his conduct or to conform his conduct to the requirements of law."[64] The difference between immaturity and insanity is that the cause of the incapacity is age, and therefore both presumably temporary and normal, rather than a "mental disease or defect." Plus, modern criminal law treats a certain age—or lack thereof—as an irrebuttable presumption of irresponsibility. So the Model Code, for example, categorically declares that a "person shall not be tried for or convicted of an offense," rather than be acquitted after a trial, "if...at the time of the conduct charged to constitute the offense he was less than sixteen years of age."[65] In other cases, the presumption of irresponsibility is rebuttable, and may even flip over into a presumption of responsibility, as when the actor falls in a gray zone between clear infancy and clear adulthood (say, during the ages of sixteen and seventeen, as under the Code[66]) or when the offense charged is particularly serious. Much of the reform of juvenile law since the Code's publication in 1962 has amounted to a downward extension of that gray zone.[67]

By contrast, the presumption of sanity is universal, and it is upon each individual defendant to rebut it. Insanity under the Code is an affirmative defense, though it should be remembered that affirmative defenses in the Code place only the burden of production upon the defendant, while the burden of persuasion remains on the state.[68]

63. § 4.10.

64. § 4.01(1).

65. § 4.10(1)(a).

66. § 4.10(1)(b).

67. For a discussion of the common law's inquiry into the responsibility of a particular defendant raising the defense of infancy, see 4 William Blackstone, Commentaries on the Laws of England 22–24 (1769).

68. § 4.03. Note that the U.S. Supreme Court has found no constitutional fault with placing the burden of *persuasion* on the defendant as well, even to the point of requiring defendants to prove their insanity beyond a reasonable doubt. Leland v. Oregon, 343 U.S. 790 (1952); see generally Clark v. Arizona, 548 U.S. 735 (2006).

In a way, it is misleading to say that article 4 on responsibility is entirely—or almost entirely—devoted to the defense of insanity. In fact, the defense is codified in a single section at the outset of the article, § 4.01. Most of the remainder of the article, in §§ 4.02 through 4.09, addresses, in considerable detail, various procedural issues related to the insanity defense, including—in rough order of appearance—the relevance of evidence of mental disease, the classification of insanity as an affirmative defense, the requirement of notifying the state of one's intention to raise an insanity defense, the form of the verdict if the defense is successful, incompetence to stand trial, psychiatric examinations of the defendant by state and defense experts, the inadmissibility of incriminating statements made during these examinations, and, last but certainly not least, the effect of a verdict of not guilty by reason of insanity ("commit[ment] to the custody of the Commissioner of Mental Hygiene [Public Health] to be placed in an appropriate institution for custody, care and treatment").[69] The vast bulk of the insanity provisions in the Code, in other words, is devoted not to defining the defense of insanity, but to an elaborate attempt to control its implementation, largely with the help of expert testimony.

Luckily, the insanity defense itself is remarkably short and to the point:

> A person is not responsible for criminal conduct if at the time of such conduct as a result of mental disease or defect he lacks substantial capacity either to appreciate the criminality [wrongfulness] of his conduct or to conform his conduct to the requirements of law.[70]

Its main features are quickly identified. The incapacity that matters is incapacity "at the time of" the crime, not before or after (most relevantly, at the time of trial). Mental disease or defect at trial—incompetence to stand trial—is measured by a different, procedural standard ("capacity to understand the proceedings against him or to

69. § 4.08(1).
70. § 4.01(1).

assist in his own defense") and affects not my responsibility for the crime, but only my "fitness to proceed," which matters only "as long as such incapacity endures."[71]

Insanity requires a different sort of incapacity, or rather incapacities: the *cognitive* incapacity to "appreciate the criminality [wrongfulness] of [my] conduct," and the *volitional* one to "conform [my] conduct to the requirements of the law." The Code drafters here responded to what they perceived as the shortcomings of the then-dominant insanity test, first set out in an advisory English opinion from 1843, *M'Naghten's Case*.[72] And so it is best to place their insanity defense side by side with *M'Naghten*.[73] Here is the *M'Naghten* test in its original formulation:

> [T]o establish a defence on the ground of insanity, it must be clearly proved that, at the time of the committing of the act, the party accused was labouring under such a defect of reason, from disease of the mind, as not to know the nature and quality of the act he was doing; or, if he did know it, that he did not know he was doing what was wrong.

Improving *M'Naghten* meant expanding it. Unlike *M'Naghten,* at least as it had entered American criminal law, the Code test does not require

---

71. § 4.03.
72. 1 C. & K. 130, 4 St. Tr. N.S. 847 (1843). M'Naghten set out to assassinate Prime Minister Sir Robert Peel, convinced that spies were following him "night and day." He killed Peel's private secretary instead, mistaking him for Peel. After M'Naghten's acquittal on grounds of insanity, the House of Lords asked for clarification of the law of insanity. *M'Naghten* was the judges' response. See generally Richard Moran, Knowing Right from Wrong: The Insanity Defense of Daniel McNaughtan (1981).
73. The drafters rejected as too ambiguous another contemporary attempt to replace *M'Naghten*, the "product" test set out in Durham v. United States, 214 F.2d 862, 874–75 (D.C. Cir. 1954) ("accused is not criminally responsible if his unlawful act was the product of mental disease or mental defect"). Commentaries § 4.01, at 173. Also rejected was Wechsler's proposed formulation: "A person is not responsible for criminal conduct if at the time of such conduct as a result of mental disease or defect his capacity either to appreciate the criminality of his conduct or to conform his conduct to the requirements of law is so *substantially impaired that he cannot justly be held responsible.*" Tentative Draft No. 4, § 4.01(1)(a), at 27 (Apr. 25, 1955) (emphasis added); see generally United States v. Brawner, 471 F.2d 969 (D.C. Cir. 1972) (en banc) (abandoning product test for MPC test).

complete incapacity—lacking a "substantial" capacity will do. Similarly, Code insanity does not require that I be incapable merely of *"knowing right from wrong,"* as *M'Naghten* had.[74] Under the Code, I may be criminally insane even if I technically "know" the difference between right and wrong, as long as I cannot be said to "appreciate" that difference. Here the Code drafters were thinking of someone who suffers from certain "emotional abnormalities" that prevent her "largely detached or abstract awareness" of the wrongfulness of her conduct from "penetrat[ing] to the affective level."[75] So I can be insane, and therefore irresponsible, if I know what I am doing is wrong, but do not know what that means, exactly. I might know the difference between right and wrong, without understanding it.[76]

More interesting, just *what* I am supposed to understand (or not understand) had been unclear after *M'Naghten*. Was I insane if I did not understand that what I was doing was illegal (or, yet more specifically, criminal), or was it enough (or required) that I did not understand that what I was doing was wrong?[77] The Code does not resolve the ambiguity, referring equivocally to the conduct's "criminality [wrongfulness]." Now, awareness of criminality and of wrongfulness tend to amount to the same thing as criminality and wrongfulness tend to coincide—what is criminal is often wrong, and vice versa (though less frequently). The formulation would make a difference, however, in cases of criminality without wrongfulness. If I cannot be insane as long as I appreciate the *criminality* of my conduct, then insane, and mistaken, beliefs in the rightfulness of concededly criminal conduct, perhaps prompted by hearing "the voice of God calling upon [me] to kill the woman as a sacrifice and atonement,"[78] would not count.[79]

---

74. Id. (emphasis added).
75. Commentaries § 4.01, at 166.
76. Id. at 169 ("broader sense of understanding than simple cognition").
77. See, e.g., People v. Schmidt, 216 N.Y. 324 (1915).
78. Id. at 324.
79. Command hallucinations can also be viewed as impeding one's *volitional* capacity to control one's conduct, rather than as a mistaken belief in the rightfulness (or at least nonwrongfulness) of the conduct. In that case, they would not be an insane mistake about a justification, but about an excuse—superior orders or, perhaps, duress. Cf. §§ 2.09 (duress) & 2.10 (military orders).

To say that I fail to appreciate the criminality or the wrongfulness of my conduct is of course but another way of saying that I am *mistaken* about its criminality or wrongfulness. In yet other words, I am committing a level one mistake (about criminality) in thinking that I am committing no crime at all, or a level two mistake (about unlawfulness) in thinking that I am justified in committing a crime. And indeed the excuses of insanity—in its cognitive prong—and of ignorance of law are closely related. As we have seen earlier, mere ignorance of law under the Code does not provide an excuse, absent a failure to publicize or reasonable reliance on an official misstatement of the law.[80] Ignorance of the law, however, does provide an excuse if it is the manifestation of an incapacity to understand the law by applying it to a particular situation, brought on by a mental disease or defect.[81] Then it is called insanity.

Note, once again, that neither the incapacity nor the mental disease or defect, by itself, is sufficient to make for insanity. The incapacity to tell right from wrong—or to keep oneself from doing wrong—may be unfortunate, but it is no excuse. Likewise, and perhaps more important, a mental disease or defect might be relevant as evidence negativing mens rea, as explained in § 4.02, but it does not make for an excuse. Insanity is no defense; irresponsibility brought on by insanity is.

The biggest difference between Model Code insanity and *M'Naghten* insanity, however, lies not in its cognitive prong, but in its volitional prong. *M'Naghten* had no volitional prong—the question of insanity was one of cognition (or knowledge) exclusively. Over the decades since *M'Naghten,* however, courts had grafted onto its cognitive test an "irresistible impulse" addendum that extended the insanity excuse to those who could not keep themselves from doing what they knew to be wrong (or criminal).[82]

80. § 15 above.
81. The Code does not define mental disease or defect, instead leaving these terms "open to accommodate developing medical understanding." Commentaries § 4.01, at 164.
82. See, e.g., Commonwealth v. Rogers, 7 Met. (Mass.) 500 (1844).

The Model Code elevated the irresistible impulse supplement to an alternative type of excuse by reason of insanity.[83] Under the volitional prong, the "reason the actor is not to be blamed for" her concededly "undesirable"[84] conduct is that it was unavoidable on account of her mental disease or defect—in other words, her insanity made her do it. Under the cognitive prong, her conduct was unavoidable, and thus excusable, because her insanity prevented her from realizing that she was engaging in criminal, or undesirable, conduct in the first place—in other words, her insanity kept her from *not* doing it.

83. Note that the Code frames the volitional prong in strictly legal terms, referring to the incapacity of conforming one's conduct to "the requirements of law," rather than of refraining from wrongful (or more specifically criminal) conduct.
84. Commentaries art. 3, introduction, at 3 (emphasis added).

CONCLUSION

The concluding section of this book features a chart that recapitulates and condenses the book, as well as the Model Penal Code, providing a quick summary of the analysis of criminal liability with citations to relevant Code sections. The conceptual flowchart should be useful not only in analyzing a case (hypothetical or not) under the Model Code, but also under American criminal law generally speaking—to the extent such a thing exists, given that there are at least as many takes on "American criminal law" as there are American criminal jurisdictions.

Here then is an analytic guideline for answering the central question in American criminal law teaching and practice: *Who is liable for what*? The basic question of liability is divided into three subquestions, which track the chapters in this book and, roughly, the articles in the Model Penal Code's general part (part I). While every question must be answered in every case, no case has nonobvious answers to all questions. This analytic guideline will not help you pick out the questions with nonobvious answers, nor tell you how to answer them (for that you will have to consult the discussion in the book). It may, however, make it less likely that you will fail to consider a question, or that you will address a question in the "wrong" doctrinal context—unless, of course, you have a good reason to do so.

§ 18 ANALYSIS OF CRIMINAL LIABILITY

1. <u>Criminality (arts. 1–2, 5):</u> Does the behavior constitute criminal conduct?
   A. What are the elements of the offense as defined? (§ 1.13(9))
      1. Conduct (§ 1.13(5))
      2. Circumstances
      3. Result
      4. Mode of culpability (as to each element)
         - purpose, knowledge, recklessness, negligence (§ 2.02)
         - none (strict liability, § 2.05)
         - rules of interpretation (§§ 2.02(3)–(4), 2.05)
   B. Does the behavior satisfy each element of the offense?
      1. Conduct
         - act (§ 2.01)
         - voluntariness (§ 2.01)
         - omission (§ 2.01)
         - complicity (§ 2.06)
      2. Circumstances
         - consent (§ 2.11)
      3. Result
         - causation (§ 2.03)
           - but-for/factual (§ 2.03(1)(a))
           - proximate/legal (§ 2.03(1)(b)–(4))
      4. Mode of culpability (as to each element)
         - mistake (§ 2.04(1))
         - intoxication (§ 2.08)
         - diminished capacity (§ 4.02(1))
      5. Inchoate crimes (art. 5)
         - attempt (§ 5.01)
         - solicitation (§ 5.02)
         - conspiracy (§ 5.03)
2. <u>Illegality (Justification) (art. 3):</u> Is the criminal conduct unlawful generally speaking?
   A. Necessity (choice of evils) (§ 3.02)

B. Self-defense (§ 3.04); defense of another (§ 3.05) & of property (§ 3.06)

C. Law enforcement (§ 3.07)

D. Public duty (§ 3.03)

E. Special responsibility (§ 3.08)

F. Consent (§ 2.11)

3. <u>Guilt (Excuse) (arts. 2, 4):</u> Is the accused responsible for her criminal & unlawful conduct?

A. Duress (§ 2.09)

B. Military orders (§ 2.10)

C. Entrapment (§ 2.13)

D. Ignorance of law (§ 2.04(3))

E. Provocation and diminished capacity (§ 210.3(1)(b))

F. Insanity and infancy (§§ 4.01, 4.10)

   – involuntary intoxication (§ 2.08(4))

TABLE OF CASES

References are to Pages.

TABLE OF MODEL PENAL CODE SECTIONS AND STATUTES

MODEL PENAL CODE

215

MODEL PENAL CODE

MODEL PENAL CODE

MODEL PENAL CODE

FEDERAL

LOUISIANA

MARYLAND

MONTANA

NEW JERSEY

NEW YORK

NORTH DAKOTA

TEXAS

RESTATEMENT (SECOND) OF TORTS

RESTATEMENT (SECOND) OF TORTS

GERMANY

INDEX

References are to pages

ACT
Act requirement. Criminal Conduct,
this index
Defined, 28–29
Voluntary, 29–30

ACCESSORIES
Complicity, this index

ACCOMPLICE LIABILITY
Complicity, this index

ACTUS REUS
Criminal Conduct, this index

AGE
Mistake as to, generally, 74–81, 83

AGREEMENT
Criminal conduct, agreement as core of
conspiracy, 124–125

AIDING ANOTHER'S CONDUCT
Complicity, 88–99

**AMBIGUOUS MENTAL STATE
REQUIREMENTS**
Rules of interpretation, 45–51

AMERICAN LAW INSTITUTE (ALI)
Model Penal Code, 7–10, 188

Revisions to the Model Penal Code, ix–x, 1n,
10n, 13n, 14n, 17n, 174n

ANALYSIS OF CRIMINAL LIABILITY
Model Penal Code, 5, 17, 23–25, 205, 206–207

ANTICIPATORY OFFENSES
Inchoate Offenses, this index

ARREST
Justification, this index

ATTEMPT
Impossibility, 118–119
Inchoate offenses, 112–123

**ATTENDANT CIRCUMSTANCE
ELEMENT**
Criminal Conduct, this index

ATTITUDINAL AXIS OF MENS REA
Criminal conduct, 59, 61–67

AWARENESS
Knowledge, this index

**BLUEPRINT FOR MODEL
PENAL CODE**
Wechsler, 8

CAPITAL PUNISHMENT
Death Penalty, this index

221

Made in the USA
San Bernardino, CA
25 September 2018